GREATER GLASGOW

AN ILLUSTRATED ARCHITECTURAL GUIDE

'All experienced visitors agreed that Glasgow was the worst of all,
where penury, dirt, misery, drunkenness and disease and crime
culminated to a pitch unparalleled in Great Britain'.
E Gauldie – Cruel Habitations

Edwin Chadwick along with distinguished Doctors Alison and Cowan made this observation during a 'perambulation' on the morning of the 24th September 1840.

Such an observation today would be inappropriate and inaccurate. Today's Glasgow is a thriving city, economically, culturally and architecturally – facing a new millennium and discarding its image as a 'mean city'.

This is a city re-born and a city regenerating whose buildings reflect a new found confidence and civic pride. If a city's architectural footprint reflects the aspirations and prosperity of its inhabitants then one look at the diversification of the Glasgow skyline can leave no visitor in any doubt that the future is bright.

Produced in partnership with RCAHMS this excellent and well-researched guide records the architectural heritage of Glasgow and encourages the reader to look anew at the 'Dear Green Place.'

DAVID DUNBAR FRIAS
PRESIDENT 2006–08
Glasgow Institute of Architects

© *Author:* Sam Small
Series *editor: Charles McKean*
Series *consultant: David Walker*
Series *cover design: Luise Valentiner,*
Trigger Press
Index: Oula Jones

The Royal Incorporation of Architects in Scotland
ISBN: 978 1 873190 326
1st published 2008

Cover illustrations
Front *Glasgow Science centre (RCAHMS)*
Back *Back Court (Ian Fleming –*
by permission of the Fleming family)

Typesetting and cover layout by Mitch Cosgrove
Picture scans and maps by the
Royal Commission on the Ancient and
Historical Monuments of Scotland
Printed by GraphyCems, Spain

British Library Cataloguing in Publication Data.
A catalogue record for this book is available from the British Library.

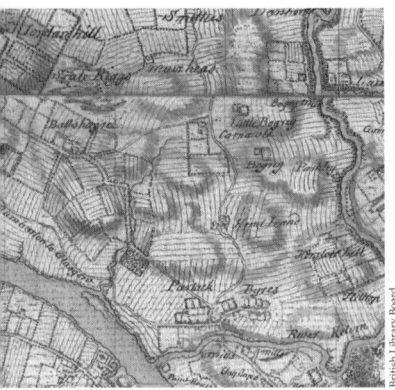

General Roy's military survey of c.1750 shows progress under way in agricultural improvements, his shading gives an impression of the NW Glasgow drumlins

British Library Board

The 'Greater Glasgow' described here is like a doughnut, a city less the hole in the middle – which has already been published as *Central Glasgow*. Greater Glasgow contains not only the dormitory suburbs, with much post-war public sector housing, but also all the civic pride of the Annexed Burghs. Posh Victorian suburbs vie for attention with tenements and industrial monuments. The contiguous suburbs north of the city, which have succeeded in remaining outside the City to avoid paying their dues to the place that supports them, are not included. The southern suburbs have been included purely to accommodate the changes in the regional boundaries since the end of the Regions in 1996. Omitted also are the ancient Burgh of Rutherglen, long a Glasgow rival, and Cambuslang – the only areas to have been absorbed and subsequently escaped Glasgow's clutches.

Pivoting around Dechmont and the Cathkins, the Clyde enters Glasgow near Uddingston. Thousands of years ago this was an estuary, which later silted up. The valley climbs fairly steeply to north and south around here, although the rim is only about 30m (98ft) above sea level. The rim of the lower valley shelves down towards the west and both valley faces are densely spotted with drumlins, boulder clay hillocks left by glaciers, some as much as 40m (131ft) high. The lively Renfrewshire White Cart Water crosses Glasgow's south boundary at Netherlee but is soon turned sluggishly west by a barrier of drumlins at Langside, to flow past Pollok towards Paisley. From the north the River Kelvin enters the City at Garscadden, deflected from its former westerly course by the rising Dunbartonshire Kilpatricks, then finds a pinball way down through Maryhill to cascade past the historic Kelvinside mills and enter the Clyde at Partick.

17TH- & 18TH-CENTURY TRADE

The northern lands within the present city boundaries were medieval church property. After the 16th-century Church Reformation, the agricultural land was acquired by some of the former churchmen, like Canon Baillie at Provan Hall and by the former archbishop's tenants, who were city burgesses rather than active farmers. Many had become heritable tenants. At that time there were only two settlements with more than a handful of tenants, Partick with

Above *Kelvin Aqueduct*
Left *Port Dundas from Garnet Hill*

11 and, also in Govan Warde, Meikle Govan itself with 41 tenants. Outwith the church lands, all on the 'Sou-side', were the ancient family seats – the Maxwells of Pollok and Haggs, the Stewarts of Crookston and Castlemilk and the Cathcarts of that Ilk – where only Pollok House remains intact on land once protected by feudal castles. By the late 17th century, prominent lawyers had bought estates and built country houses on them. In the 18th century tobacco merchants paid for improvements to make the River Clyde navigable. Water-powered cotton spinning was introduced in country areas, where mill-owners had to provide housing. Agricultural enclosures led to the Lowland clearances, with population movement into the urban centres and developing industries. Iron mining became established early in the east at Carmyle, then in Lanarkshire; coal mining in the south side at Govanhill; while 18th-century bleachfields were constructed beside waterways near Partick at Pointhouse on the Clyde and at Cathcart, Darnley and Thornliebank, all on the River Cart, or its tributaries on the south side. Canals were built to bring in cheap Lanarkshire coal and other commodities to feed industry and the population, and more industries developed along their banks. The canal terminals of Port Eglinton to the south and the more successful Port Dundas to the north were developed before steam and railways overtook both water power and horse-drawn technology. Wealthy merchants and then manufacturers also bought country estates; by 1795 the city was ringed by dozens of their mansions. Lesser businessmen next built villas within easy reach of their offices. Before 1830 there were 14 villas near the new Greenock turnpike road in the three-quarters of a kilometre (half a mile) between the mansions of Plantation and Cessnock.

Steam power was first applied to cotton spinning in Glasgow at Springfield in 1792. Power weaving sheds did not appear until 1851 at Pollokshaws. Others were built in the East End at Calton, Bridgeton and Dalmarnock and at Dennistoun and Govan. Coal mining was biggest at Shettleston and at Govanhill, an integrated works, where coal went directly to the iron-smelting furnaces. I well remember the fiery skies of Dixon's Blazes – the famously illuminated night sky, seen when the blast furnaces were opened at Dixon's Govanhill Iron Works, on Cathcart Road – seen on a cloudy night from five miles away; much better than the aurora borealis. The biggest works were McFarlane's Saracen Works, Possil; Beardmore's Forge, Parkhead; railway locomotive building, second in importance only to shipbuilding, St Rollox, Springburn and Polmadie; shipbuilding on both sides of the Clyde; and Tennant's alkali and soapworks, Port Dundas.

INTRODUCTION

Lord Provost Sir Daniel Stevenson, speaking at an International Congress in 1900, claimed that Glasgow had taken a foremost place in developing public utilities, with municipal water dating from 1855, gas from 1869, electricity from 1891 and tramways from 1894. *'Nothing short of rank socialism'* was the response of at least one delegate. Gasholders by the M8 at Provan date from 1904, and the tramways water-cooling tower on the hilltop at Pinkston was a landmark for many years, but undoubtedly the most popular survivor today is the Tramway Theatre.

19TH-CENTURY INDUSTRY

The expansion of coal and iron ore mining for the manufacture of steel and to feed heavy industries and chemical works, together with steam power and railways, concentrated workshops into even more urban locations, where property speculators built houses to rent. Labour was needed quickly in vast numbers. Between 1780 and the 1830s Glasgow's population quadrupled from 67,000 to 250,000, still drawn from the Lowland agricultural clearances and from Highland as well as Irish sources. By the 1860s the Glasgow total had risen to half a million and by the 1890s it was 850,000, including the suburban areas. Dwellings were needed on an unprecedented scale. The Scottish tenement was built by landlords in hundreds, even thousands; but not enough! Overcrowding became rife in some areas; with no water mains or sanitation at first, squalor became unavoidable and disease went through in waves. Many working-class tenement houses contained just a room and kitchen, or even the one-room 'single end'. Political reforms throughout the later 19th century encouraged measures to eradicate the slums. 'Ticketing', the noting over a house door of how many were permitted within, was introduced to control the numbers in each dwelling. Police Burghs had already been established in the north at Partick and Maryhill and at Pollokshaws and Govan, south of the river. They collected rates to pay for fresh water and drainage, introduced from the mid-century, along with isolation fever hospitals to beat the epidemics. As residential districts emerged on the south side, Burghs were created during the 1870s at Kinning Park, Crosshill, Pollokshields (West), Govanhill and finally Pollokshields (East).

Pinkston Power Station

RCAHMS

4

RCAHMS

Fairfield Yard, 1890

Food supply markets expanded, with animal lairage for all Scotland at Whiteinch, the meat market at Bellgrove and enormous granaries at Meadowbank. With new docks west of the city centre, Glasgow harbour grew beyond all recognition, providing a total of more than 18 kilometres (11 miles) of deep-water quayside by 1930 and more than 19 kilometres (12 miles) by 1962.

20TH-CENTURY CONTRACTION

The rapacious city had been engulfing its surroundings since the 1830s, swallowing up many independent burghs, frequently against their wishes. Govan, not entirely without reason, even believed it should have swallowed Glasgow. But the industrial explosion had fizzled out by the First World War and even coal was worked out by 1920. The population of the 'Second City of Empire' had topped the one million mark and the city boundary now enclosed nearly 78 square kilometres (30 square miles), more than ten times the size of the Royalty of 1636. Heavy industry had seen its day in Glasgow and these industries decayed during another half century of subsidised death-throes, taking with them most of their buildings and the ships.

Before the First World War the City was concerned with the eradication of slum dwellings, had rehoused the population from 2,500 demolished slum buildings and had labelled 16,000 as unfit for habitation, but the private sector was still expected to meet any housing shortage. The 20th century had already seen rent control kill any profit for the

The sound of the Clyde is that of a thousand hammers echoing in the empty belly of a hull; the fiendish chatter of electric riveters and a sudden squeal of metal tortured in the service of the seas. 'This is wonderful,' *I tell Jock, 'I thought the Clyde was idle!' 'It isna wonderful,' says Jock. 'It isna as guid as it looks!' He explains to me that many a ship in these days is built at cost price just to keep the yards open.*
H V Morton, *In Search of Scotland,* 1929

Old and new in Hutchesontown

In 1951, the Depute Town Clerk stated that '40 years ago there were many empty houses but few abandoned by their owners, today there are no empty houses but many are abandoned.'

The High Street, Glasgow Garden Festival

private landlord, so ending tenement building. To defuse social unrest, the Westminster government's Housing Act of 1919 required for the first time that local authorities provide municipal housing for working people. In 1935, rates were allowed to subsidise council house rents, causing the breakdown of the factoring system. The resulting lack of maintenance was followed by massive deterioration of private rented tenements.

From the 1920s the public sector assumed responsibility for social housing, to remove the vast shortage only properly identified late in the decade, as well as replacing slums with fit houses. In 1945 the City Engineer, Robert Bruce, produced a Plan envisaging more than 300,000 new houses and the demolition of 175,000 overcrowded ones, in vast clearance areas. This was scrapped when the Clyde Valley Regional Plan recommended the creation of New Towns beyond a green belt surrounding the city. Glasgow Corporation then experienced an intense rivalry. The new Town Planning Committee, created under 1947 Town Planning legislation, wanted to confine house building, often in multistorey blocks, to the 29 CDAs (Comprehensive Development Areas). It also recommended the Overspill of a quarter of a million people to other towns during the four years required to clear and build new housing in the CDAs. Meanwhile the Housing Committee built the huge peripheral schemes in the proposed green belt.

Popular protest at blanket demolitions brought better control, Listed Buildings in the 1960s and Conservation Areas in 1974. Local Government reorganisation in 1975 saw the start of the refurbishment of tenements and the re-cladding of high rise blocks, but there was little new housing. By the later 1970s, there was a new wave of low-rise brick-built houses, both public and private, to be succeeded by quasi-public Housing Associations. By 1979 the State Housing Programme had achieved its main objectives – the end of overcrowding and the eradication of slums. Overspill was stopped and rehabilitation of the peripheral schemes began in 1980. The 1988 Glasgow Garden Festival, followed by the 1990 European City of Culture and the 1999 European City of Architecture and Design, have become symbols of the regeneration of the City.

HOW TO USE THIS GUIDE
Organisation of the Guide
The territory covered extends from the outer
limits of the companion *Central Glasgow*
guide to the current City boundary, plus East
Renfrewshire to Eaglesham and Newton Mearns.
The guide has been arranged around the major
roads radiating from the centre, commencing
north of the Clyde with Dumbarton Road
and working clockwise to London Road, then
crossing the river to Carmunnock Road and
continuing clockwise to Govan Road. The 13
routes take us through the former independent
Burghs, the grand West End and 'Sou-side'
villas, to the rural settings of the Kelvin Valley
and the Forth & Clyde Canal, and beyond to the
country seats and to the villages of Carmunnock
and Eaglesham.

The companion guide to *Central
Glasgow* by Charles McKean, David
Walker and Frank A Walker (Rutland
Press, 1999).

Text Arrangement
Entries for principal buildings follow the
sequence of name (or number), address, date
and architect (if known). Lesser buildings are
contained within paragraphs. A few demolished
buildings and unrealised projects are included.
In general the dates given are those of the design
(if known) or of the beginning of construction (if
not). Text in the small column is illustrative of
less architectural aspects of the area.

Space has permitted the inclusion of only
about two-thirds of the significant buildings
in the area and I have dropped those that are
inaccessible, or concealed from public places,
plus many where the architect is unknown and
building type is duplicated many times.

Map References
The few numbers on the outline maps on pages
236–239 are for guidance only and refer to the
sequence in the text, not the pages.

Access
Although some of the buildings described are
public and easily accessible, many are private.
Readers are requested to respect that privacy.

SPONSORS
This volume would not have been possible
without the generous support of the Russell
Trust, the Landmark Trust and the Heritage
Lottery Fund through the Royal Commission of
Ancient Historical Monuments of Scotland and
the Recording Your Heritage Online Project.

Anthony Inglis and his brother John started building steam engines for ships, including the *Shenandoah,* a US Civil War coastal raider, named after the famous river. They moved to Pointhouse in 1862, building passenger ships for the Far East and South America. Their successor Dr John Inglis started building yachts, notably for the Khedive of Egypt and the Royal Yacht *Alexandra* for King Edward VII. A Board member of the North British Railway, he built four Clyde Steamers, including the first *Waverley*, lost on Royal Navy service in 1940. Harland & Wolff bought the yard in 1919.

DUMBARTON ROAD
PARTICK

The Archbishop had a summer palace at Partick, where there was a small group of church tenants in the 16th century. By the 18th century the palace was gone, but the Younger and Cumming families still represented the 'Old Rentallers'. The Youngers had owned the Bishop's Orchard, the Brewlands and part of the Mill lands during the 17th century and the rest of the Mills had become the property of the Baxters' Guild. In 1611 Partick Castle was built for George Hutcheson by the mason William Miller, whose accounts survive to this day (see *Central Glasgow* Guide). Close to the Crawford bridge that replaced the old ford across the Kelvin in 1611, on the ancient route from Glasgow to Dumbarton, the 18th-century village of Partick stretched from the Cross to the River Clyde. There was another ford here across the shallow Clyde to Govan, the biggest settlement on the Archbishop's lands. The Clyde then spread much farther north than today's channel.

Print and dye works were begun about 1800, followed by power-loom weaving. In the 1840s, shipyards arrived: Pointhouse (later to become A & J Inglis) in 1842 at the Printfield site on the east bank of the Kelvin, followed by the Meadowside yard of Tod & McGregor in 1845 on the west bank. The resulting employment required tenements to house the labourers as well as the middle-class clerks and shopkeepers. Dumbarton Road was the class divide between them: on the workers' south side coal cost 'half a crown' a bag but, on the middle-class north side it cost 'five bob'. Partick had a population of 5,000 when it became a Burgh in 1852. When Glasgow swallowed the Burgh 50 years later, its population had expanded to 70,000.

Patrick Sewage Pumping Station

Sam Small

Partick Sewage Pumping Station, 33–35 Dumbarton Road, 1904, Alexander Beith (A B) McDonald Richly carved red sandstone shell, hygienic white-glazed brick within. Glasgow was responsible for draining 104 square kilometres (40 square miles) around the city.

Willow View Court, 31–45 Peel Street, *c.*1992, Michael & Sue Thornley Lively brick and blockwork terraced housing, in scale with the residential surroundings

overlooking the West of Scotland Cricket
Ground. Modelled façade, low projecting
bay windows and some dormers breaking
the main parapet line add up to a distinctive
composition. Saltire Society Commendation,
1994 (colour page 34).

Willow View Court

Partick Burgh Halls, 3–9 Burgh Hall Street,
1872, William Leiper
Richly carved white sandstone in lively French
style. Steep mansard roof and later richly carved
timber bell tower, on two-storey galleried
main hall, well used by the public, with open
truss roof. Three John Mossman sculpted relief
panels, 'Misericordia', 'Justicia' and 'Veritas'
above the ground-floor windows. A plainer
three-storey east wing contains the Lesser Hall
above Offices. Original stained-glass windows,
including geometrical internal screen and
Burgh Coat of Arms, opulent marbled staircase,
now much better seen after remodelling and
refurbishment, 2004, ZM Architecture.

Partick Burgh Halls

Above 271–285 Dumbarton Road
Right Partick Police Court (now the Centre for Sensorily Deprived)

Partick Burgh Hall, 1853, unexecuted design by Charles Wilson. Only a single-storey Police Court building was authorised. The Police Commissioners did not construct the Burgh Halls for another 20 years, after Wilson had died and when there was more civic pride.

Right 385–405 Dumbarton Road

Frank Burnet (1846–1923) trained in the City Architect's office, working on tenement design for the City Improvement Trust. As a developer, he designed and also built many tenements and pubs around the city. His partner **William James Boston** (1861–1937) specialised in commercial and industrial projects, while **James Carruthers** (1872–1952), who trained in-house, designed most of the firm's adventurous works, including their best offices at 140–2 St Vincent Street and the St George's Mansions for the Police Board (see *Central Glasgow Guide*).

360–392 Dumbarton Road, former Hamilton Place, *c*.1860
Extremely long white sandstone tenement over ground-floor shops. Decent pattern book design but end pavilions provide inadequate punctuation. **Nos 271–285**, *c*.1905, Campbell Douglas & Paterson, tall red sandstone tenement, in the simplified and elongated baroque of the Glasgow Style.

Centre for Sensorily Deprived, 47 Anderson Street, 1853, Charles Wilson
Built as Partick Police Court. Crisp stone details in Wilson's formal classical style. The least expensive option, chosen by the parsimonious first Police Commissioners, determined to keep down the rates. Fussier first floor added 1873, John Smellie, builder and part-time Burgh Surveyor. The slick new materials of extension, 2000, Glasgow City Council, sit well alongside.

383–405 Dumbarton Road, 1903,
Frank Burnet & Boston
Red sandstone tenement on three streets. Busy with turrets and balconies at top floor, reminiscent of their St George's Mansions (see *Central Glasgow* Guide).

Sandy Road Health Centre, 2003, Gareth Hoskins
Two-storey zinc-clad box, above a fully glazed
ground floor, shielding a larger four-storey
oak-clad box; windows have oak slats to protect
against solar gain.

Above *Sandy Road Health Centre*
Below *Partick Fire Station*

Partick Fire Station, 120–124 Beith Street, 1906,
James Miller
Red brick with stone dressings, then the fashion
in London. Eighteen dwellings, arcaded engine
house entrance arches, control room and offices,
relief sculpture on gable, hose-drying campanile
behind. Conversion to 23 flats, 1988, Simister
Monaghan McKinney (colour page 35).

482–492 Dumbarton Road, former Downie
Place, *c.*1860
White ashlar tenement over ground-floor shops.
Encrusted with window cornice details. Named
after the Downie sisters, wives of retailers Wylie
& Lochhead, the developers, and perhaps by
William Lochhead who was architect as well as
cabinetmaker.

Left *Crathie Drive Hostel*

Crathie Drive, 1946, Francis C Scott
Multistorey hostel for single women, 88 flats in
eight-storey gallery access building.

DOWANHILL SOUTH
When development started on Dowanhill estate
in 1853 the southern end, entirely tenements,
was already within Partick Burgh (for Dowanhill
north, see p. 39).

St Peter's RC Church & Presbytery, 46–50
Hyndland Street, 1898, Peter Paul Pugin
Substantial gothic complex in red sandstone,
with large slate roof.

Francis C Scott was Chief Architect,
Glasgow Corporation Housing
Department in the mid-1940s under
Director Ronald Bradbury, also an
architect. He was passed over in 1948,
when Bradbury left and Archibald
George Jury, later City Architect, was
appointed Director of Housing. Scott
was soon headhunted by Sir Patrick
Dolan, ex-Glasgow Lord Provost and
now Chairman of the New Town, to
become the second Chief Architect
& Planning Officer of East Kilbride
Development Corporation. Donald
Reay, the first Chief Architect had left
when his masterplan was rejected in
favour of one prepared by the Scottish
Office in 1950.

Lawerence Place & Elgin Place

Partick East Church of Scotland, 20 Lawrence Street, 1897, John Bennie (J B) Wilson
Scottish gothic, red sandstone, octagonal stairtower links hall & vestry.

Former **Lawrence Place & Elgin Place**, 34–52 Lawrence Street, 45–49 Dowanhill Street, 29–47 Havelock Street, Hyndland Street, 1858, McCraw & Kay, builders
White stone classical tenements, alternate main door and close entrances. The church architect and academic Peter Macgregor Chalmers lived here. **Foremount Gardens**, 65–73 Highburgh Road, 1899, Peter Macgregor Chalmers. Incomplete terrace of red sandstone houses with half-timber Tudor gables. The undeveloped land became gardens for the adjoining church (colour page 33).

1**Cottier Theatre**, 93 Hyndland Street, 1865, William Leiper
Former Dowanhill Church and Halls, winner in competition, beating John Honeyman, until then the recognised United Presbyterian church architect. Leiper had trained with Boucher & Cousland, then gained experience in several offices, before entering a partnership in 1864 with Robert Grieve Melvin. Melvin had inherited James Smith's office and they now completed the latter's design for Stirling's Library (see *Central Glasgow* Guide). Soon after his competition

Cottier Theatre

success, Leiper split with Melvin to set up his own practice. Dowanhill, superbly designed in elongated gothic, is a typical Normandy church. With its fine tall steeple and spire, the church dominates the skyline from both Dumbarton Road and Byres Road. Inside is a three-sided gallery on cast-iron columns under a hammerbeam roof. Daniel Cottier stained glass and fragments of stencilled interior wall decorations. Converted to theatre, late 1980s, Ian Begg. Restored from 1997, Four Acres Charitable Trust, with drawings by Nicholas Groves-Raines. The Trust, with Lottery funding, is progressing plans to open a Cottier Study and Exhibition Centre (colour page 33).

PARTICKHILL

To the west of the estate and up to the top of the very steep hill were posh villas of city merchants and yard owners, later joined on the east side by middle-class terraced houses and some grander tenements. These tall red sandstone tenements near the hilltop were eventually completed by Duncanson & Henderson, measurers, better known for their development at Hyndland.

St Kentigern's Hostel, 10 Partickhill Road, 1843
Former Wellpark House, a large two-storey Jacobean white sandstone double villa. Decorated gables to main front. This was the first house to be built on Hillside after Russell's son feued the land.

28–30 and 2–8 North Gardner Street, 1905, Thomas Baird
Red sandstone tenement. Second-floor balcony and massive keystones emphasize central entrance to large flats. Subtle Glasgow Style details and full-height bay windows as stop-ends at Partickhill Road.

Much of Partick was held by the Craig family before the Reformation and through the 17th century. By the 1780s John Purdon, a weaver at Bridgend of Partick, was the feuar of Partickhill. In 1797 the writer James Robb acquired most of the estate and built a villa, 'Hillhead', now 64 Partickhill Road. When he died in 1815, his estate was bought by the merchant James Hamilton of Mavisbank, whose grandson, William Hamilton, a cotton manufacturer, laid out this the largest Partickhill estate for building in 1841. The Purdon family sold three smaller pieces of Partickhill after 1797: Hillside was bought in 1809 by James Russell, a papermaker at Dalsholm; Muirpark, the smallest, in 1811 by Thomas Muir, whose trustees sold to developer John Gardner, a Partick butcher; and finally Stewartville, bought in 1812 by John Campbell, a retired army captain. This last portion was eventually acquired in 1851 by the engineer James Aitken, naming the estate from his wife's maiden name of Stewart.

William Russell's Hillside House, demolished as recently as 1999, was reputedly one of three houses of the same design, the other two being Dowanhill House, c.1810 for James Buchanan and the third on the south side of Dumbarton Road, west of Balshagray Avenue. Sadly all three are lost without trace.

Left *Corner North Gardner Street & Partickhill Road*
Bottom *St Kentigern's Hostel*

13

51–59 Partickhill Road, former Hawarden Terrace, *c.*1888, possibly Robert Turnbull
Curved line of five terraced houses, good interiors with marble and Delft fireplaces and carved timber stair at No 59. **Partickhill Court** (former Woodlands), **No 52**, *c.*1856. Subdivided villa with full-height semicircular bay window.

Woodbank & Carriage House Arch

2 **Woodbank, 56 Partickhill Road**, *c.*1841, John Baird I
Elegant classical white sandstone country house with prominent Ionic columned porch and small wings guarded by stone lions. Behind a screen wall, entered through an arch surmounted by a sculpted eagle, is a stable yard and carriage house with a pigeon loft; in front, a simple grassed garden. Beyond the vestibule, a stone stair and cast-iron balustrade lead up from the hall decorated with elaborate coffered and corniced ceilings and a Corinthian columned screen.

71 Partickhill Road, *c.*1885
Sandstone two-storey villa, with attic billiard room, all converted to flats. The complete absence of carved stone detailing makes it surprisingly modern-looking. **No 74**, *c.*1870. Round-arched, two-storey stone villa, painted front. Delicate detailing and bay window.

74 Partickhill Road

5–11 Turnberry Road, 1874, probably Hugh Barclay
Four bold classical terraced houses, bay windows from basement to first floor. Cast-iron parapet. **Nos 13–15**, 1874, Hugh Barclay. Large white sandstone double villa.

1–37 Banavie Road (former Annfield Terrace), 1868. 39 two-storey terraced houses, punctuated by slightly advanced two-house central and end pavilions.

72 Peel Street, *c.*1860
Plain detached villa with trim cast-iron veranda and ground-floor bay window. **Nos 53–63** (former Hamilton Terrace West), 1875, Hugh & David Barclay. Three-storey tenement, with basement and prominent attic.

BROOMHILL
Broomhill Mansion was purchased in 1875 to become a Home for Incurables, then a suburb was developed on the gently undulating land to the north of Victoria Park, from 1890. Victoria Park had been formed by Partick Burgh to commemorate Queen Victoria's Golden Jubilee in 1887 when the unique Fossil Grove of 350-million-year-old fossilised tree stumps was discovered. The Clyde Tunnel and Clydeside Expressway have cleared the tenements to the south.

Balshagray Church, Broomhill Cross, 230 Broomhill Drive, 1907, Stewart & Paterson Fashionable Arts & Crafts gothic in red sandstone, Art Nouveau interior panelling. Stained glass, 1950, Sadie McLellan, illustrating Scottish industry.

Broomhill Trinity Congregational Church, 20 Victoria Park Gardens South, 1907, John James (J J) Burnet
Gothic, red rubble, entrance through large porch at base of squat tower.

6–10 Broomhill Gardens, *c.*1888
Curved terrace of five part-painted sandstone houses, splayed bay windows.

206–216 Broomhill Drive, *c.*1891
Terraced houses, with bracketed cornice as first-floor cill band. **Inverclyde Gardens, Nos 137–159**, *c.*1905, William McNicol (W M) Whyte. Rare Scots Baronial tenement in white sandstone.

42–56 Balshagray Drive, 2 Marlborough Avenue, *c.*1900, John Burnet & Son
Eight smart red sandstone terraced houses.

Detail of Inverclyde Gardens

Sam Small

Whiteinch Public Library

WHITEINCH

An island until the 18th-century river improvements created Glasgow harbour and drowned the ancient Clyde fords. Dredged material was deposited on the island now linked to the north bank. Barclay Curle's 1855 Clydeholm shipyard, employing 1,000, prompted more tenement building. Meadowside granaries were built in 1912 by the Clyde Port Authority and extended in the 1930s but, like the yards, the shipping has all but gone and the granaries are demolished.

Whiteinch Public Library, 14 Victoria Park Drive South, 1923, Thomas Gilchrist Gilmour of Glasgow Office of Public Works
Quietly dignified library with coat of arms over entrance.

19–29 Squire Street and **69 Northinch Street**, 1912, Peter Macgregor Chalmers
Built as Whiteinch Jordanvale Parish Church. One of Chalmers' studious revivals of the Romanesque, in red sandstone. Inconspicuously converted to residential use, 2000.

Right North British Diesel Engine Works
Below Titan Crane

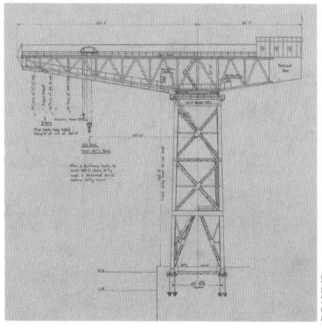

3 **North British Diesel Engine Works**, 739 South Street, 1913, Karl Bernardt, executed by John Galt
Steel-framed brick and glass building modelled on AEG turbine factory, Berlin by Peter Behrens on which the German architect-engineer Bernardt had also worked. Tall main workshop fronting river, with flattened mansard roof. Gable ends originally glazed. Large central aisle with east gallery, two layers of travelling cranes. On quayside, Titan Crane, 1920, Sir William Arrol. Original for the 'Meccano' model.

Glasgow Harbour

4 *'GLASGOW HARBOUR' PROJECT*

When the shipyards took over the riverbank
in the mid-19th century, to be followed by
the Meadowside Granaries and the animal
lairage, Partick and Whiteinch lost their Clyde
frontage. One hundred and fifty years later the
derelict banks, even more isolated by the 1960s
Expressway, are undergoing a renaissance.
The **Masterplan**, 2004, Kohn Pedersen Fox,
is a visionary linear mixed development of
business, leisure and residences on 49 hectares
(120 acres) of derelict land. A walkway is being
built along the full length of the river from the
city centre and a new rapid transit railway is to
be constructed for ease of access, linking the area
with the city centre. In addition the Expressway
is being modified to break up the barrier it has
been for nearly 50 years. **Phase One Housing**
is like a mini-Manhattan, an exciting big-city-
scale new town; but, like the post-war new
towns, it consists only of houses, and lacks other
facilities. **East Section**, 2003, RMJM (Glasgow).
Two parallel high-quality blocks of 10 and 13
storeys with opposed stepped terraced roof
profiles. **Centre Section**, 2003, Cooper Cromar.
Five dramatic blocks, seven to 19 storeys high,
containing 321 flats built around a square.
West Section, *c*.2004, RMJM (Edinburgh).
Parallel blocks. **Business and Leisure Facilities**,
including a new Museum of Transport by Zaha
Hadid, are to be built to the east across the River
Kelvin. **Phase Two Housing**, 2004, Gordon
Murray & Alan Dunlop. Located to the west of
the First Phase, on the site of the Meadowside
granaries, this development of some 770
apartments will comprise five 14- to 22-storey
towers and several seven-storey slabs to the
north.

Scotstoun House (demolished)

The Oswald family accumulated great wealth from the Virginia Tobacco trade. Glasgow was well situated to make two return sailings per annum, compared to the single trip possible from Bristol or London. The route to the north of Ireland was also much safer during the French wars. When the trade died in the American War of Independence, the Oswalds diversified into West Indian sugar. Already wine importers, they had invested in the Glasgow bottleworks in the 1740s. West Indies merchants James and Alexander Oswald were also partners in the Linwood Cotton Company at Paisley.

Above *Westercraigs Home for Girls*
Below *Victoria Park Gates*

SCOTSTOUN

The estate, with its early 18th-century mansion, was acquired from the Walkinshaw family by the Oswalds, who extended the Mansion, 1825, David Hamilton. Although Charles Connell's shipyard was started in 1861, the southern end of the Scotstoun estate was not developed for terraced housing until 1886. Yarrow's shipyard had relocated to the Clyde in 1906 because of high rates and labour costs at their former yard on the Thames, but the north of Scotstoun was still undeveloped when Glasgow Corporation bought the remainder in the 1920s to build a low-density suburban estate. The mansion survived in a small park until multistorey flats were built in the 1960s. Today Scotstoun is largely composed of an early 20th-century housing scheme of pleasant low-rise tenement houses.

Whiteinch Homes, 19 Westland Drive, *c.*1895
Modelled on English almshouses and built, in Scots Renaissance style, for the Jane Allan Trust to house elderly employees of Allan Shipping Line, it is now owned by a Housing Association. **Westercraigs Home for Girls, No 21**, 1891, Stewart Henbest Capper. A long low 17th-century Scottish orphanage, with crowstep gables, all in red sandstone. One of Capper's few buildings in Scotland, and quite unlike his narrow and lofty addition to Ramsay Garden, at the top of Edinburgh's Old Town.

Victoria Park Gates, Victoria Park Drive North, 1887, Saracen Foundry
Presented by Ladies of Partick to commemorate Queen Victoria's Golden Jubilee. Four cast-iron gatepiers with Queen Victoria medallions inset on outer and coats of arms on inner piers.

Scotstoun Leisure Centre, Danes Drive, *c.*1995, Glasgow City Architect
Popular swimming pool and integrated leisure facility, 1930s retro-style (colour page 35).

Dunronald, 55 Crescent Road, 1906
Yellow brick villa with Olde English mixture of Arts & Crafts features. One two-storey half-timbered wing contrasts with dormer windows on a wide-eaved purple slate roof above single-storey Elizabethan glazing at the other. Fine interiors.

JORDANHILL

The wide flat lands of Jordanhill belonged to the Crawfords of Kilbirnie in the 15th century. They first built a mansion in 1562. Captain Thomas was a supporter of Lord Darnley, husband of Mary, Queen of Scots; winning military successes after Darnley's murder, he became Provost of Glasgow. The family sold the estate to the tobacco merchant and banker Alexander Houston in 1750. His son rebuilt the mansion in 1782 and it was sold on in 1800 to the West Indies merchant and Glasgow Dean of Guild Archibald Smith. Smith altered and extended the house in 1824. The Smith family sold the estate for a Teacher Training College in 1912; the plain mansion survived until at least the 1960s but was subsequently demolished.

146 Southbrae Drive

Sherwood and **Ainsley, 583** and **585 Anniesland Road**, 1891. Half timbered villas with green slate roofs. **Southbrae Drive, No 146**, *c.*1890, style of Norman Shaw. Even better Arts & Crafts villa, half-timbered, multi-paned casement windows.

House for University Principal

5 **Principal's House**, Strathclyde University, Jordanhill Campus, 1997, McNeish Design Partnership
Competition winner for formal residence and hospitality facility. Simple white pavilion, double-height drum public space and private rooms in rectangular rear wing, reminiscent of Basil Spence's Gribloch but without the 'Hollywood Regency'. (See *Stirling and the Trossachs* Guide.)

Jordanhill College of Education, 76 Southbrae Drive, 1913, H & D Barclay
Another competition winner. Symmetrical courtyard-plan college, European stylistic origins with taller central and end pavilions.

Teacher Training Colleges remained under Church control until 1905, more than 40 years after the schools were taken over by locally elected School Boards. The 1872 Education (Scotland) Act made elementary education compulsory for 5- to 13-year-olds. All teachers had to be certificated, requiring at least an ordinary Arts MA, followed by a year at a Teacher Training College. Janetta Bowie, a 1920s Jordanhill trainee first experiencing teaching practice, found a post-World War I mature student, now qualified, successfully using his revolver to command class attention. She herself later discovered, apart from the register, only two things on her desk: the Bible and a strap.

Demonstration School

Jordanhill School, 45 Chamberlain Road, 1913,
Honeyman Keppie & Mackintosh
Former Training College Demonstration School.
New type of institutional symmetry, with central
administration block and rear hall, plus long
corridor access wings, for a new Education
Authority. Mackintosh's competition-winning
design was not completed and the plan was
enclosed in a disappointingly institutional
Beaux-Arts stone shell by Graham Henderson,
chief draughtsman and later a partner in the
firm of Keppie & Henderson. There are no
lightening Mackintosh touches. Mackintosh
was sacked from his partnership at this time
because his sketches for the entire Jordanhill
complex were on tracing paper and contained
many minor faults. He was accused of being a
drunk and a bad timekeeper; in reality he was
suffering a clinical depression brought about
by a sharp decline in the volume of business.
The rift may also have been partly because he
had not married Keppie's sister, with whom
there had been a longstanding friendship; she
was infatuated with him, but he had married
Margaret Macdonald in 1900.

Jordanhill Parish Church, 28 Woodend Drive,
1904, James Miller
Perpendicular gothic with flamboyant tracery,
squat bell tower, all red sandstone. Five-aisle
church unusually aligned south-north. Gallery
to south, arcade between nave and chancel, open
hammerbeam roof.

All Saints Episcopal Church, 10 Woodend
Drive, 1904, James Chalmers
Unexciting Romanesque outside, tower not
built. Rich interiors: Lorimer interior screen
and War Memorial; stained glass including
Alexander George Thomson memorial window
by Chalmers.

GREAT WESTERN ROAD
KELVINSIDE

Originally a fifth of the Ruchill estate, one of the largest bought at the Reformation by the former tenants of the Glasgow bishop's Barony, this area was inherited in 1743 by Grizel Peadie who named it Bankhead. (See also pp. 69–70 for Ruchill.) It was bought in 1750 by tobacco lord Thomas Dunmore, who built a new mansion and changed the name again to Kelvinside. The estate changed hands a few more times before it was purchased in 1839 by lawyer Mathew Montgomerie, who developed it with John Park Fleming and James Beaumont Neilson, calling it Queenstown. Land was sold for the relocated Botanic Gardens, half of the site for the Glasgow Observatory on the top of Dowanhill and plots for the first four Great Western Road terraces: their own Windsor, now Kirklee Terrace on the north and Kew, Grosvenor and Belhaven Terraces on the south. The original estate plan was designed by Decimus Burton but, to be more commercial, was later modified by James Salmon Sr.

In 1868 the Victoria Park Feuing Company acquired nearly 14 hectares (35 acres) of Kelvinside estate to the east of Horselethill, and James Whitelaw Anderson, who developed the Westbourne Gardens area, purchased 6.5 hectares (16.5 acres). Montgomery died in the same year, the Kelvinside management passing to his partner's son James Brown Montgomerie Fleming, who now sold four much larger plots: John Ewing Walker bought North Kelvinside in 1868 (see p. 57); James Buchanan Mirrlees bought 6 hectares (14 acres) in 1869 for a villa, 'Redlands', later converted to a hospital and the surroundings developed for terraced houses after 1900; in 1873, about 3 hectares (seven acres) at Kirklee Road were acquired by writer Thomas J Smellie and builder Andrew Goodall, who built 17 houses there; and in the same year, to the west of Redlands and Cleveden Road, 4.5 hectares (11 acres) were bought by ironmaster Thomas Russell, who built the large villas fronting Great Western Road.

Thereafter there were few sales, including the site for Kelvinside Academy. Land was also sold for industrial use and working-class tenements in Maryhill. Cleveden Drive and other areas to the west were developed about the turn of the century, while Kelvindale, further west, was not developed until after the First World War. West

The Great Western Road, which leads west from the North Woodside estate, was laid out after an Act of Parliament in 1836 and was completed to the city boundary about a century later. Keeping the full city width of 18m (60ft), it runs in a straight line as far as Anniesland, where it met the road from Renfrew at the junction with the route from Partick leading north to the canal and beyond. Leaving Central Glasgow halfway up the slope of the north bank of the Clyde Valley, the road climbs to a summit at Gartnavel, where there is a distant view to the Kilpatrick Hills. The road was promoted by owners of the lands adjoining the route and played a large part in opening up the West End estates.

Kelvinside House (demolished)

James Beaumont Neilson (1792–1865) became the new Glasgow Gas Light Company's Engineer in 1817 at the age of 25. He devised the bat's-wing burner, improving illumination. Experiments at Clyde Ironworks led to his 1828 patent for the 'hot blast' smelting process. Coal consumption was reduced by 50 per cent and Lanarkshire's blackband ironstone became commercially viable. His brother-in-law Mathew Montgomery, having bought the estate, set up the Kelvinside Estate Company, with himself, his law partner John Park Fleming and Neilson as the three partners, to develop Kelvinside. Approaching 60, Neilson sold his interest to his partners and bought the Queenshill estate near Castle Douglas in 1852. He retained his city house and four years later he had started the Lancefield Forge with Alexander Fulton.

of Hyndland Road, Devonshire Gardens and Terrace were built in the 1870s and 1880s, while the remainder of Hughenden was laid out about 1900.

NORTH OF GREAT WESTERN ROAD

Churchills, Kirklee Road, 2001, Zoo Architects
Two maisonettes above a shop, replacing an earlier Post Office intrusion, make a colourful contrast with the Victorian surroundings.

2 Kirklee Road and **15 Kirklee Terrace**, mid-19th century
Large Victorian villa on steep corner site, the Baronial tower with wrought-iron and glass porch added by J J Burnet about 1900, as was the billiard room. The whole concept is a light relief from the classical terraces on the main road. Art Nouveau fireplaces, and other interior details, in the style of Norman Shaw.

1–14 Kirklee Terrace

6 **1–14 Kirklee Terrace**, 1845, Charles Wilson
This magnificent Roman Renaissance palazzo, sitting high above the main road, is one of the grandest terraces in the city, rivalling in scale and position Wilson's own Park Circus of 1855 (see *Central Glasgow* Guide). Tall centre and end bays, lower links set back. Heavy rustic ground-floor details, corbels support individual first-floor balustraded balconies. Elaborate surrounds to all upper windows (colour page 36).

1 Redlands Road & 3 Kirklee Road

7 **3 Kirklee Road** and **1 Redlands Road**, *c.*1902, John Archibald Campbell
Quiet Scots Renaissance asymmetrical double villa, in red sandstone with swept eaves and central pilastered doorway. A talented pupil, like his partner J J Burnet, Campbell trained in the Beaux-Arts style at Atelier Pascal in Paris.

The partnership was dissolved in 1897. While his 1901 Todhill is Arts & Crafts (see p. 170), his 1902 masterpiece at 163 Hope Street is more vigorously renaissance (see *Central Glasgow Guide*).

7–23 Kirklee Road and **2 Redlands Road**, 1900, John Archibald Campbell
A more lively group of four symmetrical pairs of Scots Renaissance terraced houses, flanked by taller gabled end houses, each with corbelled turret. Octagonal bellcast dome at 23 and cone at 2 Redlands Road. First-floor balcony between high bay windows in central range. Details similar to adjoining double villa.

23 Kirklee Road

Mirrlees Drive
3–13 Mirrlees Drive, *c.*1906, John Archibald Campbell, Scots Renaissance terrace of six paired houses. **Nos 15–19**, same date and architect, three more Scots Renaissance terraced houses similar but smaller than his Kirklee Road houses. Good interior wood panelling and chimneypieces at No 15. **5–9 Redlands Road**, 1909, John Smellie, terraced houses, cast-iron balustrade on corbelled first-floor balcony. **2 Mirrlees Drive** (former 11 Bellshaugh Road), *c.*1902, Thomas Smellie. Scots Renaissance end-terrace house, now part of Kelvinside Academy. Bay window parapets break eaves line. **8–12 Kirklee Quadrant**, *c.*1896, Alexander Petrie. Red ashlar tenements on curved plan, main door and close entries. Finer detail at Nos 10–12, good cast-iron railings. **1–7 Kirklee Gardens**, 1877, James Thomson. Unfinished classical terraced houses, projecting two-house end pavilion, cast-iron lamp standards and railings.

8–12 Kirklee Quad

1–7 Kirklee Gardens

After the Glasgow School Board purchased old Glasgow Academy in Elmbank Street, a group of prominent lawyers, businessmen and bankers bought land in 1877 from the Kelvinside Estate Company to establish Kelvinside Academy, a school to supply education of the highest class to the growing West End suburbs. James Brown Montgomerie Fleming, owner of the Kelvinside estate, James Buchanan Mirrlees of Redlands and James Marshall of the Saracen Foundry were founding directors of the Academy Company. The new Glasgow Academy was built at Kelvinbridge and, when Hillhead School was opened soon after by Govan School Board, Kelvinside Academy suffered financial problems until the 1890s railways and the subway could attract pupils from a wider area.

Kelvinside Academy

Kirklee Bridge

8 **Kelvinside Academy**, 20 Bellshaugh Road, 1877, James Sellars
Dignified Greek Ionic temple over plain entrance podium, with severe wings and taller end pavilions (colour page 36). An early work by an eclectic architect, later using any style, Sellars was by temperament a classicist. Cast-iron lamp standards, decorated with entwined bay leaves, flank the entrance. Austere interior, hall behind the elevated entrance and between classrooms. Hugh Fraser Library, 1989, a quiet timber-clad room.

Kirklee Bridge, spanning the River Kelvin gorge from Kirklee Road to Clouston Street, 1899, Charles Forman, of Forman & McCall
Classical, inspired by Piranesi, three-arched, red sandstone with polished granite Ionic columns and balustrade.

1–6 Redlands Terrace, *c.*1925, McKellar & Gunn
Rock-faced renaissance terraced houses, sitting high and enjoying a good view across the main road to Great Western Terrace.

Lancaster Crescent
A curious mixture of villa styles, linked into an
unlikely terrace. **No 1**, 1898, Henry Higgins.
Villa, set obliquely to rest of crescent, linked to
No 2, figured pilasters at central entrance. **No 2**,
*c.*1898, James Miller. Villa linked to Nos 1 and
3. Doric porch, leaded glass fanlight and door.
Stained-glass stair window, Oscar Paterson.
Nos 3–7, *c.*1898, James Lymburn Cowan and
Nos 8–9, 1907, John Campbell McKellar, plainer
curved terraced houses, Corinthian pilastered
doors.

Above *1 Lancaster Crescent*
Below *Redlands House*

Redlands House, 11 Lancaster Crescent, *c.*1871,
James Boucher
Luxurious Italianate villa, for James Buchanan
Mirrlees. A palace, in its own huge grounds,
for another ironmaster. Conversion to hospital,
Roman Doric porch and rear extension, *c.*1924,
James Salmon.

Left *8–9 Lowther Terrace*
Below *10 Lowther Terrace*

9 **8–10 Lowther Terrace**
Three grand Edwardian houses forming an
irregular ashlar terrace, linked as a Church of
Scotland Home, 1948, Noad & Wallace. **No 8**,
1904, James Miller. Jacobean Renaissance,
simple interior. **No 9**, 1904, Sydney Mitchell.
Scots Renaissance mid-terrace polished ashlar
house. Bay windows linked by projecting first-
floor balcony. Second-floor Jacobean dormers
break roofline. Good plasterwork and first-floor
library. **No 10**, 1900, James Miller. Renaissance,
for J Cargill. Dutch Renaissance gable and attic.
Ionic features at second-floor level. Delicate cast-
iron balustraded balcony over doorway. Good
Art Nouveau railings and second-floor balcony
on west flank. Excellent interiors with Oscar
Paterson stained-glass staircase window.

Right 8 Cleveden Road
Below 5 Cleveden Road

Cleveden Road
No 4–8, *c.*1893. Symmetrical Jacobean semidetached villa, tall chimneystacks, good plaster interior. No 5, *c.*1877, John Gordon. Renaissance villa, tower at south, wide entrance porch, good interiors. No 16, *c.*1883. Dutch Renaissance villa, with tower, good entrance hall and figurative stained-glass stair window. No 31 refurbished *c.*1900 in Glasgow Style, probably George Walton.

10–28 Cleveden Gardens, *c.*1880
Town houses, stepped in pairs: Nos 10–18, John Kennedy; Nos 26–28, Alexander Tait. Simple Greek details.

15 Cleveden Gardens

10 **15 Cleveden Gardens**, 1902, Andrew Prentice Edwardian renaissance polished ashlar villa by this Greenock-born, London-based architect. Bold arched ground-floor windows, upper sections leaded. Cast-iron first-floor balcony fronts, deep bracketed eaves, attic skylights, glazed ridge lantern and cupola.

11 Winton Drive, *c.*1895, probably David
Woodburn (D W) Sturrock
Three-storey white ashlar villa, Corinthian
columned porch. **7–35 Winton Lane**, *c.*1892.
Mews Cottages. No 27, John Morrison. Rare
carved portrait of a horse at No 7.

Winton Lane Mews

Stoneleigh

11 **Stoneleigh, 48 Cleveden Drive**, 1900,
Henry Edward (H E) Clifford
Elizabethan country house with tower, for
stockbroker Joseph Turner. Main rooms,
including oak-beamed open hall leading to
majestic stair, located beside kitchen on ground
floor. Dramatic south view. Converted to old
people's home, 1950s. Original fine interiors,
including good carved timber or marble
chimneypieces, some Jacobean details, others
Glasgow Style; stained glass, Henry J Payne and
Mary Newill. Fairy-tale cameos in hall, style of
Edward Burne-Jones woodcuts, probably Mary
Newill.

Cleveden Drive
54 Cleveden Drive, *c.*1893. Classical
asymmetrical ashlar villa, tall centre bay, twin
Ionic columned porch, deep eaves, stained-glass
stair window, good interior. **Westmount, No
56**, *c.*1887, John Gordon. Symmetrical ashlar
villa, classical with Corinthian pilasters. **Amalfi
House, No 58**, *c.*1880. Classical, twin Corinthian
columned porch, rich renaissance interiors. Rear
extension, 1898, James Lymburn Cowan. **1–15
Cleveden Crescent** and **61 Cleveden Drive**,
1876, John Burnet Sr. Across Cleveden Drive
and climbing uphill is the elegant symmetrical
Crescent of substantial renaissance houses, with

1–15 Cleveden Crescent

ground-floor bay windows and even larger houses as end pavilions and a double-house central pavilion with full-height bays.

Glendoune (former Averley), **996 Great Western Road**, *c*.1876. Symmetrical classical villa, elaborate bracketed cornice above door. William Leiper later added interior panelling and a decorative plaster ceiling.

998 Great Western Road

Guy McCrone's fictional *Antimacassar City* convincingly describes late Victorian life in Kelvinside and the adjoining West End estates:

'Although the house came to her in February, it was May before Bel and her family moved into it. For anyone so house proud as Mrs Arthur Moorhouse, a shorter time would have been utterly impossible. The house [in Grosvenor Terrace] had been bought from wealthy owners and was in excellent condition. Most of the paint, even, was fresh. But its four floors had to be painted anew, from the children's flat beneath the slates to the maid's basement bedroom.'

The prevailing wind kept smog away from the sumptuous palaces and villas in this desirable area.

12 **998 Great Western Road**, 1877, James Boucher The grandest house on Great Western Road, with rich interiors. Italianate villa, for James Marshall of the Saracen Foundry. Ionic pilasters at first floor above ground-floor rustication, with flat voussoirs over windows, elaborate centre bay with balcony over Doric porch, all capped by stone balustrade. No longer St Mungo's Academy Centenary Club and maintenance is now required. Boucher often worked for people of the Saracen Foundry, including on the sumptuous interior of 22 Park Circus for Walter Macfarlane himself (see *Central Glasgow* Guide).

Nuffield House, 1000 Great Western Road, *c*.1887
Renaissance villa, original interiors, including galleried smoking room in the tower. **No 1012**, 1893. Classical ashlar villa. Later and grander version of Nos 994 and 996.

St John's Renfield Church

St John's Renfield Church, 16–22 Beaconsfield
Road, 1929, James Taylor Thomson
A competition win, sitting high on the slope
of Balgray Hill, in Thomson's simplified late
medieval gothic with openwork flèche, reflecting
his years in the USA with Bertram Goodhue.
Glass by Douglas Strachan. See also Thomson's
version of simplified Romanesque at High
Carntyne Church (see p. 89).

SOUTH OF GREAT WESTERN ROAD

Grosvenor Terrace

13 **1–17 Grosvenor Terrace**, 1855,
John Thomas Rochead
Very long Venetian palace of terraced houses,
with round-headed windows, classical columns.
Cast-iron railings to stairs and basement area.
Good interior plasterwork in Nos 11–17. Nos
1–10 now a hotel, rebuilt, using glass-reinforced
concrete panels, after fire in 1978. (See also
Central Glasgow Guide.)

Kew Terrace

1–20 Kew Terrace, 1849, John Thomas Rochead
Classical with central and end pavilions and
smaller linking sections.

1–16 Belhaven Terrace, 1866 and **17–28 Belhaven
Terrace West**, 1874, both James Thomson.
Renaissance terraced houses, Corinthian
columns and first-floor bay windows at centre
and end houses.

Great Western Terrace

Above Great Western Terrace
Below 1–3 Lancaster Terrace

Sam Small

14 **1–11 Great Western Terrace**, 1869, Alexander Thomson

The most severe and monumental of the Great Western Road terraces is a long terrace of simply detailed houses, generally of two storeys and basement, with two-house three-storey pavilions located one house from each end, visually creating the illusion of the two-storey block penetrating the taller blocks. This was a unique and successful feature adopted to visually reduce the length of the building. Projecting porches incorporate Ionic columns, deep corbelled eaves and delicate cast-iron railings to basement areas. It is built on a raised level platform. The steps and ramps at each end were cleverly adapted by William Holford & Associates when the road became an expressway. Notable interiors and top-lit galleried stairwells (colour page 35).

1–3 Lancaster Terrace, *c.*1875

Three villas linked to form a terrace, figured pilasters flank doorways, alternate square and splayed bay windows.

Westbourne House, 985 Great Western Road and 11 Hyndland Road, *c.*1873, possibly Robert Turnbull
Large white ashlar Italianate villa, clerestory windows to billiard room.

Above *Westbourne House*
Left *Westbourne Terrace*

15 **Westbourne Terrace**, 21–39 Hyndland Road, 1871, Alexander Thomson
Classical terrace, end pavilions slightly advanced. Ionic columns in continuous ground-floor podium support two more storeys, with first-floor bay windows. Whole raised above Hyndland Road by polished ashlar retaining wall; good cast-iron balustrades and lamp brackets, recently restored.

Belmont & Hillhead Parish Church

16 **Belmont & Hillhead Parish Church**, 23 Saltoun Street, 1875, James Sellars
Competition winner, beating William Leiper and John Honeyman. Delightful French Gothic,

inspired by Sainte Chapelle, Paris, but details adapted from the Lady Chapel of Saint Germer. West front rose window, large sculptured angels, twin turrets, slate roof, tiled cresting, elaborate flèche. Rib-vaulted timber roof and carved choir stalls; marble communion table; elaborate timber canopy to marble font; oak pulpit, 1924, T Taylor. Stained glass, 1893, Edward Burne-Jones; 1893–1903, Cottier & Co.; 1917, William Meikle & Sons; 1958, Sadie McLellan. Interior remodelled 1921, Dr Peter Macgregor Chalmers (colour page 35).

20–26 Roxburgh Street and **33–35 Saltoun Street**, 1897, Adam & Short
Monumental five- and six-apartment tenements, main door and close entries. Massive full-height bowed and square bay windows. Design used again at 84–98 Hyndland Road.

1–20 Huntly Gardens

The Victoria Park Feuing Company was a consortium of lawyers, accountants and builders who built terraced houses in Huntly Gardens at the interior of the plot they had purchased in 1868. On the more expensive land fronting the adjoining Byres Road and in Saltoun, Ruthven and Roxburgh Streets, they built good-quality tenements.

Huntly Gardens
1–20 Huntly Gardens, *c.*1872. Terraced houses with two-storey bay windows. The terrace rises in pairs of houses towards the old Observatory. Corinthian pilaster doorways, good cast-iron balcony brackets and balustrades to flanks. **21-34 Huntly Gardens**, *c.*1880. Terraced houses, each house stepping up the hill. Nos 30–34 have decorative ironwork and contain high-level glazing for billiard rooms.

Horselethill Road
Marleybank, 1 Horselethill Road, *c.*1840. Classical villa, the first in the area, figurative stained-glass stair window probably Daniel Cottier. **11–11A Horselethill Road**, *c.*1875. Large asymmetrical double villa, Roman Doric doors below tower feature, round-headed windows at second floor, corbelled bow and projecting square windows.

Marley Bank

RCAHMS

RCAHMS

RCAHMS

Sam Small

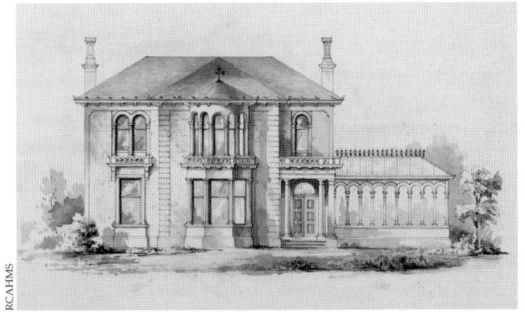

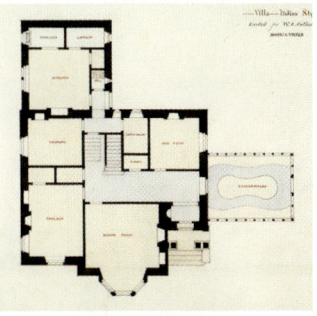

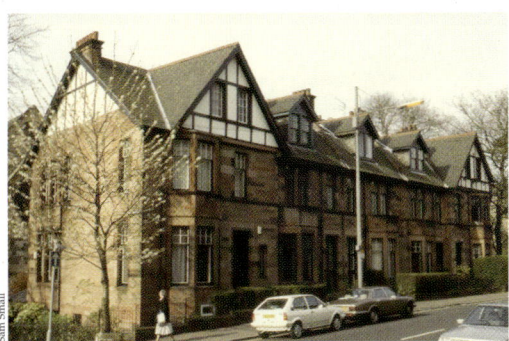

Top left *Norwood, Sydenham Road*; Top right *Principal Floor Plan, Norwood, Sydenham Road*; Above *Cottier Pulpit, Dowanhill Church*; Left *Foremount Gardens*

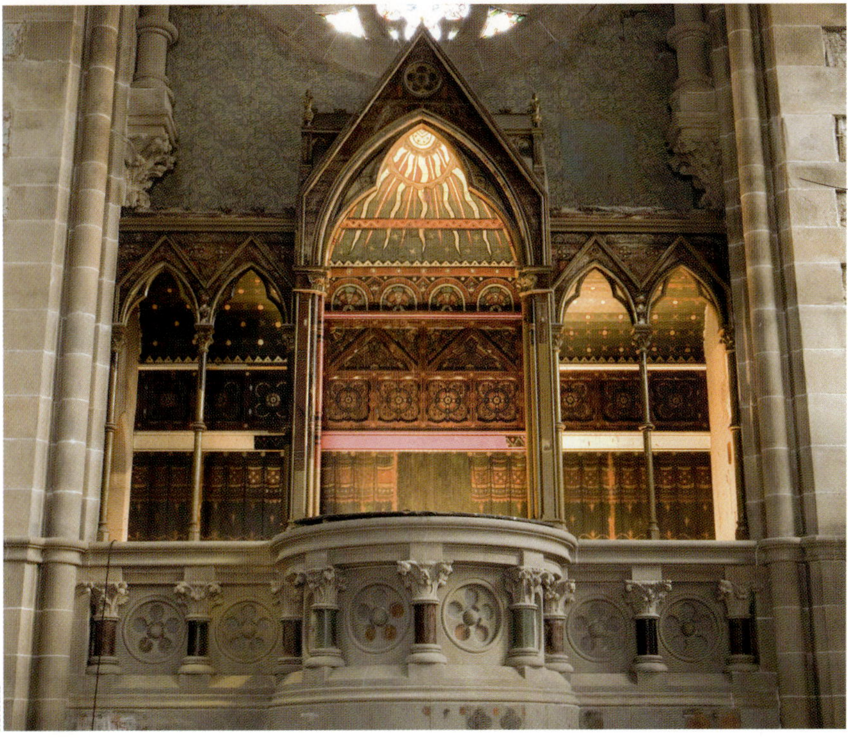

RCAHMS

Top *Crown Terrace;* Right *Stained glass of Drake by Norman W McDougall at Willowbank Bowling Club;* Bottom *Ascot Cinema in Bingo guise;* Below *Willow View Court*

RCAHMS

Sam Small

RCAHMS

Top *Belmont and Hillhead Church*; Above *Partick Fire Station*; Below *Great Western Terrace*; Bottom *Scotstoun Leisure Centre*; Below left *Westbourne Free Church – later Struthers Memorial Church*

RCAHMS

RCAHMS

RCAHMS

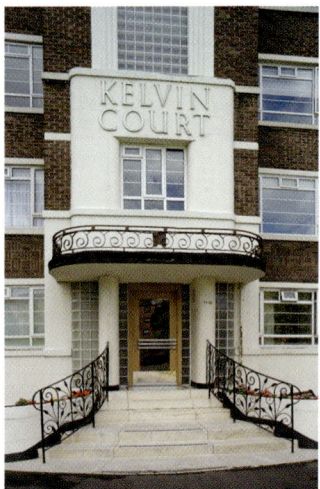

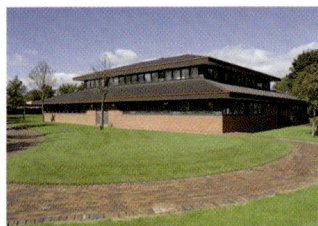

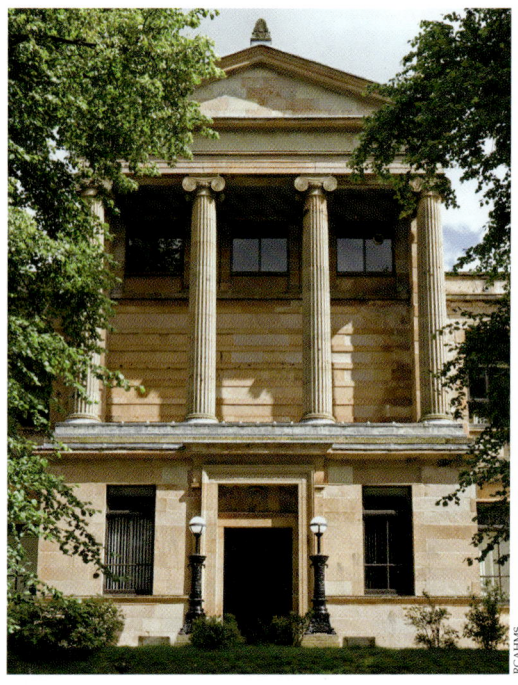

Top left *Kelvin Court*; Above *Kelvinside Academy*; Bottom *Kirklee Terrace;* Left *One Todd Campus*

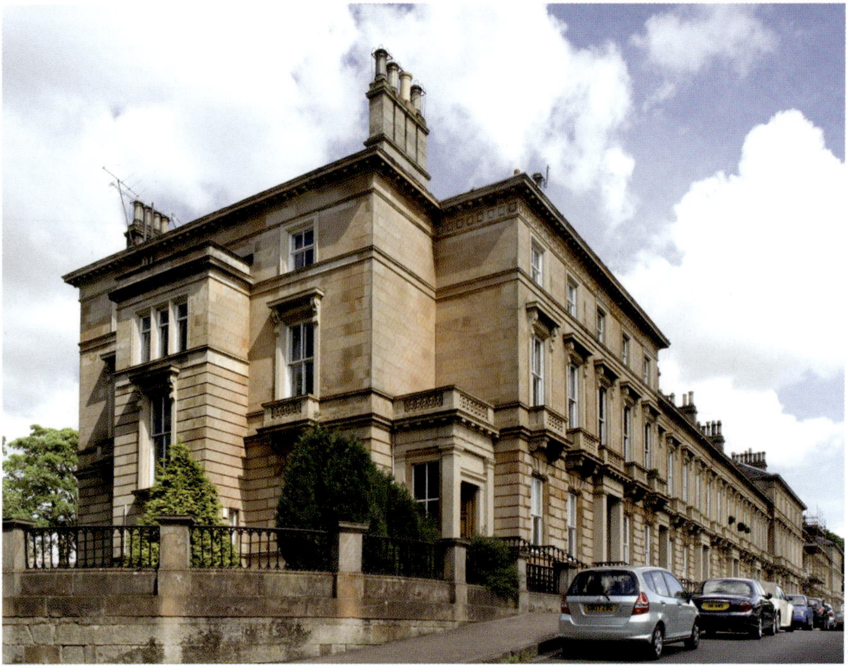

RCAHMS

St Luke's Greek Orthodox Cathedral, 27–29
Dundonald Road, 1877, James Sellars
Normandy gothic turrets flank tall lancets and
rose window, on better frontage than the same
architect's nearby Belmont & Hillhead Parish
Church. Stained glass, 1877, Stephen Adam.
Modern Byzantine screen with icons.

Observatory Road
Fern Tower, 1 Dundonald Road, 1874. Picturesque
Italianate villa, with arched windows, balcony
and attic tower feature at south east. Fine stone
and timber carvings. **1–10 Marchmont Terrace**,
Observatory Road, c.1870. Terraced houses
stepping down hill, projecting figure pilaster
pavilions, carved thistle motif over first-floor
window of No 10. **Elmslea**, 124 Observatory
Road, mid-19th century. Villa with arched
windows, unusual timber porch, some Saracen
Foundry cast iron work. Now university offices.

St Luke's

Notre Dame High School

17 **Notre Dame High School**, 160 Observatory Road,
1939, designed Thomas Smith (T S) Cordiner
Scandinavian influenced, built 1949–53 on the
site of the former Observatory. A long block in
yellow brick, concrete and ashlar, with projecting

wings, incorporating bas-relief stone panels. Mackintosh-style baluster screens on stairs. Metal sculpture on modernist flèche with cross above main entrance pavilion. Brick shrine with statue of Virgin and Child to north.

Notre Dame RC Training College, 1–7 Bowmont Gardens, *c.*1880
Former classical terraced houses raised on a platform. Converted to college *c.*1930s.

1–20 Athole Gardens, *c.*1878
Greek details, after Alexander Thomson, curved terraced houses, Saracen Foundry cast-iron railings.

Above *1–18 Westbourne Gardens*
Right *28–41 Westbourne Gardens*

Westbourne Gardens
Nos 1–18, 1872, James Thomson. Renaissance terraced houses, with taller end pavilions and corbelled first-floor windows. Extensions to rear of No 1, 1905, David Barclay, include Doric columned screen with segmental arch over wrought-iron fanlight. **Nos 28–41**, *c.*1876. Unique design of large gothic terraced houses, with taller end pavilions. Vigorous details include foliate capitals to door columns. Good cast-iron railings to steps and basement. **Nos 49–51**, *c.*1875, Alexander Thomson. Classical terraced houses, Ionic porches, ashlar first-floor balconies with good cast-iron balustrade to Nos 50–51. The end house destroyed in Second World War.

RCAHMS

18 **Struthers Memorial Church of Scotland**, 52
Westbourne Gardens, 1881, John Honeyman
Built as Westbourne Free Church. Italian
Renaissance with exceptionally delicate
detailing. Corinthian above Ionic twin columns
supporting pediment of shallow portico. Two
bell towers with ogee lead domes (colour
page 35). Good interior with galleries, deep at
back, shallow to sides, coffered ceiling, elaborate
ornament, baroque furnishings. Stained glass,
*c.*1920, Douglas Strachan and *c.*1951, Margaret
Chilton.

DOWANHILL

Dowanhill was acquired in 1853 from the
trustees for the late James Buchanan, a textile
merchant and manufacturer, by Thomas Lucas
Paterson, another textile man now turned
property developer. Paterson had already
successfully developed Newhall estate in
Bridgeton (see p. 94). The original layout plan,
prepared by James Smith, was modified to omit
several villas in the centre, making way for the
grand terraces designed by James Thomson,
around Crown Circus. Paterson worked with
several partners and suffered many misfortunes
including the collapse of several companies and
finally bankruptcy in 1888.

*Westbourne Free Church (later Struthers
Memorial)*

John Honeyman (1831–1914), having
measured and studied gothic churches
in England, was an authority on
medieval architecture and was retained
as a consultant by Glasgow Cathedral
for many years. He started his practice in
1853 and through the 1860s he designed
many gothic churches in Glasgow.
When John Thomas Rochead returned
to Edinburgh in 1870, Honeyman built
Rochead's classical design at North
Park House, when he was designing
his own classical terraced houses for
Belmont Crescent. He continued in
the classical vein with Craigie Hall
(see p. 197) and widened his repertoire
with the Venetian Ca d'Oro of 1872,
then Tudor and Italianate schools in
the mid-1870s. St Anthony's RC Church
of 1877 is Italian Romanesque and the
same year St Bonaventure was French
Gothic but, for his Barony North Church
and Westbourne Church, he reverted
to classicism. He assumed John Keppie
into partnership in 1889 and after his
retirement in 1901, to facilitate Charles
Rennie Mackintosh's partnership with
Keppie, Honeyman helped Thomas
Ross to direct the rebuilding of part of
Iona Cathedral (see *Argyll & The Islands*
Guide).

James Buchanan (1755–1844), originally
a linen merchant, became a partner in
Dennistoun Buchanan, cotton spinners
on the Gryffe near Paisley and owner,
with his sons, of the water-powered
cotton mills at Stanley, near Perth.
He bought a Glasgow estate, which
he named Dowanhill. One of his
sons endowed the Buchanan Prize at
Glasgow University, for excellence in
Theology. The Buchanan of Dowanhill
Monument in Glasgow Necropolis is
not quite the most showy of many there
commemorating the city's merchants
and manufacturers.

T L Paterson and Company traded in
Glasgow's principal imports, sugar
and cotton from America and exported
general merchandise to India. The
company collapsed in 1873 after
uninsured shipping losses. Paterson
arranged for his Trustee to release the
unfeued parts of Dowanhill, when Robert
Cassels invested substantial cash and
guaranteed a bank loan to Paterson. They
both collapsed in 1887. By the mid-1890s,
Robert Cassels' sons realised that they
could never recover the capital already
invested by the former partners and
then sold off the balance of Dowanhill
as quickly as possible, although the very
last plot was not sold until the 1930s.

Above 6–34 Victoria Crescent Road
Above right 35–37 Victoria Crescent Road

Victoria Crescent Road
Nos 6–34 Victoria Crescent Road, 1865, possibly James Thomson. Classical terraced houses, oriel windows, groups step up hill. **Victoria Terrace, 38–52 Victoria Crescent Road**, 1856, Daniel Charleston, builder. Classical terraced houses stepped down the hill in pairs, end pairs advanced, south pair taller. **King's Gate, 33–37 Victoria Crescent Road**, 1905, David Barclay. Three Glasgow Style terraced houses, the second part of King's Gate, for John Lindsay. **King's Gate, 48 Dowanside Road**, 1903, David Barclay. Another Glasgow Style terraced house, for John Lindsay, the first of the four houses built, although six were originally envisaged. **43 Victoria Crescent Road**, 1899, David Barclay. Glasgow Style terraced house, end house of Queen's Gate, entered from adjoining street.

19

1–8 Queen's Gardens

1–8 Queen's Gardens, 1879, James Thomson Large classical terraced houses for William Russell, taller end pavilions. Nos 2–4 were bombed in Second World War, rebuilt as luxury flats 2003.

Ramoyle

Ramoyle, 10 Victoria Circus, 1859, possibly Boucher & Cousland. Italianate white ashlar villa. Side extension, 1898, Alexander Skirving. **Kensington Tower, No 6**, 1858, possibly Boucher & Cousland. Italianate villa with tall tower for George Alexander. Extension, 1897, James Lymburn Cowan for publisher Blackie. **Elstow, No 5**, 1856. Baronial villa, for Henry Herbertson, measurer. Extension, 1899, Alexander Nisbet (A N) Paterson.

Sam Small

20 **11–24 Kensington Gate**, 1901–2, David Barclay
Glasgow Style houses, part of a sinuous terrace:
good glass. **2–8 Kensington Road**, 1900, David
Barclay. Glasgow Style, more good glass,
part of Kensington Gate. **3–9 Lorraine Road**,
1900, David Barclay. Glasgow Style terraced
houses, red ashlar, the first part of Kensington
Gate. **2–4 Lorraine Road**, 1899, David Barclay.
Glasgow Style double villa in white ashlar,
to a deep plan. Part of William Russell's feu
for adjacent Lorraine Gardens. **1–10 Lorraine
Gardens**, 1883, James Thomson. Grand
classical terraced houses, built for William
Russell, the estate quarrymaster, who ended in
serious debt.

Sydenham Road

Norwood, No 1, 1857, Boucher & Cousland.
Italianate white ashlar villa, with large central
bay window and conservatory. **Aytoun House,
No 3**, 1859, Boucher & Cousland. Italianate
villa, painted ashlar. Flat roof replaced original
pitched roof during the Second World War.
Refurbished and floor added 2001, Page &
Park. **Benvue, No 4**, 1859, Boucher & Cousland.
Italianate villa, in white ashlar. Repeat of
Dunard design, with steeper roof. **No 5**, former
Dunard, 1858, Boucher & Cousland. Italianate
villa, white ashlar with shallow roof pitch.
Newhall, No 8, 1858, James Thomson of West
Nile Street, not the famous Baird & Thomson.
Tudor gothic villa for Thomas Lucas Paterson,
the estate owner, named after his Bridgeton
development (see p. 94; colour page 33).

Above Kensington Gate
Below Newhall

Sam Small

James Boucher (1826–1906) and
James Cousland (1832–1866) were
both apprenticed to Charles Wilson.
In 1858 they built a double villa for
themselves at 35-37 St Andrew's
Drive, Pollokshields, known as
'Swiss Villa' (now demolished; see
p. 178). Seven Dowanhill villas are
illustrated in the Boucher & Cousland
promotional brochure; however, there
is evidence in the Dowanhill Estate
and Sasine records, based on repeat
commissions by developers or owners,
and stylistically, to suggest that they
designed at least another nine villas
in Dowanhill. Cousland suffered an
accident during the building of St
George's Church in 1864 and died
within two years. Boucher continued to
practise in and around Glasgow until
about 1891, although he had largely
retired to Coulport in 1880.

Langdale

Prince Albert Road
Linden Lodge, No 7 and Bothkennar, No 8,
1861, possibly Boucher & Cousland. Italianate
white ashlar double villa, each house entered
from a different street. **Langdale, Nos 4–6**, 1858,
Boucher & Cousland. Another Italianate double
villa, white ashlar, extended by 1900. **Holmhurst,
No 2**, 1860, possibly Boucher & Cousland. White
ashlar villa, extended 1894, David McSkimming,
builder.

2-12 Princes Terrace

21 **Princes Terrace**, Prince Albert Road, 1868,
James Thomson
Grand classical terrace of twelve houses
with round-headed dormers. Fine Italianate
ashlar details, cast-iron balustrades linking
front dormers, solid stone balustrades to rear.
Unusual bay windows to south-facing rear,
overlooking the private communal garden. Plans
are mirrored about the central pair of houses.
Interior of end terrace house, **No 1**, *c*.1880, James
Miller for ship-owner William Henderson.
Unusual double glazing system with leaded
lights, elaborate stained glass in front door.
Panelled entrance hall, with arcade screening
hall at right, itself later panelled with Baroque
overmantel. Good panelling, plasterwork and
chimneypiece details in drawing room, dining
room and billiard room.

Royston & Westdel

**Royston and Westdel, 10 Crown Road North
and 2 Queen's Place**, 1889, George Washington
Browne
Asymmetrical double villa, by Glasgow
architect, who was Robert Rowand Anderson's
partner and was now working on his own
in Edinburgh. Westdel extended, 1896, A
N Paterson. **Dowanhill Arch**, 1871, James
Thomson. Unique stone arch over service lane

links the Crown Gardens terrace to Crown Circus. The Circus and terraces on either side replaced the villas originally intended for this part of Dowanhill (colour page 34).

Sam Small

Crown Circus

22 **Crown Circus (Nos 3–10)**, 1–2 Crown Terrace and 15–17 Crown Road North, 1857, James Thomson
Grand classical painted ashlar terraced houses. Sited at the top of a steep rise from Byres Road, the building commanded a view of Gilmorehill for years. Eight convex houses with Roman Doric columns at ground floor on Nos 3–5 and 8–10; the two central houses, Nos 6 and 7, have pilasters, all supporting a Doric detailed balcony at first floor. A U-plan terrace, the two pairs of end houses face adjoining streets; details at Crown Road North as main front, whilst at Crown Terrace round-headed dormers break ashlar roof balustrade. Gardens retaining wall reinstated 2002, Glasgow West Conservation Trust, when overgrown forest trees were also replaced by smaller species.

Crown Circus was probably the 22-year-old James Thomson's first solo design, after his senior partner John Baird died. He was commissioned by the builder and lath-splitter Andrew Henderson, who feued the plots piecemeal. The houses were very slow to sell, the fourth taking 12 years. To service his loan Henderson rented houses to a bank manager, the rector of Glasgow Academy and the minister of Park Church. The 1861 Census shows some other occupants who could not have paid the rent: three labourers and a cane chair-worker – squatters, perhaps?

Kinnoul Place (Nos 2–8), 68 Dowanside Road and 2–6 Kinnoul Lane, 1891, John Smellie Plain symmetrical terrace of four houses, in white ashlar with rubble gables. **1–2 Beaumont Gate**, 1899, George S Kenneth, and **Nos 3–10**, 1902, David Barclay. Finely detailed red sandstone Glasgow Style tenements. **13–18** and **28–30, 30–32 Highburgh Road**, 1901–3, David Barclay. More finely detailed Glasgow Style tenements, taller on the main road, for John Lindsay.

Western Telephone Exchange

23 **Western Telephone Exchange**, 24 Highburgh Road and 3–7 Caledon Street, 1907, Leonard Stokes, with Colin Menzies
Arts & Crafts built in multicoloured ashlar and brick, on a strongly expressed frame grid, the severity broken by Stokes's favourite round arches at the parapet. The cornices over windows between the bays are the only classical features. Stokes built many splendid telephone exchanges, his best at Southampton and at Gerrard Street, in London's Soho. Flats were included to use fallow space built for future expansion.

38–40 Highburgh Road

38–40 Highburgh Road and 78–104 Dowanhill Street (former Queen's Gate), 1901, David Barclay
Glasgow Style red sandstone tenements, taller in Highburgh Road than in Dowanhill Street, for the mason William Miller. **106 Dowanhill Street** and **47–55 Dowanside Road** (former Albert Gate), 1900–4, David Barclay. Glasgow Style terraced houses, for the joiner John Lindsay.

57–67 Dowanside Road and 111 Dowanhill Street (former Albert Gate), 1904–7, David Barclay. Glasgow Style incomplete terrace on smaller scale, built as part of the Queen's Gate block, for John Lindsay.

Left 3–11 Crown Terrace

Crown Terrace (Nos 3–11), 1873, James Thomson Grand classical terraced house design, centre section taller, with bay windows, white ashlar. **Crown Terrace West (Nos 12–17)**, 1880, James Thomson. Late terraced house design incorporating bay windows, size cut to save cost, for Thomas Lucas Paterson.

12 Sydenham Lane, 1885, James Sellars Former two-storey stable with single-storey coach house for 12 Crown Terrace West, now converted to a house.

Above 12 Sydenham Lane, former stable
Left 1–15 Princes Gardens

1–15 Princes Gardens, 1891, Lindsay & Benzie, speculative builders
Terraced houses, with basements at end units, built as a crescent rising into the hill to reduce excavation costs and to increase the number of houses. Here the builders were reading the market better than the estate owner, who had instructed Thomson to design the much larger

The John Lindsay and William Benzie partnership first feued land in Dowanhill Street for two tenements. They next built tenements in Possil, on Walter Macfarlane's land, followed by terraced houses and tenements in Hillhead. Feuing from Thomas Lucas Paterson, they built more terraced houses and tenements in Donaldshill and Dowanhill. Next was Princes Gardens, which was slow to sell and the partnership was dissolved. Benzie went on to develop terraced houses in Hyndland while Lindsay, the entrepreneur, feued larger plots in Dowanhill, also for terraced houses. He often worked informally with mason William Miller, who likewise feued large plots of Dowanhill, mainly for tenements. With Benzie and later Miller, Lindsay built houses on nearly 19 acres, about a fifth of Dowanhill, the second largest feuing estate in Glasgow's West End.

terrace across the ridge. The builders' design was later developed by David Barclay for John Lindsay, after National Building Regulations were introduced in 1892.

HYNDLAND

This part of the bishop's lands was bought by Rae Crawford in 1799. In 1875 his descendant William Stuart Stirling Crawford had a feu plan prepared by John Carrick, later the City Architect but sold the estate the next year to a partnership, four members of an Edinburgh Bruce family. They feued two groups of plots to William Robertson, an Edinburgh builder for two terraced blocks at the top of Kingsborough Gardens: Hanover Terrace and Hanover Terrace North. Robertson died before their completion. William Benzie acquired the rest of the Kingsborough Gardens site and built the red terraced houses on most of the plots before 1910, the remaining plot being taken up by the city after the Second World War. James Barr prepared a new feuing plan for the main part of Hyndland, west of Hyndland Road, in 1897. The following year the 'measurers' Duncanson & Henderson set up The Western Property Company, which developed superior tenements there, mainly by John Campbell McKellar, and all were complete by 1910.

Royal Bank of Scotland, 162 Hyndland Road, 1934, James McLachlan
Egyptian-inspired incised Art Deco façade details.

Hyndland Branch, Royal Bank of Scotland

Hyndland Public School, 12 Airlie Street, 1912, H E Clifford
A late project, symmetrical classical design, red sandstone and clean playful stone window openings (spoiled by modern windows), by the architect of the Scots Renaissance Burgh Halls, at Pollokshields (see pp. 175–6).

84–94 Hyndland Road, *c.*1901, John Short
Simple white stone tenements with details identical to 20–26 Roxburgh Street, by Adam & Short on the Victoria Park Feuing Company's land.

24 **Hyndland Parish Church**, 79 Hyndland Road, 1885, William Leiper
Geometric gothic, red snecked rubble, with buttressed aisles. A cruciform church of nave and aisles, with transepts and chancel. Unfinished tower over elaborate porch. Figurative corbels

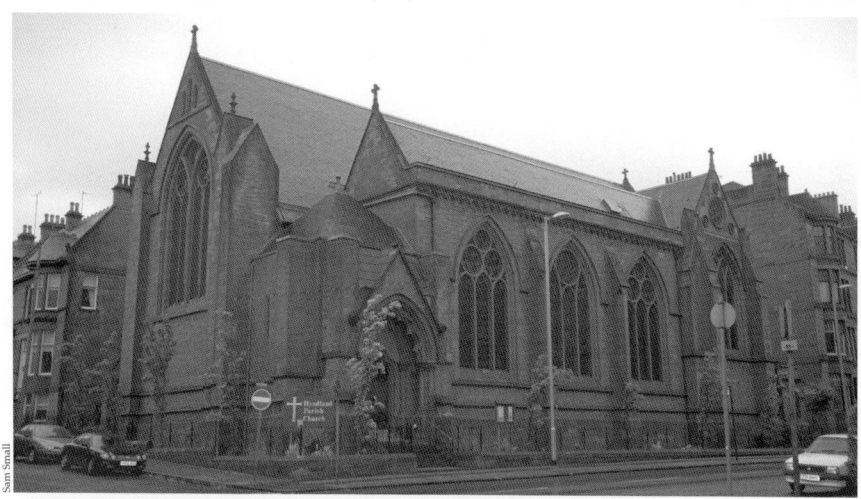

Hyndland Parish Church

carry columns and open timber roof. War Memorial east window, 1921, Douglas Strachan. Aisle windows: *c.*1940, Douglas Hamilton; *c.*1960, Gordon Webster; 1969, Sax Shaw. South transept window, 1962, William Wilson. Carved oak panelling, marble communion table and font, marble and ashlar pulpit, organ in north transept, 1887, Henry Willis. South transept converted to I J Ballantine Memorial Chapel, 1966.

St Bride's Episcopal Church, 61 Hyndland Road, 1903, George Frederick Bodley, completed 1913, Harold Ogle Tarbolton
Decorated gothic. Internal figure sculpture Eric Gill. Stained glass, 1920s. Scott Morton fittings.

Kingsborough Gardens
Nos 10–16 (former Hanover Terrace North), 1888 and **Nos 22–36** (former Hanover Terrace), 1882, William Robertson, builder. White sandstone French urban palace. The Edinburgh builder's first Glasgow terraces. At No 34, fragments of Charles Rennie Mackintosh interiors. **38 Kingsborough Gardens**, 1900, D W Sturrock. Closing Robertson's earlier incomplete white stone terrace, although in Glasgow style, rather than repeating Robertson's French details, for William Benzie. **Nos 40–46**, 1902, George S Kenneth. Two 12- and two 10-apartment red sandstone houses, following the style used in Kenneth's previous work for John Lindsay. **Nos 48–54**, 1903, D W Sturrock. Another four similar nine-apartment red sandstone houses. Opposite, **Nos 1–41**, 1899 to 1902, D W Sturrock

Below Hanover Terrace North
Bottom 19–41 Kingsburgh Gardens

Montague Terrace

Charles Wilson (1810-1863) worked for David Hamilton for 11 years until 1837 and he studied widely on the Continent. After his Tudor design won the competition for Gartnavel Lunatic Asylum, his monumental public works developed Hamilton's Italian Renaissance, often adopting almost Romanesque round headed arches, as did Alexander Thomson at this period. Wilson's grandest public building is the Trinity Free Church College (see *Central Glasgow* Guide), while his more neoclassical John Neilson Institute in Paisley is considered by some to be his best (see *South Clyde Estuary* Guide). For one of his last public buildings, Rutherglen Town Hall, he adopted the more picturesque Scots Baronial style which he had devised for his villas. They often had classical plans, which he clad with specifically west of Scotland renaissance details, again following Hamilton. After the Romanesque Argyle Free Church at Rothesay, Wilson's churches evolved into gothic, often with tall spires, notably at Eastwood (see p. 163).

for William Benzie. Large red sandstone houses, similar to Lindsay & Benzie's Princes Gardens (see p. 45).

HUGHENDEN

Montague Terrace, 10–20 Hyndland Road, *c.*1883, probably Hugh & David Barclay Classical terraced houses, with Grecian motifs, unfinished, possibly because of recent infill of old quarry. **1–7 Hughenden Terrace** and **5–6 Montague Lane**, *c.*1881, Hugh & David Barclay. Classical terraced houses and mews cottages. **Hughenden House**, 25 Hughenden Road, 1907, Burnet, Boston & Carruthers. Excellent glass and interiors. **1–5 Devonshire Gardens**, *c.*1870. Large classical terraced houses, now a hotel. Some good stained glass on stairs; cast-iron roof crest at No 1. **1–9 Devonshire Terrace** (former Marlborough Terrace) *c.*1883, James Thomson. Unfinished classical terrace of large houses.

ANNIESLAND

In 1841, the Glasgow Lunatic Asylum, or Gartnavel Royal Hospital, was built in open countryside at Anniesland. Although the Forth & Clyde Canal passed this way and was open for sea to sea navigation in 1790, the area was still predominantly farming, with some mining at Cowdenhill and Cloverhill in Knightswood, brickworks at Temple and quarrying at Garscube. By 1850 the Great Western Road was laid out from the city only as far as Anniesland Cross. In the later 19th century industry expanded with the 1871 Partick, Hillhead and Maryhill Gas Works at Temple; the 1874 Saw Mill on both sides of the canal; and the 1890 Iron Works. The North British Railway station opened in 1886, encouraging some tenement building around the Cross, villas from 1890 in Claythorn and more in Edwardian style from 1903.

25 **Gartnavel Royal Hospital**, 1055 Great Western Road, 1841, Charles Wilson
Soon after leaving David Hamilton's office, Wilson won the competition to replace William Stark's 1807 Parliamentary Road Lunatic Asylum with a new one at Gartnavel. A large Tudor-style hospital, two detached E-plan ranges with taller central and end pavilions. The west range was for the wealthy; the east was the charity wing, for the less fortunate. Superintendent's flat at centre of west range, four-storey over entrance,

Left *Gartnavel Royal Hospital*
Above *Blood Transfusion Unit*

male and female dormitories on either side. East
wing simpler detail, two domed pavilions link to
garden wall, plain interiors. Wilson's Chapel and
linking arcade were never built. **Chapel**, 1904,
J J Burnet, domestic looking. **Nurses' Home**,
1935, Norman Dick, of John Burnet, Son & Dick.
Three-storey dark red brick, flat-roofed series of
linked geometric buildings, in distinctive 1930s
style with horizontally divided metal windows.
Tom Wheldon Building, Beatson Oncology
Dept, 2000, Wylie Shanks. Tall glazed reception,
glass canopy and oversailing lightweight roof.
Blood Transfusion Unit, 2000, W S Atkins.
Crisp concrete- and metal-clad block, glass block
stairtowers.

Kelvinside Railway Station, 1051 Great Western
Road, 1897, J J Burnet
Charming, very finely detailed Italianate villa
style, with wide central bay at ground floor and
Doric frieze at eaves. Converted to restaurant
1980, rebuilt as Stazione Restaurant 1998 after
fire.

Kelvinside Railway Station

11 Whittinghame Drive

26 **11 Whittinghame Drive**, 1907, John Ednie
Asymmetrical Arts & Crafts ashlar villa with
baronial details, crowstep gables and corbelled
bays. High-quality original panelling and
plasterwork interiors. Excellent stained glass to
hall and vestibule door, Oscar Paterson.

Westwood and St Brendan

Westwood and **St Brendan, 3** and **5 Arnwood
Drive**, 1903, Neil Campbell Duff
Substantial, individually designed villas, both
with drum towers in red rubble and ashlar
dressings. Westmorland green slate roof and red
tile ridges.

Kelvin Court

Kelvin Court, 1–52 and 53–100 Great Western
Road, 1938, James Newton Fatkin
Two H-plan, six- and seven-storey blocks of
flats. The only scheme of inter-war mansion
flats of this scale in Scotland, using outrageous
Newcastle red brick. Echoing 1930s London style
with metal windows, vertical glass blocks at
entrance stairtowers and curved cantilever rear
balconies (colour page 36). Some flats retain their
1930s details such as fireplaces.

1544 Great Western Road, 1939, Charles James (C J) McNair
Former Ascot Cinema. Art Deco, with two semicircular monumental faience stairtowers. Façade incorporated into new flatted housing, 2001, Holmes Partnership (colour page 34).

Above *Ascot Cinema frontage today*
Left *Anniesland Court*

27 **Anniesland Court**, 833–853 Crow Road, 1966, Jack Holmes & Partners
A principal landmark of western Glasgow since its construction. Twenty-two-storey narrow rectangular-plan tower block on commercial podium, with adjoining three-storey block to south. Cladding to podium and three-storey block altered 1984. Podium shops linked by covered walkway to upper terrace and enclosed lift/stairtower to residential tower block. Glazed stair linked to tower at enclosed access deck every third floor. Mosaic faced pre-cast concrete cladding strips alternate with horizontal glazing, gables red brick faced. Refurbished early 2000s.

Temple Anniesland Parish Church and Hall, 859–869 Crow Road, Church 1904, Badenoch & Bruce
Large red sandstone, Lancet style, Early English gothic. **Hall** (original Church), 1898, Alexander Petrie, in plain gothic.

KNIGHTSWOOD

Knightswood was the City Council's prize development, built to a very high standard on land they had acquired outside the old Royalty; a large low-density semidetached cottage-type housing estate along the extended Great Western Road from 1923. They built a further scheme between 1937 and 1942.

Bearsden Road

Bearsden Road, 1937, William B McNab, Glasgow Corporation Housing Department Modernist three-storey stone-faced tenement flats, part of the better-standard Great Western Road housing scheme of 433 dwellings.

St Margaret's Church, 1996 Great Western Road, Knightswood Cross, 1928–32, Lorimer & Matthew St Margaret's was Sir Robert Lorimer's very last church, completed posthumously by J F Matthew in Lorimer's Scottish style with Baltic-inspired profile. Hipped end roof and Arts & Crafts interior features. Stained glass, Alexander Russell. **Hall**, 1925, Jeffrey Waddell. Original red sandstone hall built, as often, before the church.

St Margaret's Church

St Ninian's RC Church & Hall, 206 Knightswood Road, Knightswood Cross, 1956, C H Purcell of Pugin & Pugin, completed by S Stevenson Jones
Traditional gothic, with Decorated tracery, pink brick and cream stone dressings.

Knightswood Secondary School

Knightswood Secondary School, 60 Knightswood Road, designed 1938, redesigned by new blood and built 1954, Gillespie, Kidd & Coia Scandinavian-influenced, cream brick, large windows and flat roof. Good period interiors. This style further refined at Kirktonholm Primary School, East Kilbride.

St David's Church, 66 Boreland Drive, 1938,
George Hunter Gardner-McLean of Gardner &
Gardner-McLean
Traditionally planned church, in trim rustic
brickwork with striking entrance tower. Concrete
arches inside. Hall by same architects, 1929. The
same firm's neo-Georgian Maritime House, for
the General Council of British Shipping, corner
of Broomielaw and James Watt Street, 1958, now
demolished.

Former Glasgow University Sports Pavilion

Former **Glasgow University Sports Pavilion**,
Kingfisher Gardens, 1936, Thomas Harold
Hughes
The leading modernist sports pavilion in
Scotland. Art Deco with classical touches, in
white-rendered brick. Long main front, with
metal windows and horizontal glazing bars
to original changing rooms. Projecting glazed
central entrance with square stairturret leading
to semicircular balcony over tearoom. Hughes
was briefly a partner of Burnet Tait & Lorne
before taking up an appointment as Professor of
Architecture at Glasgow University, where he
was considered an outstanding teacher. Smartly
refurbished and converted to residential use,
1990s.

DRUMCHAPEL
The undulating lands of Garscadden were
obtained from the Erskines by Patrick Galbraith
in 1444. They passed to Wallace of Dundonald
in 1611, then to the Colquhouns in 1655.
Garscadden House was built sometime after
1664 and enlarged about 1747. Coal mining
was begun around 1870 near the village of
Drumchapel, on the south-east of the estate.
The railway station was opened in 1891 and
a sprinkling of middle-class villas followed.
In 1938 the City built 40 flatted dwellings at

From the canal, the path takes us through the pretty suburban district of Drumchapel, which is entitled to boast an artistic golf course and a first class lawn tennis court. Garscadden lies but a short distance further on. The fine gates, which lead to the well-kept and beautifully wooded policies, were erected in 1789 from designs by Charles Ross, a Paisley architect.
T C F Brotchie, *Some Sylvan Scenes near Glasgow*, 1910

In former days the Kilpatrick lairds were famous for their convivial meetings, and it is told that on one of these occasions, after a long course of hard drinking, someone observed, '*Is na Garscadden lookin unco gash?'* '*Deil mean him,' said a brother laird; 'he's been with his Maker this twa hours. I saw him slip awa, but didna like to disturb good company by saying ought about it.'*

Drumchapel to rehouse overcrowded families. They purchased the whole estate in 1939 and the 1951 post-war plan included 7,500 mainly three- and four-storey tenement dwellings, housing 35,000 people at the peak in 1961, when it was nicknamed 'The Drum'. The estate meanders around a cluster of small drumlins on the lower slopes of the Kilpatrick Hills, merging with those of the Campsies. The Arndale Shopping Centre, 1962, Gerald M Baxter, was followed by an industrial estate. The shops were extended in 1971, not long before the population declined through overspill and other migration looking for work. Drumchapel today is becoming a much more interesting place to live, with fresh refurbishment of some of the bland mid-1950s housing and considerable variety in the private sector replacements, all enhanced by the hilly setting.

The hilltop Garscadden was a symmetrical Georgian Mansion, with a fine classical portico at first-floor level, reached by twin quadrant stairs. Long demolished, the site is occupied by Garscadden Policies, three multistorey blocks of flats, 1965, A Buchanan Campbell. Nearby is the family memorial at Linkwood Crescent, while part of the estate wall survives on Maryhill Road, with massive 19th-century cast-iron gates, at the West of Scotland Science Park.

Above *St Laurence (Martyr) RC Church*
Below *Church of Jesus Christ of Latter Day Saints*

St Laurence (Martyr) RC Church & Presbytery, 215 Kinfauns Drive, 1954, Reginald Fairlie & Partners
Spanish Hacienda style, white rendered with arcaded loggia and dark pantile roof at the foot of the hill. L-plan, concrete A-frame ribs and painted brick inside.

Achamore Drive, 1980s, ASSIST Architects
Low-rise housing for housing co-operative, on cleared upland site. Lively arrangement of varied heights, bay windows, balconies and highlighted close entrances, using a pallet of brick, cast stone and render. A more stimulating environment than the former bleak post-war uniformity.

Church of Jesus Christ of Latter Day Saints, 436 Kinfauns Drive, 1961, John Easton
Red buttresses on white painted walls, shallow pitch metal roof. Remarkable tapering tower, with horizontal Art Deco fins, now Kinfauns Family Resource Unit.

42–52 Jedworth Avenue, 1992,
Simister Monaghan
Refurbishment of three-storey flats, atop another
drumlin, for Housing Association. Saltire Society
Commendation, 1994.

St Pius RC Church & Presbytery, 4 Bayfield
Terrace, 1954, Alexander McAnally
Simplified Romanesque, aisleless red brick
church. Cream stone entrance and dressings
with slender copper-capped campanile. Fine
modern timber and marble interior. Stanley
Spencer-inspired painted Stations of the Cross.

Campbell Colquhoun Burial Ground,
Linkwood Crescent
Remains of three-sided 17th-century rubble
enclosure and simple iron railings on top of
another rise. Carved stone details include a
frieze of diamond bands, window mouldings,
corbels and two heraldic shields.

MARYHILL ROAD
NORTH WOODSIDE
This western part of North Woodside was sold,
along with Keppoch, by Janet Campbell in 1702
to William Stirling, younger brother of James
Stirling of Keir. William, like his brother, was a
substantial sugar merchant, with several estates
in Jamaica. One of their descendants bequeathed
the money to build Stirling's Library and another
married the Maxwell daughter of Pollok. Several
feus were sold in the latter 18th century. When
William Gillespie, owner of South Woodside
Cotton Mill (see *Central Glasgow* Guide), found
that he was unable to use the North Woodside
flour mill, he quickly sold the estate again. By
the 1820s there were a few villas along the steep
climb up Garscube Road, with coal and clay
pits and brickworks nearby. Industry now grew

The writer William Colquhoun,
of Camstradden, descended
from a younger brother of Robert
Colquhoun of the Luss family, bought
Garscadden in 1655. William's elder
son Andrew inherited Garscadden
and built the house but, when his line
ran out, the estate passed through
Andrew's younger brother Lawrence,
who had purchased Killermont,
and his daughter Agnes. She had
married John Coates Campbell of
Clathie in Perthshire, and their son
Archibald Campbell Colquhoun,
of Killermont and Clathie, thus
inherited Garscadden. Archibald was
a partner in the Thistle Bank, Sheriff
of Perthshire, Lord Advocate and
Lord Clerk Register, as well as MP for
Dunbartonshire.

Tower Buildings

on the hillside between Maryhill Road and the Forth & Clyde Canal until the 1860s. Tenements followed in the eastern section after the estate was laid out by the City of Glasgow Bank and the 100-year-old mansion was demolished in 1869 for terraces to the west.

Tower Buildings, 2–14 Possil Road and Farnell Street, 1875
At the foot of a steep hill, once known as Garscube Cross, renaissance three-storey warehouse above shops, for ironfounder James Allen of Elmbank Foundry on the canal. Corner emphasised by conical roof. In the 1930s the top floor became the Tower Ballroom.

St Columba of Iona RC Church

28 **St Columba of Iona RC Church**, 74–76 Hopehill Road, 1937, Gillespie, Kidd & Coia
Basilican plan with low aisles and bold central entrance tower at west, featuring Italian Romanesque details adapted for West of Scotland climate. Concrete portal frame, glass and brick, steep tiled mansard roof. Stone

features at entrance and to adjoining brick presbytery. Painted panels of *Stations of the Cross* brought here from the Empire Exhibition, Hugh Adam Crawford. Marble altar screen and carved crucifix, Benno Schotz.

Queen's Cross Church

29 **Queen's Cross Church**, 870 Garscube Road, 1896, Charles Rennie Mackintosh
Art Nouveau details on tapering medieval tower contrast with traditional perpendicular gothic gables. Rectangular plan with transepts and porch, red sandstone ashlar, slate roof and red ridge tiles. Timber barrel vault tied with steel beams. Some Mackintosh interior furnishings; screen below east gallery, 1939, Thomas Howarth. West window coloured lights, 1960, Gordon Webster. Now Headquarters of the Charles Rennie Mackintosh Society. *Open to the public.*

NORTH KELVINSIDE
This estate, on the western edge of North Woodside, was bought by John Ewing Walker in 1868 from James Brown Montgomerie Fleming, by then owner of the principal Kelvinside estate. Walker formed the Kelvinside Feuing Company and started the development with villas and terraced houses overlooking the River Kelvin gorge, subsequently continuing with middle-class tenements. After he died, his Trustees continued the business for more than ten years, then in 1886 sold the unfeued land to the North Kelvinside Feuing Company, which developed working-class tenements in the Burgh of Maryhill.

When he bought North Kelvinside, John Ewing Walker was a substantial second generation coachbuilder and proprietor of large livery stables, two of them being 'Greek' Thomson buildings. His father had operated a horse-drawn bus service, subsidised by the Kelvinside owners. John moved into Kelvinside House and had started to lay out the estate overlooking the Kelvin when he died suddenly in 1875. The Kelvinside manager, James Brown Montgomerie Fleming, thought Walker *'ruined the view'* by cutting down the trees, but he was wrong to say that John had *'ruined himself'*: the bankrupt coach-builder was a different John Walker.

St Charles' RC Church

143–165 Wilton Street

30 **St Charles' RC Church**, 9 Kelvinside Gardens,
1959, Gillespie, Kidd & Coia
Original plan by Coia, developed by Andy
MacMillan. Elegant modern church on dramatic
hillside site. Rustic brick, clerestory lighting,
exposed concrete frame and tall freestanding
skeletal bell tower. Sanctuary lamp and
modelled terracotta frieze of *Stations of the Cross*
on concrete beam inside, both Benno Schotz.

Wilton Street
Nos 65–107, *c.*1860/65. First terraced houses
on the estate. Charles Wilson-style details, long
white ashlar gently stepping terrace, round-
arched doors and windows, pilastered reveals.
Late 19th-century Glasgow Style wrought-iron
railings at No 87. **Nos 143–165 and 167–205**,
*c.*1860. Overlooking the Belmont Street climb
up from the river, with backs to the Kelvin, two
convex crescents of large luxurious terraced
houses in white ashlar.

31 **Kelvin Stevenson Memorial Church**, 62
Belmont Street and 93–99 Garriochmill Road,
1898, J J Stevenson
Dramatically sited on steep bank of Kelvin
gorge. Designed by a Glasgow architect on a visit

Sam Small

Kelvin Stevenson Memorial Church

from his London office, which became a gateway for many other Scots in London. Scottish gothic red sandstone church, with crowstep gables, tall tower and open crown steeple. Entered from Belmont Street at high level. Good interior, with north aisle arched arcade and gallery over, continued to west, fine detailing. Stained glass mid-20th century, Gordon Webster. Halls and caretaker's house entered from Garriochmill Road at lower level.

Belmont Bridge, Belmont Street, *c.*1870
Adjacent to the Kelvin Stevenson Memorial Church. Part-promoted by the City of Glasgow Bank to provide access from Great Western Road, thus opening up development of their North Woodside estate. Single-span high-level bridge on tall piers. Rustic lower stonework, ashlar parapet and voussoirs. Smaller north span replaced in concrete, 1971.

Lanarkshire Regimental Drill Hall

Below The 66 Steps
Bottom 13 Kelvin Drive

Lanarkshire Regimental Drill Hall, 21 Jardine
Street, 1894, Robert Alexander Bryden
Massive red brick Tudor, with timber-framed
upper floor and double gables. Central corbelled
chimney breast, carved armorial, main entrance
to right in tall corniced ashlar panel, arched
windows to basement and ground floors.

1–11 Doune Gardens, *c.*1865
White ashlar terraced houses, arranged in
stepped pairs on the side of a steep slope above
the Kelvin. Corinthian door pilasters, some with
carved owl capitals. Etched glass inner doors,
stained glass at No 5, Daniel Cottier-like side
panels at No 10.

'The 66 Steps', Kelvinside Terrace West, 1870,
Alexander Thomson
Massive stairway with rubble retaining walls
and Greek details, originally the link from the
Wilton Street plateau to a now demolished
bridge over the Kelvin. 301 Wilton Street and
2 Kelvinside Terrace West, *c.*1901. Italianate,
asymmetrical picturesque large double villa on
corner site, bold bow windows at north and west
corners.

Kelvin Drive
Nos **4–14**, *c.*1865. Smaller white ashlar terraced
houses, facing deep gorge hidden by overgrown
trees, later cast-iron veranda at No 8. Conical
tower alongside mansard attic roof at No 13,
over bold bay replacing original window;
another large conical tower at the three-full-
storey No 14. **1–15 Botanic Crescent**, *c.*1870.
Elegant Italianate crescent of houses, climbing
around the hill. **Lismore, 115 Kelvin Drive**,
*c.*1860. Picturesque Italianate villa, tall entrance
tower and bay window. Built on edge of

cliff, for Johan Keif, German Consul. **251–261 Kelvin Drive**, *c.*1895, David Wyllie. Red ashlar tenements, reminiscent of those by David Barclay in Highburgh Road, Dowanhill (see p. 44). Distinctive dormer bows, conical roofs over bowed bays, overhanging eaves, coloured glass to upper window sashes. **36–42 Clouston Street** and **1–5 Sanda Street**, *c.*1865. L-plan block, Alexander Thomson-style details on white ashlar tenements, good cast-iron railings remain.

Left *1–15 Botanic Crescent*
Above *Lismore*

MARYHILL

Maryhill Road, previously known as Gairbraid Street, was built as a turnpike in 1753, when the only industries were textile manufacture, bleaching and calico printing. Gairbraid was one of the large estates dating from the Reformation. The Forth & Clyde Canal crossed the Kelvin on Whitworth's famous aqueduct in 1787 and the Glasgow branch canal reached Port Dundas in 1790. Mary Hill, heiress of Gairbraid, feued land along the canal and the turnpike in the 1790s, but the population of her development, supposedly named after her, was only about 2,000 in 1841. By 1856 railways

Gairbraid House (demolished)

The old house of Gairbraid *now stands naked and forlorn amidst a wilderness of free coups, broken bottles and bricks, pools of dirty water, clothes lines fluttering with coloured rags and all the abominations of a new suburb. Instead of the singing of birds and the music of the soft flowing Kelvin, which of yore, pleased and refreshed the passer-by, the air is now vocal with the discordant voices of rough men, scolding women and greeting bairns, with the clang of machinery and the hiss of the steam engine.*
J Guthrie Smith, *Old Glasgow Houses of the Old Gentry*, 1878

were beginning to overtake canal transport and the Burgh was established. The 19th century saw rapid industrial development, with iron foundries on both sides of the canal, most others to the east. Several saw mills; glass and bottle works in the 1870s; Alexander Ferguson's Lead & Colour Works, 1874; George MacLellan's Glasgow Rubber Works, 1876; and several chemical works from the 1880s. The population had grown to 24,000 in 1881, and when Glasgow absorbed the Burgh in 1891 it had reached nearly 40,000. By then Maryhill Road was lined with sandstone tenements. Many more were built by John Campbell McKellar's speculative building company from 1890 to 1910. Slum clearance in the 1930s was followed in the 1960s by demolitions for the lower-density Comprehensive Redevelopment of North Woodside and for the construction of an Expressway to remove a bottleneck on the commuter route from Bearsden and Milngavie (which is also the tourist route to the Trossachs), leaving a population dramatically reduced to around 25,000.

Hathaway Lane, *c.*1978, McAllister, Armstrong & Partners
Early tenement refurbishment for Glasgow District Council. Saltire Society Commendation, 1980.

Stow West Keltec Project, 75 Hotspur Street, *c.*1905, Robert Alexander Bryden
Built as Garrioch School for Maryhill School Board. Baroque-detailed red ashlar. Designed after Bryden left Clarke & Bell, where he was the partner responsible for the extension to the Christian Institute in Bothwell Street (see *Central Glasgow* Guide).

Above *Garrioch School*
Right *Craigen Court*

Craigen Court, Shakespeare Street, *c.*1989, Ken MacRae, with McGurn, Logan, Duncan & Opfer
Winner of the RIAS/Maryhill Housing Association Competition for the 21st Century Tenement, 1984. Brick-faced, split-level flatted dwellings. Saltire Society Commendation, 1990.

Ruchill Parish Church, 15 Shakespeare Street,
1903, Neil C Duff
Perpendicular gothic, red Locharbriggs
sandstone, buttressed south-west tower, Art
Nouveau glass. United Presbyterian Church built
before reunification with the Church of Scotland.

Ruchill Parish Church and Hall

32 **Ruchill Parish Church Hall**, 17 Shakespeare
Street, 1899, Charles Rennie Mackintosh
Built as mission halls for Westbourne Free
Church before the adjacent United Presbyterian
Church. Tall Art Nouveau halls and janitor's
house around tiny courtyard. Internal walls
two-thirds panelled, typical Mackintosh glazed
door panels, curved stair with cut-out design on
landing balustrade.

Maryhill Barracks, 1876
Garrioch Barracks, as they were originally
called, were built on 12 hectares (30 acres) of the
Ruchill estate, to house an infantry regiment,
a squadron of cavalry and a battery of field
artillery. The City Council had been petitioning
the government since the early 1800s for more
military protection from their fear of 'riot and
tumult' in the growing industrial areas. Higher
quality than normal, the barracks seem to have
reduced vandalism and engendered a sense of
community.

Glenfinnan Drive, Wyndford Estate, 1960, Harold Buteux, Scottish Special Housing Association
Sensitive, mixed high- and low-rise housing development within the old barracks walls. Saltire Society Award, 1968.

Maryhill Burgh Halls

Maryhill Burgh Halls, 10 Gairbraid Avenue, *c.*1878, Duncan McNaughtan
French Renaissance urban palace looking down Maryhill Road. Corinthian columns support parapet over entrance porch, clock in pediment above. Slender ventilator, ogee roof and finial. Large hall to rear, similar features. McNaughtan was better known for his tall Baltic Chambers (see *Central Glasgow* Guide). After some years as a community centre, refurbished, 2005, JM Architects.

Maryhill Public Baths & Washhouses, 64 Burnhouse Street, 1896, A B McDonald
Edwardian renaissance polished ashlar, on steep site, iron truss-roofed laundry, Ionic dwarf columns in windows. Proposed conversion to swimming pool, 2005, Glasgow City Council.

Maryhill Public Library

Andrew Carnegie (1835–1919) gifted £100,000 for 14 libraries in Glasgow on 15 May 1901. Seven of the buildings were designed by James Rhind, of Inverness and previously Montreal, who won with them in competition: Woodside, Maryhill, Dennistoun, Bridgeton, Parkhead, Govanhill and Hutchesontoun.

Maryhill Public Library, 1508 Maryhill Road, 1902, James Robert (J R) Rhind
Rich renaissance details and sculpture on narrow frontage. Two top-lit reading rooms with original timber screens.

Forth & Clyde Canal Aqueduct, Maryhill Road, 1881
Massive masonry structure, replacement for Robert Whitworth's 18th-century original.

2064 Maryhill Road, 1875
One-and-a-half-storey H-plan double villa, first-floor dormers. Estate houses for demolished Killermont House.

Aqueduct Bridge

33 **Forth & Clyde Canal Kelvin Aqueduct**,
Skaethorn Road, 1787, Robert Whitworth
Four heavy masonry arches, each 15m (50ft)
long, on buttress piers, resembling cutwaters,
though only one in the river. Overall spectacular
structure 122m (400ft) long, 23m (70ft) high
above bed of the River Kelvin carrying the Canal
over the Kelvin valley. Rustic masonry at lower
courses, polished ashlar above. Adjoining the
river crossing, to the east, is another Whitworth
major feature of his western stretch of the Canal,
an elegant stairway of five locks and associated
oval basins, raising the navigation level nearly
12m (40ft) to reach the Glasgow Branch into
Port Dundas. These are among the finest canal
features in Britain.

GARSCUBE
In 1687 the Campbells of Succoth bought
Garscube estate which remained in their
possession until early in the 20th century.
Glasgow Corporation formed Dawsholm Park
in 1921, while Glasgow University acquired the
rest for its Department of Veterinary Science,
the latter closed to the public (for security).
Subsequent University developments include
the West of Scotland Science Park, a joint venture
with the Scottish Development Agency (SDA).

Business Units, facing Maryhill Road, *c*.2000,
Bradford Robertson Architects
Three-storey slick glass- and metal-clad,
articulated office blocks with external metal
spiral escape stairs, for Scottish Enterprise,
Glasgow.

[Garscube is] a very comfortable
place, with the air and the reality of real
luxury, in everything about it. Considering
the odious manufacturing country that
surrounds it, its principal excellence is
its singular seclusion within the dressed
ground of the place – the stranger could
never suspect, while admiring its trees,
beautiful grass, well kept walks, its garden,
stream and mansion house, that if he
ventured to raise his head above the slopes
that enclose him, he would see groves of
chimneys, the obelisks of manufacturers,
polluting the atmosphere on every side.
Henry, Lord Cockburn, writing in
Circuit Journeys, 1843, of the great
Tudor-Jacobean house designed by
William Burn in 1827 and demolished
by the University.

Old Garscube House (demolished
before 1827)

One Todd Campus, West of Scotland Science
Park, 1981, William Gillespie & Partners
Symmetrical stepped red brick, grey steel
pagoda roof and tinted glass clerestory lighting
(colour page 36). **Industrial Units**, Kelvin
Campus, West of Scotland Science Park, 1981,
David Harper Mann, SDA. Three crescents of
red brick, top-lit, metal-roofed industrial units.
Observatory, Glasgow University Astronomy
Department, Acre Road, 1964, Keppie
Henderson & Partners. Sculptural concrete roof
over long brick block, ending in copper-domed
tower in bleak hilltop surroundings.

Killermont (Garscube) Bridge, Maryhill Road,
1925, Thomas Somers, City Engineer, with
Considère Construction
An elegant double-span reinforced concrete
segmental arch over the River Kelvin, replacing
an earlier triple-span masonry bridge. Solid
granite abutments and parapet.

BALMORE ROAD

Carron Wharf, Port Dundas

*We come to the most surprising
phenomenon which I ever witnessed
on any part of the earth's surface – a
Harbour on a Hill! Looking up from one
of the openings in Argyle Street, I saw,
or fancied, a grove of masts far above the
highest steeple in Glasgow! After half an
hour's laborious ascent, scrambling from
flat to flat, and from factory to factory,
among cotton and carbon, sulphur and
soda, I reached a lofty eminence that
overlooked the great western metropolis,
and found myself in – 'Port Dundas!' This
eccentric Port was crowded with shipping.*
James Johnston, *The Recess, or Autumn
Relaxation in the Highlands and
Lowlands*, 1834

PORT DUNDAS

Port Dundas marked the end of the Glasgow
branch of the Forth & Clyde Canal. It was
completed in 1790 and named after Sir
Lawrence Dundas, Governor of the Canal
Company. At the end was a timber seasoning
basin and a distillery. Other industry soon
followed: granaries, sugar refining, chemicals,
iron founding and engineering. The Canal
water level, 41m (156ft) above sea level at Port
Dundas, is 35m (135ft) above the Clyde Street
carriageway. The contemporary Monklands
Canal linked the Lanarkshire coalfields to the
Forth & Clyde at Port Dundas by a 'cut of

junction'. A series of four locks, constructed in 1785 at Blackhill, raised the navigation level of the Forth & Clyde Canal by some 29m (96ft) to the level of the Monklands Canal.

Above *Canal Offices (drawing)*
Left *Canal House following restoration*

Railway Swing Bridge, Mid Wharf Street and North Canal Bank Street, *c.*1890. Single-track Caledonian Railway swing bridge, with hand-operated gear. Bow-sided plate girder, stone abutments. **Bascule Bridge**, Mid Wharf Street, North Canal Bank Street and North Speirs Wharf, early 19th century. Sole survivor of standard Forth & Clyde Canal type. Two timber lifting spans, with hand-operated cast-iron mechanism and balance weights, attached to hollow stone abutments. **Canal House**, 2 Speirs Wharf, *c.*1800. Attractive two-storey Georgian office, with central pediment and Roman Doric columned porch, restored 1989. **City of Glasgow Grain Mills**, 4–38 Speirs Wharf, *c.*1851. Four large blocks, five- and six-storey white ashlar, with former loading doors capped by open pediment hoods. Converted to flats and private leisure suite, 1989, Nicholas Groves-Raines. **Port Dundas Sugar Refinery**, 40–50 Speirs Wharf, 1866. Seven-storey, classical pediment above three projecting centre bays, end pairs also project. White ashlar front to canal, red and white brick other walls. Converted to flats 1991, James Cunning, Young & Partners. The entire Port Dundas complex restoration for Windex, including the adjacent Wheatsheaf Building, won both a Civic Trust Award and a Europa Nostra Award in 1991. **Forth & Clyde Canal Workshops**, Applecross Street, *c.*1800. Long range of whitewashed rubble buildings, brick at west end, also two-storey house.

City of Glasgow Grain Mills

Port Dundas Sugar Refinery

Top *Possil House (demolished)*
Above *Saracen Works (demolished)*
Right *St Teresa of Lisieux RC Church*

POSSIL

Industry on the lands of Possil was encouraged by the Canal, which had reached Hamiltonhill in 1777. Lower Possil estate and mansion were acquired by Walter Macfarlane before 1878, when his relocated Saracen Foundry was already in business. There he laid out a splendid suburb, where Lindsay & Benzie built many tenements before moving across to Hillhead and the West End. The City's new Housing Department built hundreds more dwellings during the 1920s.

Passing 'the Harbour on the Hill' and emerging to the northward from the urban labyrinth by the Possil road, the morning air is clear and cool. A gentle breeze is playing over the spiky fields of wheat. About a mile out we pass Possil House, the residence of our respected sheriff, Sir Archibald Alison, Bart. The house is large and substantial but withal plain edifice and is surrounded by finely timbered policies of considerable extent.
Hugh MacDonald, *Rambles Round Glasgow*, 1854

Walter Macfarlane (1817-1885) started his first iron foundry in 1859, at Saracen Lane, off Gallowgate, where he made cast-iron plumbing and architectural products. He moved to a larger site at Washington Street, Anderston in 1862, before making his final move to 73 Hawthorn Street, Possil. There the Saracen Works, designed in 1869 by James Boucher, grew to become the largest architectural iron foundry in Europe, casting a vast range of items from rainwater goods and domestic mantelpieces to public shelters, fountains and bandstands. The works were demolished in 1967.

34 **St Teresa of Lisieux RC Church**, 86–90 Saracen Street, 1956, Alexander McAnally
The dominant public building of Possil. Romanesque T-plan church, red brick, cream dressings, round-arched openings, relief of St Teresa on tower, aluminium spire. Rich high-quality timber and marble interior; stained glass, Guthrie & Wells. Fire-damaged hall replaced by new stepped range of barrel-vaulted, glazed timber function rooms constructed inside, 1995, Page & Park: Europa Nostra Award, 1996.

Possilpark Library, 17 Allander Street, 1911, George Simpson
Baroque features, single-storey, top-lit. Internal features remain, including Glasgow School of Art student classical figure paintings: *Art*, Helen Johnston; *Astronomy*, Alma Assefey; *Commerce*, Robertson Weir; *Geography*, Archibald McGlashen; *Poetry*, Tom Gentleman; *Science*, Josephine Cameron.

Possilpark Library

Ruchill House (demolished)

RUCHILL

Early in the 18th century James Peadie, a sugar merchant and one-time Provost of Glasgow, became owner of the estate of Ruchill. Allan Dreghorn, an early Virginia 'tobacco lord', bought the estate from the Peadies in 1749. Although part was soon to be alienated as Bankland (see Kelvinside, pp. 21–24), the estate remained rural until the East India merchant William James Davidson sold the remainder to Glasgow Corporation in 1892. The City built Ruchill Fever Hospital on gently rising ground to the north. Treating the then killer diseases of scarlet fever, measles, whooping cough and tuberculosis, the hospital was 'isolated' by the 21-hectare (53-acre) hilltop Ruchill Park and the adjoining Golf Course to the south.

Mondriaan Housing, 2005, Holmes Partnership
Built by the canal, on the site of MacLellan's Rubber Works. Façade design inspired by the works of Dutch neo-plasticist painter Piet Mondriaan (1872–1944).

Sir Archibald Alison (1792–1867) was a historian, a sheriff and among the first Honorary Fellows of the Architectural Institute of Scotland. A Tory advocate for the resistance of popular intimidation, he all but strangled the Scottish trades unions at birth, to prevent the weavers' riots leading to civil war. He also raised his voice against the distress caused to children of the able-bodied unemployed. He wished the law changed but his judgements were overturned by the Court of Session.

Water Tower at Ruchill Hospital

35 Water Tower, Ruchill Hospital, 520 Bilsland Drive, 1892, A B McDonald
The magnificent focal point, and the best of the cocooned remains, of an infectious diseases hospital with many separate ward blocks. Tall square red brick and stone tower on pedestal, with decorated two-stage body and complex three-stage head resembling a Flemish bell tower. Octagonal turrets, bell-roofed with onion finials to corners of first stage; another octagonal tower with pyramid roof, drum of columns, cupola with foliage top and finial to top stage of head (colour page 103).

LAMBHILL
Lambhill estate and the House, north of the Canal and outside the City boundary, was the property of Robert Graham in 1795. The canal stables, now ruinous, date from the early 19th century. The Lambhill Iron, later Engineering Works, of R Laidlaw & Son, on the south of the canal, next to the old Possil quarries, dates from 1881. Coal pits at Cadder, about 2 kilometres (1.25 miles) north of the bridge, were closed in 1913 after a fatal accident, when the owners, the Carron Company, were found negligent in not providing safety equipment. The original Canal bridge of 1790 was replaced in 1930 by a steel bascule bridge, after Glasgow's Housing Department built some 230 dwellings in Hawthorn Street and 70 more at Lambhill, in 1919; all later transferred to the city. In 1947, over 100 more houses had been started, of the 850 planned by the Corporation for Cadder Road.

Greenview School

Greenview School, 165 Glenhead Street, 1929, John Austen Laird
Built as Balmore Public School. Queen Anne, long splayed wings, central hall. Decorative glass enclosing corridors, 1962, R W K C Rogerson.

Chirnside Primary School, 284–288 Ashgill
Road, 1950, Ninian Johnston
Early example of post-World War II school,
reinforced concrete, brick and glass skin, very
shallow pitched roof. L-plan en-suite janitor's
house.

St Augustine's RC Church

St Augustine's RC Church & Presbytery, 393
Ashgill Road, 1954, Reginald Fairlie & Partners
Spanish Colonial, white harl with green
Westmorland slate roof, parabolic concrete
arched interior. Carved panels of St Augustine
and the Loaves and Fishes over entrance.

St Agnes RC Church, 694 Balmore Road, 1893,
Pugin & Pugin
Large, perpendicular gothic, towerless, red
Locharbriggs sandstone. Lavish gilded stencilled
interior, 1913, Pugin & Pugin. Outstanding
alabaster pulpit, Stations of the Cross, 1906,
Bruges.

Lambhill Cemetery Entrance

690 Balmore Road, 1880, possibly Pugin & Pugin
Built as St Agnes School. Central gable and
bellcote, red sandstone, cocooned.

Lambhill Cemetery Entrance Arch, 1035
Balmore Road, 1880, James Sellars
Severe classical triumphal arch in banded ashlar,
good cast-iron gates. Former Lodges behind
flank walls, demolished 1991.

Crematorium, Western Necropolis, 19 Tresta
Road, 1893, James Chalmers
Built for Scottish Burial Reform & Cremation
Society. Gothic, red sandstone, short nave, large
unfinished tower and stairturret. Memorial
plaques inside, stained glass, 1950 Harrington
Mann and 1965 Gordon Webster.

SPRINGBURN ROAD
GARNGAD
To the east of St Rollox, on the Rosebank estate, Charles Tennant II, son of Charles Tennant of the St Rollox Chemical Works, opened Garngad Copperworks in 1866. He already owned the Tharsis Copper Mines in Spain. This was just one of many industries to develop in the area after 1860. Tenement houses were built nearby and on the Garngadhill drumlin. Garngad and Garngadhill were renamed Royston and Roystonhill by Glasgow Corporation in 1942.

*Townhead & Blochairn Parish Church
Spire (only the spire now remains)*

Royston Hill

36 **Townhead & Blochairn Parish Church Spire**, 176 Roystonhill, 1865, Campbell Douglas & Stevenson
Very tall geometrical gothic tapering tower and spire, grey rubble, on dramatic hilltop setting, centrepiece of Spire Park, created on the site of the demolished church.

Roystonhill, 2000
Imaginative refurbishment of four-storey flats climbing around the hill high above the M8 motorway.

Royston Primary School, 102 Royston Road,
1906, Duncan McNaughtan & Son
Built as St Rollox School. Renaissance with
Mackintosh-inspired details. Projecting gabled
hall across corridor.

200–284 Royston Road, 2000
Fresh new four-storey flats for housing co-
operative, a sign of the renewal of a badly run-
down area.

ST ROLLOX
St Rollox is a corruption of St Roche. By 1795
the mansion of Rollocks, just north of the Cut
of Junction canal, was owned by A Warren,
but it was soon displaced by Charles Tennant's
massive chemical works started in 1799. The
famous Tennant's Stalk, built in 1842 to disperse
smoke and chemical fumes, was 133m (435ft)
high and 12m (40ft) wide at the base. It was
demolished in 1922. On the site of the chemical
waste dump Crudens built the Sighthill
multistorey flats in 1961.

St Roche the Confessor was the patron
of plague sufferers. A chapel was
founded, in 1508, in the muir outside
the north gate of Glasgow, by Thomas
Muirhead, Rector of Stobo and Canon
of Glasgow Cathedral. He was a
nephew of bishop Andrew Muirhead,
who died in 1473. The cemetery
adjacent to the chapel was used in the
Glasgow plague epidemic of 1445–6.

Cowlairs House (demolished)

RCAHMS

Across Springburn Road from Tennant's
Chemical Works, the Caledonian Railway built
St Rollox Works in 1856. Like the Edinburgh &
Glasgow, the 'Caley' works built and repaired
locomotives, carriages and wagons until, as
the last surviving Springburn railway works,
they were closed in 1987. The late 18th-century
Scott family mansion of Cowlairs was rebuilt
by the distiller James Gourlay, but in 1841 the

Above Wheelwright Shop, St Rollox
Right St Rollox (Caledonian) Offices

Edinburgh & Glasgow Railway Company built
their Cowlairs Works on the estate, next to their
46m (150ft) drop 'inclined tunnel' into Queen
Street Station. In 1865 the Edinburgh & Glasgow
was absorbed by the North British Railway
Company. The works closed in 1968, when
British Rail stopped using steam locomotives.

St Rollox House, 130–132 Springburn Road,
1887, Robert Dundas, engineer
Former St Rollox Railway Works Offices.
Long red brick block, with yellow dressings,
round-arched windows in pilastered bays, for
Caledonian Railway Company. Now occupied
by Scottish Enterprise, Glasgow North.

Sighthill Cemetery, 201 Springburn Road,
opened 1840
19 hectares (46 acres) on a dramatic hill site.
Lodge and Gateway to Sighthill Cemetery,
Springburn Road, 1839, John Stephen. Greek-
detailed miniature temple acts as lodge at
gateway to Cemetery; modern iron gates and
railings. **Martyr's Memorial**, 1847 to John Baird
and Andrew Hardie, the hanged leaders of the
Radical uprising of 1820. Tall classical pedestal,
relief sculpture on one face, grey sandstone,
bellcast cap, draped urn. Many tombstones by
John Mossman and others, commemorating the
architect William Leiper, the shipbuilder Robert
Curle and Bailie James Moir, a Parliamentary
reformer. The Mitchell Library has his book
collection and named the James Moir Hall in his
memory. **Gateway**, Keppochhill Road, with the
original decorative cast iron.

Lodge at entrance to Sighthill Cemetery

SPRINGBURN
Climbing further up the steep Kirkintilloch Road
there were three small villages, housing weavers,
agricultural labourers and quarry workers before
the heavy industries reached here. The first,
at Springvale, was built to accommodate the
workforce of Joseph Findlay's cotton-spinning

mill and the others were located at Springburn
Cross and Balgrayhill. The Petershill mansion,
built for Alexander Williamson, survived
through the 1890s to the north of St Rollox Works
and south of the two Springburn locomotive
works. North of the railway works, Mosesfield
was one of the villas here at the end of the 18th
century.

Near Petershill was the Barony Poorhouse,
built by Glasgow Parochial Board, who imposed
austere conditions on the destitute, infirm or
aged inmates. It was later called the Barnhill
Institute and then Foresthall. Beyond the
Springburn Park, the Barony Parish Board built a
Poor Law Hospital. It opened in 1904, with 1,867
beds, and is now the Stobhill General Hospital.

Numerous steep drumlins underlie this
area; Balgray Hill, at 107m (351ft), is nearly the
highest point in the city, after Carmunnock. The
new expressway of the 1970s CDA completed
the destruction of Old Springburn, of which a
few gems survive.

Springburn Public Halls

Springburn Public Halls, 46 Keppochhill Road,
1899, William B Whitie
Whitie is better known for his Mitchell
Library (see *Central Glasgow* Guide). Italian
Renaissance, round-headed window between
Ionic columns supporting a big pediment, all
red ashlar. Original interior galleries and organ
in wide plaster-vaulted main hall. A James Reid
benefaction, built after his death in 1894, the
seating capacity was 1,600. Converted to Sports
Centre, 1963, now apparently abandoned and at
risk.

Elmvale Primary School, 104 Elmvale Street,
1901, H E Clifford
Handsome, tall red sandstone Board School
with Art Nouveau details. Deep curved eaves,
slate roof and leaded ventilators. Janitor's house
recalls Salmon or Charles Rennie Mackintosh.

The Blocks, Ratho Terrace (demolished)

North Glasgow College – former North British Locomotive Company

Walter Neilson (1818–1889), son of James Beaumont Neilson, moved his Hyde Park Works to Springburn from Finnieston in 1861. He sold out to his partner James Reid, but in 1884 he opened a new business across the railway line, later bought by Sharp, Stewart & Co., who renamed it Atlas Works. These two businesses, plus the Queen's Park Works at Polmadie, were amalgamated to form the North British Locomotive Company in 1903. For a while they were the biggest locomotive company outside America, with a capacity to build 600 locomotives per annum and they employed 7,570 people. The Company became bankrupt in 1962 and the Administration building is now part of North Glasgow College.

37 **North Glasgow College**, 120–136 Flemington Street, 1908, James Miller
Former North British Locomotive Company offices. Four tall blocks around courtyard. Edwardian grand baroque, Ionic columned projecting central entrance and end pavilions, red ashlar to street, other walls brick, polychrome-glazed to courtyard. Impressive baroque decorated entrance hall, and lavish principal rooms. First World War Memorial windows above main stair, William Meikle & Sons. Converted to College 1962.

Springburn Library & Museum, 179 Ayr Street, 1902, William B Whitie
Edwardian baroque, top-lit single-storey red ashlar with baluster parapet, Ionic entrance, round-arched doorway.

Springburn Library

St Aloysius RC Church & Presbytery, 6–10 Hillkirk Street, 1881, John Leck Bruce, of Bruce & Sturrock
Early English gothic in cream ashlar, gabled west front, porch to north, original baptistery to south. Interior more decorative, stained glass by Hooper.

Trustee Savings Bank Building, 247–255 Springburn Way (former Springburn Road), 1893, Robert Ewan
Renaissance details, sculpted friezes, big cornice on brackets.

38 **Redclyffe**, 140–142 Balgrayhill Road, 1890, Charles Rennie Mackintosh
Immature Mackintosh for his cousin James Hamilton. Symmetrical double villa with massive outer bay windows, smaller inner bays

Redclyffe

beneath swept-down slate roof, on brackets. Coarse red ashlar, polished dressings, stone mullions, small-pane upper sashes, leaded at No 140. Wrought-iron gates and railings to low boundary wall.

104–138 Balgrayhill Road, *c.*1975, Baxter Clark & Paul
Early low-rise, brick-built housing, breaking Glasgow's high-rise pattern. Saltire Society Commendation, 1977.

Balgray Tower, 52 Broomfield Road, 1820, Moses McCulloch
For James Duncan of Mosesfield House. Gothic, battlemented villa, with octagonal stairtower on harled rubble block.

Immaculate Heart of Mary RC Church, 166 Broomfield Road, 1950, T S Cordiner
Design influenced by Jack Coia. Triangular concrete trusses, low eaves, brick walls, gable wheel window and sculpture of Our Lady.

Springburn Park was formed on high ground gifted in 1892 by James Reid of the locomotive works. He also gifted a bandstand and a house, New Mosesfield, for a museum. Column, formerly part of a fountain, late 19th century. Re-sited from Balgray Pleasure Ground. Mannerist-style glazed terracotta, painted Ionic column, with thistle and other motifs representing nations of UK and Ireland and capped by a unicorn and St Andrew's Cross. Statue of James Reid, 1903, Sir William Goscombe John. Bronze figure of James Reid of Hyde Park Works and female figure plaques on granite plinth. Art Nouveau touches on wrought-iron enclosure.

Below *Balgray Tower*
Bottom *Immaculate Heart of Mary RC Church*

Winter Gardens

Superintendant's House & Water Tower, Stobhill

39 **Winter Gardens**, Springburn Park, 1899, Simpson & Farmer, hothouse builders 55m- (180ft)-long glasshouse gifted by James Reid. Frame made by William Baird of Temple Ironworks. Elegant glazed cast-iron arched roof, carried by mild steel girders on tall red brick walls, with round-arched windows. Low clerestory across ridge, decorative thistle crest. Internal gallery all round, cast-iron stairs with decorative cast-iron balustrades. Today a skeleton, awaiting funding for restoration

Colston Wellpark Church, 1378 Springburn Road, 1915, H E Clifford
Bland gothic with flamboyant traceried east window, red rubble and ashlar dressings with hammerbeam roof. Burning Bush east window, *c*.2000, Alex Moffat. Stained glass executed by Colston Glass Project (colour page 102).

Stobhill General Hospital, 133 Balornock Road, 1900, Thomson & Sandilands
Symmetrical, columned porch and broken pediment over projecting centre, gable-ended pavilions, in red brick and ashlar. Very prominent red ashlar water tower displaying clock face. Late 19th-century Arts & Crafts half-timbered villa, former **Superintendant's House**, now staff dining room.

McKinnon House, Stobhill Hospital, 1990s, Matheson Gleave Architects
Intimate, domestic-scale, cruciform-plan Psychiatric Care Unit. Three wings of self-contained ward accommodation, the fourth for more intensive treatment. Brick-faced, timber frame, large glazed areas overlook landscaped courts.

BALORNOCK

South of Springburn Park is Balornock, an interwar Corporation estate of about 2,000 houses. Further south is Barmulloch, another post-war scheme in the area. The Scottish Special Housing Association built 2,000 non-traditional houses, including some Swedish timber and other prefabricated types.

Red Road High Flats

High Flats, Red Road, 1962, Sam Bunton
26- to 31-storey, steel-framed flats, built by the City's Direct Labour Organisation. When constructed, they were the tallest flats in Europe. 1980s refurbishment includes vigorous coloured patterns on elevations. Having acquired a notorious reputation, now to be demolished.

ROBROYSTON

Wallace Monument, Robroyston Road, 1900, McGlashan sculptors
Tall pink granite Celtic cross, on plinth, derived from St Martin's, Iona. William Wallace was reputedly captured here in 1305; the site now near Robroyston Mains farm cottages.

EDINBURGH ROAD
BELLGROVE

James Graham, one-time owner of the Saracen's Head Inn, tried to sell 22 plots for a suburban housing development at Graham Square before 1778. He was not successful until the city moved its cattle market to Bellgrove in 1817. The City Architect roofed over the cattle market after the Glasgow Markets and Slaughterhouses Act of 1865, extending the roof to cover the meat market ten years later.

After the 18th century, the principal route to the east travelled along Gallowgate from Glasgow Cross, passing through the flat lands of Bellgrove, then along a low shelf on the gentle slope of the Clyde Valley, through Parkhead and Tollcross before climbing steeply out of the valley up to Bellshill and on to Kirk o' Shotts.

Above *Entrance to former Cattle & Meat Markets*
Right *Matador*

Graham Square
14–28 Melbourne Street, former Slaughter House, *c.*1910, A B McDonald. Gateway, with two massive piers and wrought-iron gates bearing City crest. **Moore Street**, former Meat Market, *c.*1875, John Carrick. Classical round-arched opening, between giant Ordered frames (colour page 37).

40 **Graham Square**, west side, *c.*1997, McKeown Alexander. Office block and 20 flats for Housing Association screened by and supporting another entrance arch of similar size and style, which led to the Meat Market from the Cattle Market. Scottish Architectural Award, 2000. **Graham Square**, former Cattle Market main entrance, *c.*1866, John Carrick. Enormous central columned Roman Doric archway, flanked by

41 pedestrian openings. **Market Hotel**, 4 Graham Square, east side, renovation and new build *c.*1997, Richard Murphy Architects. Residential complex, with external steel stairs, steel balconies and glass canopies; linking two rebuilt 19th-century harled end pavilions by Carrick,

42 now forming 17 flats. **Matador Building**, Graham Square, east side, *c.*1995, Page & Park (colour page 102). Twenty-four flats for Housing Association. Civic Trust Award, 2000; Regeneration of Scotland Award, 2000. **Bellgrove Street**, *c.*1999, McGurn, Logan, Duncan & Opfer. New four-storey flats for Housing Association. **Bellgrove Street**, *c.*1866, John Carrick. A second, smaller, heavily rusticated opening in the channelled ashlar boundary wall led from the North British Railway cattle pens to the former cattle handling sheds beside the Cattle Market.

DENNISTOUN

Easter and Wester Craigs belonged to George Hutcheson in 1652. Alexander Dennistoun built Golfhill House on part of the Craigs and, c.1850, he commissioned James Salmon to prepare a feuing plan for a private housing suburb called Broom Park, on the lands of Craig Park and Whitehill. Work started two years later, with villas at Wester Craigs, but the plan was soon abandoned, terraces and tenements being built north of Duke Street uphill towards Alexandra Parade, in the estate now called Dennistoun. Ten years later he bought lands of Annfield and Bellfield, parts of the Craigs south of Duke Street, from trustees for the late John Reid, to continue his development. These villas had been named after the wives of the original owners. The junction of Duke Street and Belgrove Street, shown on maps as King's Cross, has always been known locally as Bellgrove. Just beyond the eastern boundary of Dennistoun's lands, across Cumbernauld Road, Netherfield Chemical Works had been established by R & J Garroway on Haghill lands in 1817. They were major producers of sulphuric acid but now make cat litter. They were followed by other industrial works, the Glenpark Tan Works of 1864, Thomas Hinshelwood's Paint, Varnish and Oil Works in Glenpark Street, 1878 and Beattie's 1886 Dennistoun Bakery in Paton Street.

Annfield House (demolished)

St Anne's RC Church

43 **St Anne's RC Church & Presbytery**,
17 Whitevale Street, 1931, Gillespie, Kidd & Coia
Coia's first church, a small-scale blend of early christian and Italian Romanesque, inspired by a study tour in 1923 (colour page 103). Concrete frame, red brick, red roof tiles. Cross over entrance carved by Archibald Dawson. Vaulted nave and narrow side aisles, brick piers, carved capitals and *Stations of the Cross*, Archibald

Duke Street, Sword Street, Annbank Street

Dawson. Asymmetrical presbytery to south, arched head entrance, broad eaves, prominent chimneys, small-paned windows. Decorative wrought-iron gates and railings in brick perimeter walls

Duke Street, Sword Street, Annbank Street, 1993, Elder & Cannon

Yellow brick tenement flats for Housing Association, unconventional layout with living rooms facing south over private square (colour page 37). Saltire Society Award, 1994.

247–249 Duke Street, *c.*1904, Alfred Hessell Tiltman, London

Former Duke Street Women's Hospital, gatehouse block. French Renaissance red sandstone façade, elaborately detailed arched windows and vehicular entrance. Dutch gabled central bay. Converted to flats, 2000.

George Macintosh had started his own shoemaking business in King Street, having left the Tanwork Company on the Molendinar, where he had trained as a clerk. Within a few years both companies were employing 300 shoemakers. About 1770, with partner John Glassford of tobacco fame, he brought Cuthbert Gordon's Cudbear Works to Ark Lane, off Duke Street, from Leith. The process made a dyestuff from lichen. George built a house next door, called Dunchattan.

George Mackintosh's Cudbear Works at Ark Lane, used 2,000 gallons of urine a day, collected from 1,500 casks dispersed in the houses of Glasgow and suburbs. Rev. John Burns, *Statistical Account of Barony Parish*, 1794

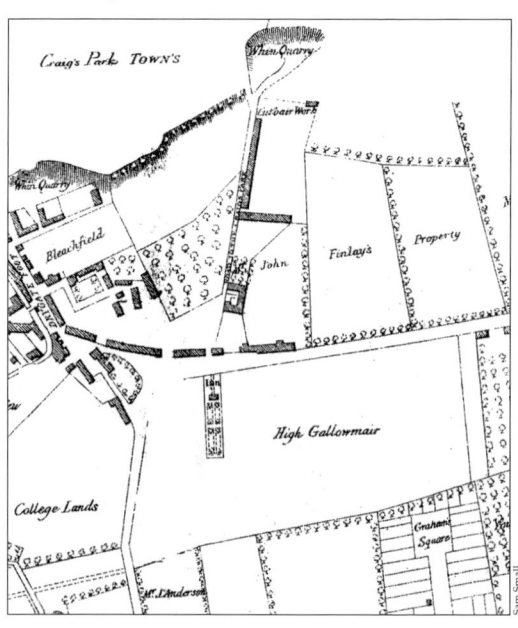

Cudbear Works

Westercraigs Court, Westercraigs, 1988, D Toner & Ker

Conversion of Campbell Douglas & Sellars' redundant German Renaissance 1876 Blackfriars Church to flats. Neat transition between adjoining tenements and smaller-scale terraced houses climbing the hill towards Alexandra Parade and the road to Cumbernauld and Stirling.

35–37 Westercraigs, late 19th century
Symmetrical semidetached Italianate double
villa. Ashlar fronted, shallow-arched porches,
columns with swagged caps with slate roof and
deep eaves.

23–49 Broompark Drive, late 19th century
Unassuming pleasant two-storey south-facing
terrace on the higher slopes of Dennistoun.
Good example of middle-class Dennistoun
character. Symmetrical, punctuated by
distinctive paired round-arched doorcases.
Heavy cast-iron details.

Golfhill Public School, 1–13 Circus Drive,
1902, A N Paterson
Baroque pilasters and arched windows at centre
of symmetrical red sandstone Board School.
Paterson was best known for his Liberal Club,
later the first Royal Scottish Academy of Music,
54 West George Street (see *Central Glasgow
Guide*).

6 Broompark Circus, late 19th century
Substantial L-plan villa, grander than most
in Dennistoun. First-floor arched windows,
sculpted panels, Corinthian columned porch.

An East End Industrial Exhibition was
organised in 1890–1, in the 1836 former
Reformatory for Boys building at Duke
Street, attracting nearly three quarters
of a million visitors and making a
substantial profit. Another was held
in temporary buildings in 1903–4 but,
despite attracting even more visitors,
made very little profit. One of the
attractions at both was Buffalo Bill's
'Wild West Show'. There was a skating
rink nearby in those days but in 1922
the site was transformed into a Palais
de Danse. The enormously popular
'Denny Pally' had the biggest dance
floor in Glasgow and was rebuilt after
a fire in 1938 but closed after 1962; the
site is now a supermarket.

Above *6 Broompark Circus*
Left *Our Lady of Good Counsel RC
Church*

44 **Our Lady of Good Counsel RC Church**, 73
   Craigpark, 1964, Gillespie, Kidd & Coia
   Splayed plan fits the wedge-shaped site. Huge
   copper-clad roof, raked in two directions, deep
   fascia at eaves, wedge-shaped plan. Brown brick,
   eaves glazing to east, doors at each end, glazing
   band on west between high and second low
   copper roof. Internal concrete columns support
   main beams, sloping pine ceiling, west gallery
   over sacristy and confessionals.

Former Dennistoun Baths, Craigpark

Snooker Club, 164–166 Craigpark, late 19th century
Built as Dennistoun Baths. French Renaissance, surprisingly domestic-looking for a swimming club, with a bay window and large sculpted panel (colour page 102).

WD & HO Wills Tobacco Factory

WD & HO Wills Tobacco Factory, 368 Alexandra Parade, 1946, Imperial Tobacco Company Engineer
1930s-style, massive square brick courtyard block. Symmetrical north front, central entry and services tower and corner towers. Extended and refurbished as City Park, providing 28,000 square metres (300,000 square feet) of office space, Cooper Cromar, 2001. Four Regeneration Awards, 2006.

Alexandra Parade Public School, 540 Alexandra Parade, 1896, Macwhannell & Rogerson
Arts & Crafts red sandstone Board School, Art Nouveau decorated entrance. T-plan, symmetrical front, inscription at central gable. Parapets and ventilators on slate roofs.

Craigpark House (demolished)

Craigpark
No 22, *c*.1870. L-plan villa, round-arched, bowed bay in gable to right. Compare with 74 Partickhill Road (see p. 14). **1–16 Annfield Place** and **1–2 Craigpark**, 1851. The first terrace in the estate. Italianate terraced houses, four altered for shops *c*.1931.

Dennistoun Library, 2a Craigpark, 1903,
J R Rhind
Edwardian Baroque, in pale sandstone, sculpted
figures top end dome. Reading room top-lit.
Much altered 1967, Rogerson & Spence.

Dennistoun Central Church of Scotland, 9
Armadale Street and Roselea Drive, 1874,
James Salmon & Son
Built as a Free Church. Early English gothic, with
ungainly square corner tower, 46m (150ft) high
stone spire and four pinnacles. Gallery on cast-
iron columns; organ, Willis of London. Salmon,
a Liberal Town Councillor and Free Kirker, lived
nearby in his own suburb.

St Denis RC Primary School, 129 Roselea Drive,
1883, James Salmon & Son
Built as Dennistoun Public School. Scots
Renaissance, grey sandstone. Early version of the
standard plan, with classrooms around central
staircase hall, entered here through a ground-
floor arcade.

Dennistoun Library

637–647 Alexandra Parade

637–647 Alexandra Parade and **81 Alexandra
Park Street**, 1874
Carefree French mansard end pavilions on plain
ashlar tenements.

Drinking Fountain, at Park gate, *c.*1870
Figure fountain in raised basin, four columns
carry ornate dome. Example of 19th century
mass production.

Walter Macfarlane Fountain, Alexandra Park,
1901, David Watson Stevenson
Greek-detailed cast-iron monument, with high-
quality entwined dolphins and four classical
females representing Art, Literature, Science
and Commerce on plinth, set in basin. A copy
of Athens's Choragic Monument of Lysicrates

The site for Alexandra Park was
bought by the City in 1866, mostly
from Walter Stewart of Haghill,
although Alexander Dennistoun gifted
five acres to give an entrance from the
Parade. The Parks Superintendent soon
reported that pollution from Provan
Gasworks and Blochairn Steelworks
was damaging much of the planting.
Paddle boating was once popular on
the pond now reserved for bird life.
There was a bandstand on the site of
today's paddling pool and model yacht
racing took place on another pond.

on top, with small basin over (colour page 101). Originally centrepiece of the 1901 International Exhibition in Kelvingrove and re-sited afterwards. Refurbished 2000.

St Andrew's East Church

45 **St Andrew's East Church**, 681 Alexandra Parade, 1902, James Miller
The best of Miller's churches. Arts & Crafts variation on perpendicular gothic. Bridge link between massive twin towers perhaps inspired by some northern Scottish tower houses (colour page 103). Plain barrel-vaulted interior, gallery three sides. **Hall**, 1898, John Gaff Gillespie of James Salmon & Son. Gillespie used a simple late gothic design with subtle carved Art Nouveau touches, reminiscent of Charles Rennie Mackintosh's hall at Ruchill (see p. 63). Iron railings to street. Hall restored, 2001, Page & Park.

St Andrew's East Church Hall

RIDDRIE
Gartcraig House was one of the grandest mansions in the area before demolition in 1929 for the Corporation Scheme of 1,046 houses at Riddrie. About a third were tenements, the other two-thirds cottage style, all built on the slope climbing up the straightened Cumbernauld

Road to cross over the Monkland Canal near the 29m (96ft) high Blackhill Locks. The new road was too steep for the trams which continued to use the old Smithycroft Road.

Riddrie Supercinema, 726 Cumbernauld Road, 1937, James McKissack
One of McKissack's best cinema designs, built for George Smith and James Welsh, pioneer cinema promoters, with 1,750 seats. On an open site, the bulk of the auditorium was partly disguised by good use of the sloping site. The streamlined forms, developing the concept of differing volumes arranged in proportion to each other, built up to the central entrance, topped with the name. Opened in 1938 as the Riddrie Picture House, it became one of George Singleton's Vogue Cinemas in 1950, was sympathetically converted to a bingo hall in 1968 and remains the flagship of NB Bingo. Much of the interior decoration remains intact.

St Thomas the Apostle RC Church

St Thomas the Apostle RC Church,
826 Cumbernauld Road and Smithycroft Road, 1954, T S Cordiner
Red brick cruciform church, with large relief of Doubting Thomas on east gable. Entrance at left, baptistry opens from vestibule projecting from gable. The adjacent plain hall was the original 1924 church.

MILLERSTON
On the undulating plain above the rim of the Clyde Valley, most of Millerston is private housing recently built on the sites of Mossbank Industrial School (1869) and of Robroyston Infectious Diseases Hospital (1917). The latter was built to remove patients further from a populous area, near Belvidere Hospital, where smallpox was formerly treated.

The Tower

The Tower, Castlefield Court, *c.*1890. Scots Renaissance imitation of 17th-century tower house; crowsteps, rounded corners, corbelled to square at attic. Refurbished as part of housing development, 2000.

CRANHILL
A City Housing Scheme of two-storey flats built south of the Monklands Canal after 1945, with pre-cast foam slag made at Tollcross. The extension area of 1962 consists of three 18-storey blocks, G Bowie, Crudens.

Stepps Water Tower

Fastnet Street, 1980s, Alan McAllister & Associates
Refurbishment of the Crudens High Flats. Barrel-vaulted roofs emphasised by neon rim lighting, the best high flats refurbishment in Glasgow, clearly visible from M8 motorway.

Stepps Road, Water Tower refurbishment and floodlighting, 1998, Chris Stewart
Just across the Edinburgh Road in Ruchazie and built post-World War I, a white sectional water container, supported on 16 tall circular columns, with mushroom tops. Required to store water pumped up to a level high enough to supply the large new estates on this elevated site, which enjoys spectacular views across the Clyde Valley to the hills on the south. Regeneration of Scotland Award, 1999. Project Neptune, four wire sculptures of water deities, 2000, Andy Scott, sculptor (colour page 103).

Queenslie, post-war Industrial Estate, now looking very sad.

Wright Business Centre

46 **Wright Business Centre**, Lonmay Road, 2006, Elder & Cannon
A very trim office and conference centre by this prize-winning practice, setting a high standard for the regeneration.

CARNTYNE
Carntyne Hall was built in 1802 for Robert Gray. John 'Iron' Gray sold the land to the Corporation for Carntyne Housing Scheme of nearly 3,000 houses, two thirds being tenements built in the second phase. This part of the new Edinburgh Road was laid out in the 1920s to serve Carntyne, reaching Baillieston during the 1930s. It was later to serve the post-war Queenslie Industrial Estate.

High Carntyne Church, 358 Carntynehall Road,
1931, James Taylor Thomson
Simplified Romanesque, in brick with stone
dressings and slate roof. Nave, low south aisle,
transepts and chancel, leaded east window.
West gable front, three-light gallery window
set in round-arched panel. Thomson designed
the Church of Scotland Pavilion, the Palace
of Industries, West and the Concert Hall at
the 1938 Empire Exhibition. The Concert Hall
especially, designed under Thomas Smith (T S)
Tait's guidance, shows Thomson's transition to a
simplified modernist style.

Calvay Crescent, 1983, McGurn, Logan, Duncan
& Opfer
One of the first housing co-operative
refurbishments, comprising four-storey flats.

SHETTLESTON
A mining and weaving village on the original
low-level road to Edinburgh. The Grays of
Carntyne and the McNairs, owners of Greenfield
since 1759, were the principal coalmasters for
several generations, Gray using wind-pumps
before steam-driven pumps were introduced
after 1768. The McNairs also owned Shettleston
House, on the north side of Old Shettleston Road,
opposite McNair Street. In 1904, the site became
the North British Bottleworks, which closed in
1983. McFarlane Lang's 1925 biscuit factory in
Clydeford Drive became part of United Biscuits
in 1966 and is now McVitie's factory, employing
about 1,000. Greenfield Colliery, like the others,
was worked out by the 1930s. Part of the estate
became a golf course, part is built on and the rest
is Greenfield Park, north of Old Shettleston Road.
Another local pit, known as 'Auld Prickie', was
at Prickliesmuir. Shettleston was brought into
Glasgow in 1912.

Portland Arms

Portland Arms Public House, 1169 Shettleston
Road, 1937, Thomson, Sandilands & MacLeod
Important interior, with stylish 1930s period
chrome and veneers, oval bar and central gantry.
Retaining traditional layout of glazed screens to
ladies' snug and private sitting room on either
side of entry vestibule.

John Wheatley College, 1346–1364 Shettleston
Road, 1894, John McKissack
Built as Eastbank Academy. Tall red ashlar
school, symmetrical front with big Flemish gables

(colour page 37). The academy was renamed John Wheatley College after refurbishment and a quirky brick extension *c*.1986.

Eastbank Academy Extension, 2001, PJMP
Extension to an unexciting replacement Academy built in 1986. One of the better examples of the 3ED projects for the construction of schools throughout Glasgow.

Eastbank Parish Church

47 **Eastbank Parish Church**, 679 Old Shettleston Road and 9 Annick Street, 1897, William Gardner (W G) Rowan
Gothic, with Glasgow Style stone carving around doorway and on the excellent gallery front and other timber furnishings.

Shettleston Old Parish Church, 99 Killin Street, 1895, William Forsyth (W F) McGibbon
French Gothic, gable front to street. Rock-faced red sandstone exterior, smooth grey inside. Slate roof to massive hammerbeam roof; four stained-glass chancel windows *c*.1950, Alfred Webster; west window, 1962, Gordon Webster.

St Paul's RC Church

St Paul's RC Church, 1651 Shettleston Road, 1958, Gillespie, Kidd & Coia
Basilican church plan, portal frame, red brick, low-pitched copper roof. Tower incorporating entry porch; copper crucifix on open frame above, Jack Mortimer, sculptor.

EASTERHOUSE
Last of all the Edinburgh Road housing schemes
is Easterhouse on the higher broken ground
north of the Monkland Canal. One of the big
four peripheral townships, each for upwards
of 25,000 people. Some parts enjoy views of
Bishop's Loch and beyond to the distant Kilsyth
Hills and the Campsie Fells. The estate became
known to some as 'The Holy City', because pre-
Reformation Barlanark was an episcopal canon's
prebend with Provan Hall as his seat.

48 **Provan Hall**, Auchinlea Road, late medieval
North block pre-Reformation, linked by screen
walls to 18th-century south block, enclosing
inner court. Rubble walls, harled at south
block. North block late 15th-, possibly 16th-
century, renaissance details, crowstep gables,
pedimented gables to dormers. North-east
angle, conical-roofed drum turnpike stairturret,
shot holes. Forestair at east end of courtyard.
Symmetrical south front to south range, steps
to exposed stone architraved, pedimented
central entrance. Hip-roofed dormers, sash
windows. 18th-century timber internal stair,
fine interior. Wide renaissance moulded arched
gateway in centre of courtyard wall, 1647
pediment, Hamilton family crest and initials.
Refurbishment 2005, Glasgow City Council
(colour page 104). *National Trust for Scotland,
managed by Glasgow City Council, open to the
public*

Glasgow Fort, 2004, Cooper Cromar
Part of the Auchinlea Park was given up
for this large shopping centre and bleak car
park, supplementing the inadequate 1970s
Easterhouse Centre, benefiting from direct
access to the M8 motorway.

Easterhouse Community Health Centre, 2003,
Davis Duncan
Splendid, much needed facility: Scottish Design
Award, 2004 for Best Publicly Funded Building.

St Benedict's RC Church & Presbytery, 755
Westerhouse Road, 1965, Gillespie, Kidd & Coia
One of the simplest of their churches but the
most distinguished building on the estate. A
rectangular harled block, arranged around a
raised central altar. Clerestory windows in large
split-pitch copper roof. Restored 2006, DTA
Architects.

St Benedict's RC Church

91

49 The Bridge, Wardie Road, c 2005,
Gareth Hoskins
An award-winning theatre and library linking
college to swimming baths, "a spectacular
and brilliant space, already an important
attraction for the community", Rab Bennets,
jury chairman, RIBA Regional Awards. RIBA
National Award 2007. Architecture Grand Prix,
Scottish Design Awards 2007 (colour page 103).

John Wheatley College Annexe, Wardie Road,
2000, Parr Partnership
Colourful four-storey college overlooking
playing fields.

Blairtummock House, 20 Baldinnie Road, *c.*1840
A plain mansion, with 18th-century features,
extended late 19th century with high-quality
neoclassical details and French iron-crested
roof. Walled garden and garden house, re-using
rescued classical stone features. Restoration and
conversion to Social Enterprise Centre, *c.*2005,
Simpson & Brown, for Greater Easterhouse
Development Co. Ltd.

Blairtummock House

Gartloch West Lodge, 1890, Thomson &
Sandilands
Scots Baronial entry to what was then called
a lunatic asylum, located in a large wooded
estate.

Gartloch Asylum

50 Asylum Section Gartloch Hospital, Gartloch
Road, 1889, Thomson & Sandilands
Competition win for the City of Glasgow
District Asylum, by Alexander 'Greek'
Thomson's son John and his Beaux-Arts-trained
partner Robert Douglas Sandilands. A luxury

asylum for 500 paying mental patients, with central administration offices and huge water towers, plus less elaborate scattered annexes for the mentally ill poor and for the original nurses' homes, dining and recreation areas, workshops and other facilities. French Renaissance with Scots Baronial details. Jacobean internal stair balustrades, Art Nouveau leaded glass stair windows. Ground-floor dado-panelled and elaborately decorated Boardroom, with Jacobean fireplaces. Inset bronze plaque lists members of the City of Glasgow Lunacy Board. Similar baronial ornamental details on dining and recreation block and exterior of boiler house and workshops block. Closed 2002 and partly demolished, awaiting new use.

Gartloch Nurses' Home, 1937, Thomas Somers
Three-storey horizontal striped brick and harling block, ending with projecting semicircular glazed ground-floor lounges.

Phoenix, Easterhouse Road, 2000, Andy Scott
Wire sculpture, symbolic of Easterhouse regeneration.

Phoenix *sculpture*

Heavy Horse, M8 Motorway, south side, 1999, Andy Scott
Wire sculpture of Clydesdale horse, part of public art project to enliven motorway environment. Regeneration of Scotland Award, 2000.

BAILLIESTON
Garrowhill was part of the Maxwell estate of Baillieston, with the Camp Pit located there. From 1934, J M Scott Maxwell of Baillieston started selling land at Garrowhill for private houses. By 1939 the population was 4,000, living in 13,000 recently built houses. At Baillieston itself, there had been a Maxwell Mansion since the 1600s; rebuilt before 1816, it was demolished after a fire in 1964. After the Monklands Canal arrived in 1790, the mining village developed, working Cuilhill Pit, Bargeddie from that date and Barrachnie Pit from 1804. In 1795 there were 75 colliers at Barrachnie village and in 1830 the population was about 3,000, all employed in the coal or iron trades. During the 1920s and 1930s, Lanark County Council built houses at Baillieston, which had a population of 6,000 in 1939. Calderbank was the last local pit to close in the 1950s.

Top *Baillieston Old Church*
Above *Baillieston Health Centre*

10 Muirhead Road, 1880s
Asymmetrical villa, Alexander 'Greek' Thomson-style window details, central gable entrance, deep eaves. White ashlar, red dressings and pointing.

Baillieston Old Church, 35 Church Street, 1833
The first Chapel of Ease built under the Church Extension Scheme. Simple rectangular harled box, with classical facade. Cast-iron gates and railings to enclosed churchyard, containing McCall and Buchanan family monuments.

Baillieston Health Centre, 20 Muirside Road, extended *c.*2004, Page & Park
Exciting new entrance and added facilities to small-scale complex.

LONDON ROAD

Leaving Glasgow Cross, London Road skirts the low-lying links of the Clyde to follow the north bank round into Lanarkshire, thence south into Dumfriesshire.

Old Dalmarnock Bridge (demolished)

The Scottish Development Agency (SDA) promoted the Glasgow East Area Renewal (GEAR) project from 1976 to 1987. This was a major integrated development, not only housing, but industrial units to generate employment, with large-scale environmental improvements and landscaping as well. The agency also promoted the regeneration of owner/occupier properties and the sale of Council houses. The SDA pioneered many light industrial and business parks. Leiper's 'Doge's Palace' has been refurbished and converted to a business centre (see *Central Glasgow* Guide). There were many large gap sites left in the East End, although centres had been developed around Bridgeton Cross and other focal points.

BRIDGETON & DALMARNOCK

Barrowfield Dyeworks had been established at Dalmarnock in 1785 and subsequent power-loom weaving and other factories developed nearby in the area now called Bridgeton. Nearly 2.5 hectares (6 acres) of Newhall were bought in 1856 by the partners of William Inglis, Scott & Co. from the West Indies sugar planter Alexander Allan of Dalmarnock. Thomas Lucas Paterson, the managing partner for the Newhall development, sold 1 hectare (2.5 acres) to Newhall Weaving Company and another 1.4 hectares (3.5 acres) to Newhall Cotton Factory, both in the first year. The remainder of the estate, totalling more than 3.6 hectares (9 acres), was sold before 1871 for tenements and a few shops. Newhall House was sold to William Hussey, a Manchester cotton-spinner, whose son married Henry Holdsworth's daughter. The house was demolished in the 1860s. By the mid-19th century, heavy industry spilled over from Bridgeton into Dalmarnock, once the most fertile land in the Barony Parish.

Entry to former **Bridgeton Central Station**
and tenement, 587–601 London Road, *c.*1897,
T R Peacock of Thomson & Turnbull, for North
British Railway
Tall tenement over shops; lower arcaded station
entry with cornice and pediment at centre, steep-
roofed pavilions at ends, red ashlar.

Bridgeton Public Library, 23 Landressy Street,
1903, J R Rhind
Edwardian Baroque in white ashlar, Ionic
pilasters, figure sculpture, first-floor Venetian
window. Two pedimented end pavilions with
Ionic columns over entrances. Good original
interior. One of 14 libraries endowed by Andrew
Carnegie in Glasgow. A post office now occupies
the original reading room.

Trustee Savings Bank building, 40–42 Bridgeton
Cross, 1894, John Gordon
Two-storey granite fronted banking hall, decorated
with coat of arms above and seemingly entered
from next door. Tall chimneys above flat-roofed
drying area for upper-floor flats.

Tenement, 32–38 Bridgeton Cross, 1871,
James Thomson
French Renaissance flats and shops, first-floor
oriel in giant arched panel.

51 **Shelter**, Bridgeton Cross, 1874, George Smith &
Co., Sun Foundry
Octagonal cast-iron shelter, on cast-iron columns,
gifted by the Foundry and known as the 'Umbrella'.
Red shingle roof, square clocktower, weathervane
(colour page 102). The Cross was a redevelopment
formed by the City Improvement Trust in the 1870s.

Buchanan Square, Greenhead Street, 2000,
Carrick & McCormack Architects
Residential development incorporating
refurbishment of Greenhead House and Logan
Domestic Science School. **Greenhead House**,
Greenhead Street, 1846, Charles Wilson. Italian
palazzo for Duncan McPhail, later the Buchanan
Institution. Dining Hall with figure added above
window, 1873 (colour page 104). Conversion
to Greenview School, 1904, Macwhannell &
Rogerson; interior remodelled 1913, Ninian
Macwhannell. Former **Logan Domestic Science
School**, 7 James Street, 1890, James Thomson.
Domestic-scale renaissance, red rubble, squat
entrance tower, oriel above door.

Below Trustee Savings Bank
Middle 32–38 Bridgeton Cross
Bottom Greenhead House

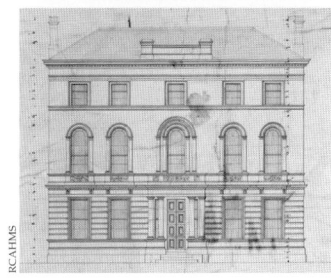

The McPhail brothers built Greenhead
spinning mill in 1824 and built
Greenhead House next door in 1846. It
was sold to the Buchanan Institution
in 1859, as a home for destitute boys.
The Logan and Johnston School of
Domestic Economy, on the corner of
James Street, was founded in 1890
by William Logan and his wife Jean
Johnston for destitute girls.

Greenhead power loom weaving factory

The Dalmarnock Turkey-Red Dyeworks were opened by the Frenchman Pierre Jacques Papillon, in partnership with George Macintosh, about 1779. With David Dale, Macintosh became a founding partner of the short-lived Balnoe Company, opening the Spinningdale Cotton Works at Cleish in Sutherland. George's son later sold the French Street dyeworks to Henry Monteith and the works survived until 1873, shortly to be succeeded by the Barrowfield Dyeworks. George's son, Charles Macintosh, a distinguished chemist, achieved lasting fame as inventor of the 'macintosh' waterproof fabric.

Sir William Arrol's Dalmarnock Iron Works employed from 4,000 to 5,000 men at Dunn Street between 1872 and 1986. Arrol is most famous for building bridges and cranes, including the second Tay Bridge, both Forth Rail and Road Bridges, the North Bridge in Edinburgh, London's Tower Bridge and the Humber Bridge, as well as the Titan Cranes at several Clyde shipyards. He developed new construction techniques and invented new machines to carry them out.

Former **Greenhead power loom weaving factory**, 89 James Street, 1888, Ninian Macwhannell
Large red & white brick factory, for Thomas Thomson, gable to street. Five low weaving sheds added, 1900.

Tenements, 97–113 Greenhead Street, 1865
Tall Italianate tenements, white ashlar, with continuous frieze and cornice above ground floor. Stone-architraved, corniced windows and roof balustrades. Similar details round the corner in James Street and at 117 Greenhead Street and Tullis Street.

Finnart Street, 1986, V Monaghan & D McMillan
Early terraced housing scheme for the Glasgow East Area Renewal Project.

103–111 French Street and **34–66 Dora Street**, 1889, Miles S Gibson
Built as Barrowfield weaving factory. Enormous polychrome brick, tall central pedimented block alongside simple smaller block.

Bridgeton Free Church, 231 Dalmarnock Road, 1901, John Campbell McKellar
Built as Dalmarnock Congregational Church. Art Nouveau details in bell turret, tracery, doorway and side porches. **Hall**, 1911, McKellar, Davis & Gunn.

52 **RC Church of the Sacred Heart**, 50 Old Dalmarnock Road, 1909, Charles Jean (C J) Menart
Stern red sandstone exterior to Roman basilica. Internal concrete vault brilliantly lit from Venetian-windowed clerestory. Marble features in the chancel. Charles Baillie fresco, restored, 1954, William Crosbie; over the altar, *Figure of Christ*, 1954, Jack Mortimer; *Stations of the Cross*, 1954, William Crosbie. Jack Coia altered the ceiling in 1953. (See also this Belgian architect's more lavish St Aloysius, Garnethill, *Central Glasgow* Guide.) **Presbytery**, 1890, Pugin & Pugin. Plainer, rubble with ashlar dressings, top floor set back above main cornice, gabled dormer heads.

East End Sawmills, Dalmarnock Road, 2005, Nord Architects
Ingenious fire-rebuild for a sawmill, using standard components.

47 Broad Street, 1896, Andrew Myles
Former Mavor & Coulson Engineering Works.
Tall block with side aisles and galleries on cast-
iron columns. Fine arched window on gable,
originally a door.

146 Crownpoint Road, *c.*1929
Ferro-concrete framed factory, brick clad, with
large glass area, lower levels now protected.
Shallow end pavilions to main front, built
around shallow bend.

Mavor & Coulson

Camlachie House (demolished)

PARKHEAD

A little north of the river the land passing on to
the inclined shelf of Shettleston Road becomes
imperceptibly elevated, noticeable only on
the radial roads leading back towards the
Clyde. Camlachie House was built in 1720 for
Walkinshaw, and was leased to Lt Col James
Wolf of Quebec when he visited Glasgow in
1749. A mining community with a population of
674 in 1794, Parkhead became another weaving
village before the arrival of heavy industry.
John Napier's Camlachie Foundry of 1812 was
an early one. Other 19th-century industries
included clay pits as well as brickworks and
potteries, latterly supplied by clay imported
from southern England.

Jeanfield House, named for Robert McNair's
wife Jean Holmes, was reputedly an ugly
building, demolished about 1847, to become the
site for the Eastern Necropolis, a large private
cemetery. Westthorn House was built for distiller
Thomas Harvie, who bought the estate in 1819.
To the east Westmuir Colliery was operated by
Robert Gray of Carntyne. Camlachie Distillery of
1834, later Loch Katrine Distillery, was enlarged
before Bulloch & Co. produced 300,000 gallons
of malt spirit per annum. Parkhead Forge,

*The foundry was then [1880s] the
Cinderella of the engineering trade. The
conditions under which the moulder
worked were vile, filthy and insanitary. The
approach resembled that of a rag and bone
shop. The entrance was usually strewn
with all kinds of scrap iron and rubbish.
The inside was in keeping with the outside.
Smoke would make the eyes water. The nose
and throat would clog with dust. Drinking
water came from the same tap as was used
by the hosepipe to water the sand. An
iron tumbler or tin can served as drinking
vessel until it was filthy or broken before
being replaced by a new one. The lavatory
was usually placed near a drying stove and
consisted of open cans that were emptied
once a week – a veritable hotbed of disease.*
Tom Bell, *Pioneering Days*, 1941

David Napier bought Parkhead Forge in 1841, bringing in William Rigby as manager. Rigby improved the Nasmyth steam hammer and equipped the Forge with massive hammers and rolling mills for steel plate used by Napier's brother Robert at his Govan shipyard. William Beardmore was persuaded to buy the Forge in 1861. His son, later Lord Invernairn, took over when William died in 1877. Two years later he introduced steel-making to Parkhead, then bought even bigger steam hammers: the 100-ton Samson, 1881, then the 600-ton Goliath, which cracked adjacent buildings. Although at its peak in 1893, massive output went to the war effort in 1914, but diversification was needed later and it was only profitable again during the Second World War.

David Kirkwood (1872–1955), the 'Red Clydesider' trained as an engineer, becoming a trade union leader. In 1916, he was transported to Edinburgh for causing trouble while acting as a shop steward at Beardmore's Parkhead Forge. He later returned and his squad became the most productive in the works. An Independent Labour Party member from 1922 to 1955, he was MP for Dumbarton Burghs, becoming a Labour cabinet minister, and was later elevated to the Lords as Lord Kirkwood of Bearsden.

established in 1837 by a former Carron Company ironmaster later of Cramond, John Reoch and his brother Andrew, soon overshadowed Napier's Foundry and, under William Beardmore, came to dominate the East End of Glasgow. The 13-hectare (32-acre) Forge was the largest employer in the west of Scotland by 1914, with 8,000 men. The works closed in 1983 and the site is now the Forge Shopping Centre.

Eastern Necropolis, 1264 Gallowgate, *c.*1860 Harled gatepiers, iron gates and railings on curved plan, in stone enclosing walls. Many 19th- and 20th-century monuments and L-plan pedimented classical lodge.

The Forge Shopping Centre, 1221 Gallowgate, 1981, Scott Brownrigg & Turner
Modern, high-profile glass pyramids and metal cladding to covered shopping mall.

Right Parkhead Forge Shopping Centre
Below Eastern Necropolis
Below right Former Employment Exchange

New Life Church, 179 Shettleston Road, 1930, J Wilson Paterson, HM Office of Works
Built as Employment Exchange. Red brick and ashlar dressings with giant Ionic order.

Parkhead Cross tenements, 1435 Gallowgate and Duke Street, 1902, Burnet, Boston & Carruthers
Baronial corner tower over balconied bank entrance, flanked by red ashlar tenements with central oriel windows. **Parkhead Cross tenements**, 1361 Duke Street and 1–15 Westmuir Street, 1905, Andrew Rennie Crawford & Veitch. Scots Renaissance flats over shops, square corner tower with bell cupola. Good Art Nouveau close tiles at No 1361.

1448–1456 Gallowgate and **Burgher Street**, 1908, Honeyman, Keppie & Mackintosh
A late Beaux-Arts work by the Atelier Pascal-trained John Keppie. Flamboyant baroque tenement above former Glasgow Savings Bank with renaissance window details and rich interior. Sculpture, Archibald McFarlane Shannan, over door in tall corner tower at Parkhead Cross.

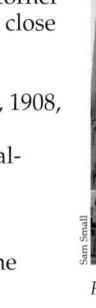

Former Glasgow Savings Bank

Careers Office, 135 Westmuir Street, 1878, Hugh H MacLure
Built as Parkhead School. French Renaissance with mansard roof and bell turret. Alterations and extension, 1889, Charles H Robinson.

Tollcross Road & Sorby Street

Sorby Street and **Tollcross Road**, c.1990, ASSIST Architects
Competition winner, for Housing Association. Tenement of 71 flats and two shops, red brick and cast stone, oriel windows. Glazed staircase pediments break eaves line.

Enterprise East, 64–80 Tollcross Road, 1905, A B McDonald
Built as Public Baths & Wash House. Renaissance red ashlar front to Tollcross Road, brick to rear.

Parkhead Library, Tollcross Road and Helenvale Street, 1904, J R Rhind
Another Carnegie Library, red ashlar with dome at corner. 'Prudence Strangling Want' sculpture, Kellock Brown.

Flats, Westmuir Street, 2002, Michael & Sue Thornley
Small four-storey tenement gap site infill complex.

Calton Parkhead Church, 122 Helenvale Street, 1934, Hutton & Taylor
Simple red brick Romanesque with corner belfry, tall barrel-vaulted nave with tie beams, on the gentle slope towards the river. Circular stone piers carry internal brick arcade. Stained-glass Crucifixion in chancel, 1970 and St Luke, in aisle window, 1971, Gordon Webster.

London Road Primary School, 1139 London Road, 1907, Thomson, Turnbull & Peacock
Typical Board School layout, with central hall surrounded by classrooms. Edwardian baroque, with Venetian windows in pedimented end pavilions.

Parkhead Stadium, 95 Kerrydale Street, 1929, Archibald Leitch
The original Celtic stand (see also Leitch's contemporary stand for Rangers, p. 196) and the 1988 extension by Lang, Willis & Galloway are lost in the redevelopment, c.1994, Percy Johnson-Marshall & Partners. Remodelling of the covered football stadium, 60,000 all-seated capacity, with cantilevered external structure. Since the club moved next to the graveyard, Celtic Park has been known to the fans as 'Paradise'.

Celtic Park Stadium

Sam Small

TOLLCROSS
The Tollcross estate was in the Corbett family for centuries before they sold part in 1792 to James Dunlop of Garnkirk, son of Colin Dunlop, tobacco merchant. In 1812 he bought the Clyde Iron Works, started in 1786 by Thomas Edington and William Caddell. Tollcross passed by James' son, also Colin, to his nephew James Dunlop, who developed Fullarton coal mine and employed David Bryce to build a new Tollcross Mansion in 1848. The undulating 32 hectares (80 acres) of Tollcross Park were acquired by the city in 1897, with the Dunlop Mansion. The Tollcross Burn, dividing Tollcross from Shettleston, runs in a surprisingly deep ravine.

Top *Former Meat Market (Moore Street)*; Below *Duke Street Flats*; Bottom *MacFarlane Fountain*; Middle left *Graham Square Offices*

RCAHMS

RCAHMS

Top *Shelter, Bridgeton Cross;*
Right *Alex Moffat Stained Glass, Colston
Wellpark Church;* **Bottom** *Matador
Building;* **Below** *Former Dennistoun
Baths (now a snooker club)*

Sam Small

RCAHMS

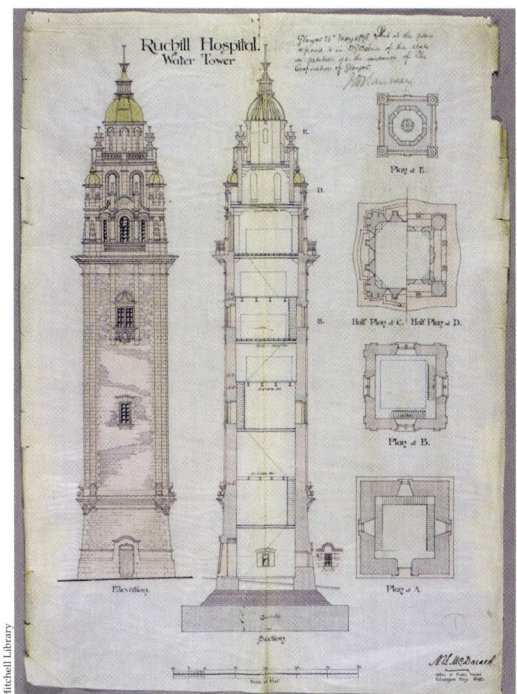

Mitchell Library

RCAHMS

Sam Small

Sam Small

RCAHMS

Top left *Water Tower, Ruchill Hospital*;
Top right *St Anne's RC Church*;
Middle right *The Bridge, Wardie Road*;
Above *Stepps Road Water Tower*;
Left *St Andrews East Church*

Below *Daldowie Dovecote*; Right *Dining Room, Greenhead House*; Bottom *Provan Hall*

Tollcross House, 591 Tollcross Road, 1848,
David Bryce
Scots Baronial country house for James Dunlop.
Asymmetrical, ashlar, crowsteps, pedimented
dormers, cone-roofed turret on low service
wing. Converted to Children's Museum,
1905, Glasgow Corporation. Refurbished and
converted to sheltered housing, *c.*1992, Nicholas
Groves-Raines. Saltire Society Commendation,
1994. **Lodge**, *c.*1858, crowstep gables, rubble,
ashlar dressings. **Conservatory**, Latin-cross
plan, dome at crossing, semicircular ends, cast
iron and glass. Tent-like extension, tensile fabric
structure, 1990s, Glasgow City Council. The Park
is also home to the National Rose Collection.

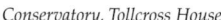

Conservatory, Tollcross House

Tollcross Leisure Centre, Tollcross Park, *c.*1995,
Kerr Robertson, Glasgow City Council
Swimming pools, sports halls and much else,
replacing the original Shettleston swimming
pool within the Park. Long single roof, with
ridge rooflight and large glass areas.

371–411 Wellshot Road, 1999, Elder & Cannon
Four-storey flats, for Housing Association.
Modelled front, featured top-floor windows
at south-west corner. Saltire Society
Commendation, 2000.

Above *Leisure Centre, Tollcross Park*
Below *St Margaret's Tollcross Church*

St Margaret's Tollcross Church, 179 Braidfauld
Street, 1900, W G Rowan
Characteristic broach spire and swept-down
roof on squat tower of full-blown Arts & Crafts
church, with half-timbered south porch. (See also
Rowan's Eastbank Parish Church, p. 90.)

The Clyde Iron Works was established in 1786 by Fife merchant John MacKenzie, with Thomas Edington, the manager of Cramond Malleable Iron Works and son-in-law of William Caddell. William Caddell, a founding partner of the Carron Iron Company, who had bought Cramond from the Carron Company in 1770, later bought shares in the Clyde Iron Works. In 1810 Clyde Iron Works was sold to the Dunlop tobacco family. James Beaumont Neilson's 'hot blast' process (see p. 21) was adopted in 1828. The Dunlops' Clyde Iron Works merged with David Colville in 1930, was nationalised in 1947, and was modernised in 1953, to become the main pig iron plant of the four remaining in Scotland, output going directly to Clydebridge Steelworks across the Clyde. Both works closed c.1970.

CARMYLE

The Bishop of Glasgow owned grain mills at Carmyle in the 13th century. About 1741 a muslin weaving settlement was established; bleachworks came later. In 1762 coal mining was started, ironstone was found in the mid-1780s and the Clyde Iron Works was established in 1786 by Thomas Edington, who bought Carmyle House, demolished c.1960. John Sligo of Carmyle employed William Burn to build Carmyle Cottage in 1836. By the 1920s Mud Row still provided some local artisan housing but Lanarkshire County Council soon replaced it with improved local authority housing.

First Ford Showroom, London Road, 1990s, McInnes Gardner & Partners
Dramatic car showroom and service centre on traffic roundabout. Horizontal and vertical metal-clad, glazed tubes.

Clydesmill Place
Spicer's, Fullarton Drive, Cambuslang Investment Park, 1990s. Lively office frontage to flat-roofed distribution depot. **Glossy Business Units**, Clydesmill Place, 2000, Scottish Enterprise, Glasgow. More like showrooms than offices. **Standard Industrial Units**, Clydesmill Place, 1980s, David Harper Mann, Scottish Development Agency (SDA). Butterfly roof and upper cladding float on clerestory glazing above brick base.

Carmyle Cottage

Carmyle House, 138 Carmyle Avenue, 1836, William Burn
Small asymmetrical Jacobean, former Carmyle Cottage. Pedimented ashlar gable entry, bay windows, dormers. Some interior features remain, including good cast-iron stair balustrade.

Carmyle Church, 135 Carmyle Avenue, 1906,
Alexander Petrie
Rectangular red ashlar gothic church,
hammerbeam roof. Chunky battlemented tower,
with perpendicular octagonal belfry and ogee
dome.

MOUNT VERNON

Mount Vernon was bought by George Buchanan,
a major tobacco merchant, who named the estate
after Admiral Vernon. The Palace Pit, on an
extensive coalfield, was Buchanan property. In
the 1860s they sold the land for private house-
building.

Kenmuir Mount Vernon Church, 2405 London
Road, 1883
Lancet-style gothic, rubble built with octagonal
turret, belfry and metal finial to spire.

Daldowie House (demolished)

DALDOWIE

The Daldowie lands belonged to the Stewarts of
Minto in the 17th century. Sir Ludovic Stewart
sold the estate and house to James Wardrop
Jr of Dalmarnock in 1653. He sold on to James
Muirhead of Bredisholm in 1671, and the
Glasgow merchant George Bogle bought them
from Muirhead's grandson in 1724. Bogle built
a new mansion and doocot in 1745. George
Brown of Langside inherited the estate from the
Bogle female line and immediately sold on to
John Dixon of Calder Iron Works. The Glasgow
merchant James McCall bought the estate in 1830
and extended the mansion, demolished c.1960s.

Daldowie Crematorium, Hamilton Road, 1950,
William Watt, Lanark County Architect
Symmetrical butterfly layout, with wide
entrance vestibule to domed centre block and
round-headed windows to twin chapels.

*Ascending to the brow of the bank, a
prospect of great beauty meets our gaze.
Far below, the Clyde is seen between
the ivied trunks, which bristle the steep,
quivering in a sunny ripple, or stretching
in wandering loveliness around the green
tree-studded haughs of Daldowie on the one
hand and towards the wood-fringed banks
of Carmyle on the other.*
Hugh MacDonald, *Rambles Round
Glasgow*, 1854

Daldowie Crematorium

53 Daldowie Dovecote, Hamilton Road, *c.*1745
Immense rubble and ashlar cylinder, keystoned
flat lintel to doorway. Flight holes to nesting
boxes below eaves, above a continuous string
course, with slated bellcast roof over (colour
page 104). Surrounded by sewage works,
neglected and vandalised, it was relocated 1
kilometre (0.5 mile) north and restored, including
an internal timber revolving ladder access
system, 1999, Design Practice, for Paterson's
of Greenoakhill Ltd and partly funded by the
Landfill Tax Credit Scheme.

CARMUNNOCK ROAD
LITTLE GOVAN
The pre-Reformation Little Govan – or Bridgend,
named after a 14th-century bridge – was feued
by the Church in 1579 to the merchant Provost
George Elphinstone, who built a house in his
barony there on the flat plain by the river.
The City, together with the Trades House and
Hutchesons' Hospital, bought the barony, which
was ruled by a Glasgow bailie until annexed
by the City in 1846. In 1790 the barony was split
between the three owners: the City taking the old
Gorbals village and land around Main Street;
the Trades House took lands to the west, from
Eglinton Street as far as West Street, for **Tradeston**
(see p. 190); while most of the land to the east of
Eglinton Street, as far as Oatlands and Polmadie,
were taken by Hutchesons' Hospital, much
becoming **Hutchesontoun**. The Hospital Trustees
later sold some land to the west of Crown Street
to James Laurie, for **Laurieston** (see p. 187).

*St Ninian's Chapel and Elphinstone's
Tower (demolished)*

An isolation leper hospital was
founded in this part of Govan in 1350,
dedicated to St Ninian. Canon Thomas
Muirhead, who founded St Roche's
plague hospital north of Glasgow
(see p. 73), established a chapel at St
Ninian's before 1510. The hospital
was still in use in 1610 and the chapel
survived, latterly as a pub, until the
1870s. The name was perpetuated until
the 1960s in Hospital Street.

OLD GORBALS
Gorbals in the 1840s was such a hotbed of
quarrels and disturbance that it became known
as 'Little Ireland'. In the 1870s Glasgow City
Improvement Trust demolished the old Gorbals
village, Elphinstone's Tower and St Ninian's

Chapel, building new tenements, designed by Alexander Thomson, around a new Gorbals Cross. They also provided a central clock tower and underground public toilets. Population had grown rapidly, reaching 40,000 in the combined areas by 1890 and, with the arrival of vast numbers of destitute immigrants, 'made down' or subdivided tenements became the norm, alongside 'back to back' building on back lands. The population in the 1930s reached 90,000. Redevelopment, following slum clearance in the 1960s, was not successful; much of that has also gone, and with it much of the population.

Glasgow Sheriff Court, Gorbals Street, 1980, Keppie Henderson & Partners
Plush modernist marble-clad complex of courtrooms on several levels, with access balconies overlooking top-lit atrium. Office suites, for the busiest court in Europe, overlooking River Clyde. Relief of St Mungo above main desk, Jake Kempsell.

Glasgow Central Mosque & Islamic Centre, Gorbals Street, 1983, W M Copeland & Associates, with Coleman Ballantyne Partnership executive architects
Tall minaret and multifaceted dome adorn an effective distillation of Islamic forms (colour page 138).

Citizens' Theatre, 119 Gorbals Street, 1878, Campbell Douglas & Sellars
Built as Her Majesty's Theatre. New façade with John Mossman statues, rescued from the old parapet, above the entrance and foyer, 1989, Building Design Partnership. The red elephants were part of Joseph Sharp's 1887 fairground-style redecoration. Brilliant refurbished auditorium interior of cast-iron columns, ornate capitals and box fronts, with rich panelled plaster ceiling.

Jeff Torrington evocatively describes the demolition and redevelopment of Old Gorbals, which he witnessed first-hand, in his 1992 book *Swing Hammer Swing!*:

Now, the buildings they go up
Just as high as the sky
But me, I'm feeling low enough
Like I could die.
They say they're building this city
Fresh from the start
But there's a demolition party
Working down in my heart.

I'm a man to pity
Got the blues, South City
Nothin' to gain
Nothin' to lose
That's how it is with them
South City Blues.

Left *Glasgow Central Mosque*
Below *Elephants in Citizens' Theatre Foyer*

The Citizens' Theatre opened as Her Majesty's Theatre in 1878, with 1,440 seats. Later named the Royal Princess's, the theatre always maintained a live programme of music hall, pantomime and plays. Saved from closure in 1945, it became the second home of the ever-popular Citizens' Theatre, founded two years before by Dr Honeyman, director of the Kelvingrove Art Gallery, and Dr O H Mavor, a.k.a. James Bridie, the playwright. Under the chairmanship of the latter, the Citizens' produced some outstanding talent, including Duncan Macrae and the incomparable actor Stanley Baxter. *The Observer* once described it as 'the most cosmopolitan, idiosyncratic, mischievous and wilful theatre in Britain'. Giles Havergal was appointed artistic director in 1969. Although he outraged some locals, he is acknowledged to have built an international reputation.

*British Linen Company Bank carving on
162 Gorbals Street*

54 **162–170 Gorbals Street**, 1897, James Salmon Jr
The last remaining Gorbals tenement, designed
just before Salmon's elevation to the partnership.
Arts & Crafts iron balcony over bay window;
tower at the other end with small windows and
steep pediments, the original turret missing.
Scroll inscribed 'British Linen Company Bank'
above entrance to former ground-floor bank,
which was provided with a very atmospheric
Glasgow Style interior by the 'Wee Troot', as
Salmon was affectionately known. Compare
with the contemporary Govan Cross Bank by
John Gaff Gillespie, Salmon's colleague and
future partner (see p. 217). Awaiting new use,
abandoned and at risk.

HUTCHESONTOUN & NEW GORBALS
Hutchesontoun was the largest portion of
the old Elphinstone Barony. Several streets
were laid out to a feuing plan of 1793, the first
buildings erected in St Ninian Street by the next

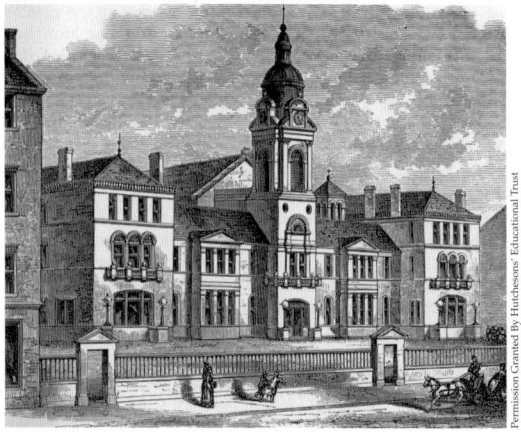

*Hutchesons' Boys' Grammar School
(demolished)*

year. Such severe restrictions were imposed on feuars that, in ten years, only five streets around the principal thoroughfare, Hospital Street, had buildings on them. Crown Street became the commercial centre, lined up with the new bridge in 1805, now replaced by Albert Bridge. In 1820, the Trustees changed their policy: abandoning ideas of grandeur, they now permitted mills and factories. By 1840, working-class flats were allowed within the four-storey stone tenements. Industry was also encouraged, later encroaching on much of the housing. The biggest works were Govan Iron Works, 1839 and the United City Bakeries Society at 12 McNeil Street, 1886. The New Gorbals, begun on site about 1990, continues to grow in this area, after the old names were blurred in the 1960s. Great enthusiasm has been shown by New Gorbals Housing Association tenants and house purchasers alike.

Glasgow College of Nautical Studies, Ballater Street, 1962, RMJM
Distinctive white-tiled modernist block, in Lever House-type composition of a block sitting on a broad podium, with a domed planetarium alongside the squat tower, as at Skidmore, Owings & Merrill's 1952 Lever House, New York.

Interior Design Annexe, Glasgow College of Building & Printing, 85 Adelphi Street, 1894, Thomas Lennox (T L) Watson
Built as Adelphi Terrace Public School. Large square-plan renaissance red ashlar Board School. Watson was apprenticed to Boucher, then worked in London for Alfred Waterhouse & Sons, preferring the classicism of the son Paul, to the terracotta gothic of the father (see also his Wellington Church, *Central Glasgow* Guide).

City Housing Neighbourhood Office, 187–203 Old Rutherglen Road, 1816
Former cotton mill for Robert Humphries. Main mill six-storey; L-plan south wing four-storey. With a cast-iron frame, this is the oldest surviving fireproof mill in Glasgow. Converted to offices, 1998.

High Flats, Ballater Street, 1958, RMJM
Four elegant 17-storey blocks. Saltire Society Award, 1964. Now sadly capped by lightweight pitched roofs.

Adelphi Terrace Public School

St Ninian's Terrace

Crown Street Regeneration Project: Masterplan, 1989, Piers Gough, CZWG
900 terraced and flatted housing units now replace poorly constructed post-war foreign system-built gallery access flats, which were themselves built on the site of tenements and the former Hutchesons' Boys' Grammar School, 1839, David Hamilton, at 211 Crown Street. **8–16 Benny Lynch Court** and **147–167 Old Rutherglen Road**, 1990s, Cooper Cromar. Intimate group of two-storey courtyard houses and four-storey flats, by what has become a high-profile practice. **St Ninian's Terrace**, Ballater Street and Laurieston Road, 1990s, Holmes Partnership. Two crescents of brick-built four-storey flats, articulated by projecting porch entrances and cap featured stair glazing. **Tulip Hotel**, Ballater Street, 1999, ADF Partnership. Sympathetic plan for 114 bedrooms and 39 student residences, acknowledging the crescent across Laurieston Road. The stone cladding panels and corner features again respond to St Ninian's Terrace across Laurieston Road. **Crown Street, Nos 187–213**, *c*.1992, Page & Park, five storeys of flats over shops with enlarged corner blocks and **Nos 221–235**, *c*.1992, Elder & Cannon, 26 mixed flats and maisonettes with stone end pavilions, both Saltire Society Awards, 2001. **Nos 224–230**, *c*.1992, Cormack Gracie Architects. Four-storey flats, with emphasised five-storey corner, all set on a defensive low podium, providing privacy for the ground-floor residents.

224-230 Crown Street

Malta Crescent, 2000, Hypostyle. City block of 203 owner-occupied homes over four storeys. Articulated crescent form, with deep recessed entrances marked by suspended sculptures.

55 **The Gatekeeper**, Kidston Terrace, 2001, Hypostyle. Appropriately monumental and vigorously modelled four-storey block of flats on prominent corner site, marking the southern gateway to the New Gorbals with more suspended sculpture (colour page 137).

56 **1 Caledonia Road**, 1856, Alexander Thomson
Former Caledonia Road UP Church. A mere
fragment of Thomson's first large church, burnt
out in 1965. A magnificent tower, unadorned apart
from the bell openings and clock on top. The
Greek 'temple' alongside on the plain base,
reminiscent of the Athens Acropolis (colour page
137). A satisfyingly balanced composition with the
bulk of the church behind and originally lit by
clerestory windows. Thomson became an elder
of this congregation, declaring later that Religion
had been the soul of Art from the beginning. A
classicist, he argued in his lectures and publications
that gothic was a barbarian interloper. Awaiting
a settled environment for incorporation into
what deserves to be a major public project.

Gorbals East Project: Masterplan, 1994,
Page & Park
200 mainly terraced houses. **Hayfield Court**,
Moffat Street, 1990s, Simister Monaghan. Three-
storey flats, with advanced stone-clad bay
supporting a roof terrace at the front of a four-
storey corner. **Moffat Gardens**, Hayfield Street,
Page & Park. Three- and four-storey flats and
two-storey red brick and cedar-clad terraced
57 houses. **Hayfield Street**, Elder & Cannon. 'The
Villa', a four-storey eliptical, copper-roofed unit,
interlocking with a three-storey cube, together
containing 14 flats.

Top *Hayfield Court & Moffat Street*
Above *The Villa, Hayfield Street*

Queen Elizabeth Square Project: Masterplan,
2000, Hypostyle
The second part of the Gorbals Regeneration
Project, for 500 housing units, built on the site of
the award-winning High Flats, 1960, Basil Spence.
More sophisticated designs by more mature
and confident architects, a decade after phase
one. **Queen Elizabeth Gardens**, 2003, Elder &
Cannon. A delightful four-storey block of flats
at the Cumberland Street end of the Gardens, in
their own distinctive precisely detailed style.

High Flats, Gorbals (demolished)

Paragon, Old Rutherglen Road, Sandyford
Street and Queen Elizabeth Gardens, 2004,
Piers Gough, CZWG
A large 127-apartment project, on the site of
Spence's original square, with eight storeys at
the south-west corner, stepping down to six on
the east and a two-storey curved mews above
garages, facing Friary Court on the south. The
higher buildings here provide an important focal
point for the project.

58 **Friary Court**, 2004, Page & Park
Seven very private five-storey wedge-shaped
flatted buildings, the narrow end facing a
semicircular garden. Ground floors open to the
garden, while balconies above overlook the side
of St Francis Church.

Above *Friary Court*
Right *Moffat Gardens*

St Francis Centre, 405 Cumberland Street, 1868,
Gilbert Blount
Built as St Francis RC Church and Friary. Very
tall church rebuilt 1870, Pugin & Pugin, in their
characteristic Decorated gothic. Converted to
community centre 1996, Page & Park. Elegant
three-storey timber and glass suite of function
rooms inserted within the church (colour
page 139). Original Blount Friary converted to
high-quality flats for the elderly, 1996, Page &
Park. Glasgow Institute of Architects Award,
1997. Civic Trust Award, 1998. Shortlisted for
Regeneration of Scotland Award, 1998. (See
also Page & Park's similar insert at St Teresa of
Lisieux, p. 68.)

Hutchesontoun Public Library

Gorbals Economic Development Centre, 192
McNeil Street, 1904, J R Rhind
Built as Hutchesontoun Public Library. Beautiful
red ashlar stone carvings of fine renaissance
swags and even better reliefs of St Mungo and
other figures carrying Glasgow's symbols above
the main door.

Southern Necropolis

Southern Necropolis, 316 Caledonia Road, 1848,
Charles Wilson
Massive castellated Norman arched gateway,
tall stairturret to one side. Necropolis extended
twice in ten years. Charles Wilson was himself
buried here. Neat and trim but the back of
the gatehouse is collapsing, from want of
maintenance.

POLMADIE
Oatlands was a miners' village, serving Dixon's
Govan Collieries. When Henry Dubs set up
the Queen's Park Locomotive Works in 1864 at
Polmadie (see North British Locomotive Co.,
p. 76), tenements quickly took over the two
low-lying areas close to the Clyde links. Alley
& MacLellan prefabricated ships at Jessie Street
from *c*.1880, and steam lorries until production
was relocated to Shrewsbury in 1917. Tenements
along Rutherglen Road were among the first in
the city to be refurbished some years ago but
were subsequently demolished and the area now
awaits the M74 extension.

Sentinel Works, 61 Jessie Street, 1903, Brand &
Lithgow, with Archibald Leitch, engineer
Four-storey clear-span patternmaking shop
and offices for Alley & MacLellan, engineers.
The earliest reinforced concrete building in
Glasgow, using the Mouchel-Hennebique
ferro-concrete system. Concrete panel walls
with classical cornice, large metal windows and
flat roof, anticipating the Modern Movement.
Cantilevered rear fire escape stair carried
on ornate cast-iron brackets. A disgraceful
shell, derelict since the 1960s and at risk from
continuing vandalism.

Sentinel Works

110 Polmadie Road, 1895, Peter Macgregor Chalmers
Former St Margaret's Polmadie Church & Halls. Free-style gothic, in grey rubble with red dressings. Church to east of two-storey hall.

KING'S PARK

Between 1920 and 1923 Mactaggart & Mickel built 1,300 two-storey houses for commuters at King's Park, on the adjoining undulating Aitkenhead estate, formerly in Renfrewshire but transferred to Lanarkshire.

Aitkenhead House

The barony of Aitkenhead belonged to a cadet of the Hamiltons of Torrance, East Kilbride, in the 17th century. The Glasgow merchant James Hamilton was several times Provost of the City in the early 17th century and his son built the first mansion. A later generation produced two Rectors of Glasgow University, before the family sold Aitkenhead to Colin Rae, who extended the house. By 1795 it belonged to Mr Scott, who sold it on to a West Indies merchant, John Gordon, who built the present mansion in 1806, adding the outer wings by David Hamilton in 1823. Gordon's town house was probably one of the first to be built in Buchanan Street. It is interesting to conjecture whether David Hamilton had designed that as well (see also his contemporary Hutcheson's Hall, *Central Glasgow* Guide).

Sundial, Aitkenhead

59 **Aitkenhead House**, King's Park, Carmunnock Road, 1806, probably David Hamilton
The mansion sits in a hollow among several small drumlins perched on the steep slope rising from Polmadie through King's Park towards the Cathkin Braes, which form the southern lip of the Clyde Valley. Neoclassical pink ashlar two-storey main block, with hipped slate roofs and a fine Corinthian porch on west front. Top-lit stair hall with cantilevered stone steps and cast-iron balustrade. Deep one-and-a-half-storey wings, protected by giant pilasters, added 1823, David Hamilton. Converted to flats 1985. **Gatepiers**, early 19th century, probably David Hamilton. Four-panelled ashlar, part-painted piers, quadrants link outer pair to four inner. Modern wrought-iron gates. Early 19th-century brick-built **walled gardens**. Massive 1885 mannerist two-tier ashlar **sundial**, on elaborate base with a tall obelisk finial. One of three 19th-century reproductions of the 1635 Newbattle sundial. **Stable block**, probably David Hamilton. Three classical ranges around courtyard, closed on south by screen wall and entered from Croftpark Avenue.

King's Park Secondary School, Fetlar Drive, 1956, Gillespie, Kidd & Coia
Built as Simshill Secondary School. On a dramatic site with extensive views to the north over the city and to the hills beyond and set

within a post-war housing area to the west of
Carmunnock Road, which creeps over a ridge
into a fold on the slope up to Castlemilk. A
courtyard complex of three buildings, large
glazed areas with controlled daylighting and
circulation concentrated at staircases. Concrete
structure, originally exposed inside and out, and
blue engineering-brick gable infill, all now clad
in lightweight panels. A four-storey classroom
block faces the single-storey administration
block, which sits over a two-storey gym on the
hillside below, part roofed with lightweight clad
steel roof trusses. The third building is the two-
storey workshop block. Alongside the gym is a
part-buried boiler house, with sculpted concrete
ventilators and a tall chimney.

CROFTFOOT
Adjoining King's Park, on the Castlemilk estate
in Lanarkshire, Croftfoot was another suburban
development built about the same time.

Croftfoot Parish Church & Hall, 318 Croftpark
Avenue, 1934, John Keppie & Henderson
Byzantine, white-pointed dark red brick with
ashlar dressings inside as well as out. Cross
finial to bell tower. Hall to west linked to church
by a low wing and an open passageway fronting
a courtyard. Undergoing a Lottery-funded
restoration, 2007.

Croftfoot Parish Church

CASTLEMILK
Castlemilk estate was the biggest property in
the parish of Carmunnock. The estate, which
was in the Stuart family from the 13th century,
was sold to the City in 1938 for one of the huge
peripheral housing estates built after 1954.
Castlemilk House, which dated back to the late
medieval period but had been greatly altered
and extended in simple baronial style from the
18th century, was then demolished.

Castlemilk House (demolished)

Stables for demolished Castlemilk House, 59 Machrie Road, *c*.1800
Converted 2006, Elder & Cannon, to offices for Housing Association. GIA Supreme Award 2007. Four one-and-a-half-storey ranges around a courtyard, with octagonal gothic tower over pend at north. Gothic single-arch **bridge** with crenellated ashlar parapets, remodelled 1833, probably David Hamilton. The Burn, known downstream in 19th-century Burnside as the Citiford, fed the reservoir of the Burnside Weaving Factory, then became the West Burn before merging with Molls Myre Burn to discharge into the Clyde as the Polmadie Burn.

Castlemilk Youth Complex, Ardencraig Place, 1980s, Ian Burke Associates
Blank brick walls enclose a tough building suited to a tough environment.

Barlia Sports Pavilion, Glenwood Path, 1980s, Glasgow District Council
Rugged striped block-work with defensive eaves to protect metal deck roofing.

60 **St Margaret Mary's RC Church & Presbytery**, 99 Dougrie Road, 1959, T S Cordiner
Concrete portal frame carrying high barn-like slated roof and clad in buff brickwork. Entry through wedge-shaped lobby, which links integral bell tower to church and to hall below.

Below St Margaret Mary's RC Church
Below right Linn Crematorium

Linn Crematorium, Lainshaw Drive, 1962, T S Cordiner
A Beaux Arts-influenced modernist complex in a peaceful parkland setting, comprising two ceremonial chambers, each with its own waiting facilities and flanked by curved cloistered remembrance gardens.

St Martin's RC Church

St Martin's RC Church & Presbytery, 201
Ardencraig Road, 1959, Gillespie, Kidd & Coia
The always softening and enhancing trees have
now gone from the steep slope above Ardencraig
Road at Templecross, near the top of the Cathkin
Braes. Modern harling, now decayed, conceals
the original pearl brickwork and exposed
concrete. The three-storey Presbytery sits into
the hill, with the plain box church behind,
approached by ceremonial ramp and stairs.
Inside the tapering pearl-grey brick chamber
directs attention to the elevated altar. Glazed
north-light trusses direct soft daylight, again
focussing on the altar. Furnishings are simple
and coloured glass in small side windows
illuminate the *Stations of the Cross*.

Castlemilk Drive, 2000
Lively designs for two- and three-storey terraced
housing. Better than the average speculative new
builds, which are replacing many of the drab
post-war flats.

Stravanan Road and **Castlemilk Drive**, *c.*2003
Attractive new flatted dwellings, whose
distinctive decorative perforated metal balconies
sit easily within a restrained palette of materials.

CARMUNNOCK
Carmunnock, part of the former Castlemilk
estate since the 17th century, remains a charming
village centred on some 17th-century cottages
around the green. Some neat villas were built
on the edges in the 1930s. Incorporated into
Glasgow at the 1975 Local Government Reorganisation, it is the only rural village in the
City. Agriculture, hand-loom weaving and, from
the mid-19th century to the 1930s, linen washing
for city restaurants and well-off households,
were the sources of employment.

*It is a very pretty little village,
retaining in its main features the rural
atmosphere of long ago. Its streets have
the abiding charm of possessing no
defined plan, affording the city eye a
contrast to miles of mathematically lined
thoroughfares. The kirk, which stands on
a knoll is curious and comparatively old.
Quaint and comfortable hostelries extend a
friendly invitation to the traveller on a hot
summer's afternoon. But Carmunnock's
chief glory is the View.*
T C F Brotchie, *Some Sylvan Scenes near
Glasgow*, 1910

Carmunnock Kirk

*The 1840 Statistical Account stated,
which must fill with envy the assessment-
crushed unfortunates of our city parishes,
that hitherto there had been no levy for
poor rates and the Parish Minister, with
justifiable complacency, expressed his
belief that such a thing as a compulsory
assessment for the support of the poor is
not at all likely ever to be required. What
a delightful little city of refuge this must
appear to the pauper-ridden denizens of
St Mungo; what an oasis in the desert, far
away from the persecuting tax-gatherer,
who, on some pretence or other, is eternally
prying into our books, and making town's
talk of our most secret affairs.*
Hugh MacDonald, *Rambles Round
Glasgow*, 1854

Carmunnock Parish Church, Kirk Road, rebuilt
1762
T-plan, two forestairs, 1819 vestry, Stuart aisle,
18th-century bellcote, rubble and ashlar dressings.
First World War memorial stained glass,
Norman Macleod MacDougall. **Churchyard**,
18th-/19th-century headstones and table tombs.
Watch-house, beside gate, simple, contains
1828 Instructions for Watch. An irregular cluster
of 18th-century vernacular houses survives,
huddling protectively around the church.

Kirk Road
Begg's House, No 8, 1780s. Two-storey, rubble
and ashlar dressings, forestair at rear, swept-
roof slate dormers. Restored 1984. **No 22**, *c*.1850.
Rebuilt white-painted cottage, harled with ashlar
dressings. **No 24**, 1762. Two-storey, end-terrace
house, crowstepped, whitewashed rubble and
ashlar dressings. **No 34**, *c*.1780. Two-storey, end-
terrace house, whitewashed coursed rubble and
ashlar dressings.

The Barracks, 8–10 Busby Road, 1790s
Much altered, rubble, ashlar dressings and
forestair. **Miln Flat, Nos 68–70**, 1750s. Pair of
one-and-a-half-storey cottages, crowsteps and
white harl.

145 Waterside Road, 1930s
One of a few Art Deco houses in Carmunnock.
There are others in Kittochside Road.

Carnbooth House

Carnbooth House, 80 Busby Road, 1900,
Alexander Cullen
Impressive large renaissance house with 17th-
century Scots details, white harl and red ashlar
dressings (colour page 140). Good interiors.
Cullen's vast 1890 Ross House for Col. Robertson
Aikman, near Hamilton, was also designed
in traditional Scots Renaissance style, as was
Heathery Park, Wishaw. Carnbooth is currently a
residential school for the blind and deaf.

CATHCART ROAD
GOVANHILL

High-quality densely packed bright stone tenements with excellent local shopping on Victoria Road and several other streets.

There was a colliers' village, known as 'Fireworks', astride Cathcart Road from the 1770s, after William Dixon leased the Little Govan colliery. Dixon bought the gently undulating Govanhill estate in 1820 and coal was worked until the late 1860s, when his grandson, the third William Dixon sold the land for feuing. The area became known as 'No Man's Land', stuck between Glasgow and Crosshill when Crosshill became a Burgh in 1871, until population growth allowed Govanhill to obtain its own Burgh status in 1877. Govanhill is now host to a large Asian community.

William Dixon, already owner of several Lanarkshire collieries and of Calder Iron Works when he came to Glasgow, built a waggonway from Little Govan to Windmill Quay to facilitate coal exports to the Clyde coast and Ireland. He died in 1824 and his son William (II) Dixon extended the waggonway to form the Pollok and Govan Railway, later incorporated in the Caledonian Railway's main line into Central Station. It was this William Dixon who opened the Govan Ironworks, half a mile north of Fireworks village, in 1839. The population had grown to 600 within two years. He worked local ironstone in seams running towards Polmadie. The five blast furnaces produced pig and malleable iron.

176–194 Butterbiggins Road, 65–73 Inglefield Street, *c.*1888
White sandstone tenement in the style of Alexander Thomson, first- and second-floor windows corniced and linked by stepped moulding.

Annandale Square

61 **Butterbiggins Road** and **Annandale Square**, 1994, Elder & Cannon
Three blocks of four-storey flats. Competition winner for Housing Association, achieving a Saltire Society Award, 1995.

Right Glasgow Samaritan Hospital for Women
Below 85–95 Govanhill Street
Bottom Batson Street School

Glasgow Samaritan Hospital for Women, 67–69 Butterbiggins Road, 1893, Macwhannell & Rogerson
Arts & Crafts with some Art Nouveau details on administration block. White rock-faced sandstone, with red dressings (colour page 137). The same architect designed the baronial-style nurses' home on the corner of Victoria Road. All converted to Housing Association dwellings, 2002, Vernon Monaghan.

85–95 Govanhill Street, *c.*1982, Simister, Monaghan, McKinney, McDonald
Three stepped pairs of block-built three-storey flats for Housing Association. Neat gardens controlled like large window boxes.

74–104 Batson Street, *c.*1992, Manson Associates
Brick-built two-storey terraced housing, with three-storey flatted feature at one end. Saltire Society Commendation, 1994.

Batson Street School, 291–311 Calder Street, 1874
Scots Jacobean revival, central crowstep gable and two pairs of spiral chimneys.

Govanhill Picture House, 47 Bankhall Street, 1925, Eric Sutherland
Egyptian front, Hindu domes, lotus-bud columns in tiled centrepiece, now a warehouse, but at risk of demolition and redevelopment. An exotic change from Sutherland's conventional gothic churches or classical banks, such as his Royal Bank, 471 Gallowgate (see *Central Glasgow Guide*).

Holy Cross Primary School, 318 Calder Street, 1914, Andrew Balfour
Built as Calder Street Public School. Edwardian Baroque, red rock-faced base, channelled ashlar over. Ionic pilasters to end bays. Art Nouveau railings round playground.

Above *Govanhill Picture House*
Left *Govanhill Parish Church*

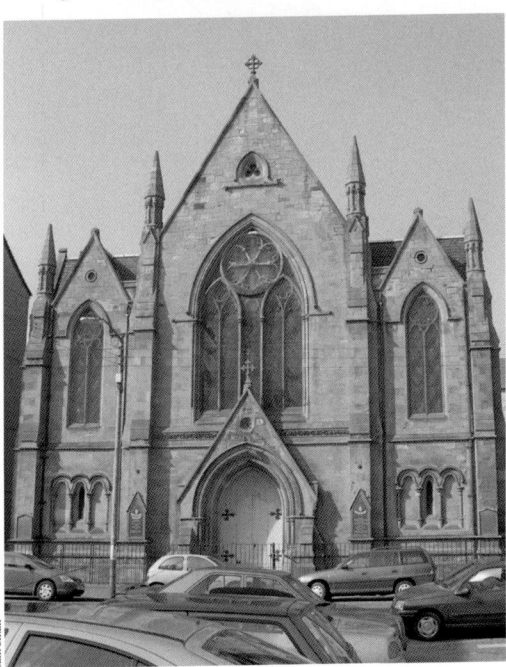

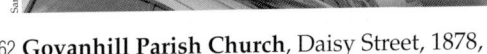

62 **Govanhill Parish Church**, Daisy Street, 1878, Robert Baldie
Geometric gothic, white ashlar, horseshoe cast-iron gallery, double-stair pulpit. Organ, 1912, Abbott & Smith, Leeds.

Govanhill Library, 170 Langside Road, 1902, J R Rhind
Edwardian baroque, paired columns, sculpted figures atop emphasised corners, copper figure on entrance dome.

Top *265–289 Allison Street*
Middle *Victoria Cross Building*
Bottom *Holy Cross RC Church*

Calder Street Public Baths and Washhouse,
99 Calder Street, 1912, A B McDonald
Red ashlar Edwardian baroque, with finely
carved city arms and window embellishments
over Roman Doric twin-column pedimented
doors. Two top-lit pools. Closed 2001 amid
popular protest. Community Trust seeking funds
to re-open the large pool, with new uses for
other areas, 2005, Nord Architects.

Annette Street Primary School, 13 Annette
Street, 1886, Hugh & David Barclay
Built as Govanhill Public School. Italianate
palazzo, elegant three-storey with pilastered
axial entry.

265–289 Allison Street, 1875,
Alexander Thomson
Finely detailed speculative tenement built by
Thomson's partner Robert Turnbull, when prices
had dropped after Thomson's death. Main
front to Allison Street, sides plain. Upper-level
details change halfway along; the left hand is
probably Thomson's original, the right simpler.
Wide pilasters to ground-floor bays support
deep entablature, with framed windows over
and pilastered top-floor windows supporting
deep main entablature. Anthemion decoration
in recessed panels between top-level windows
provides the most distinctive Thomson feature.

Victoria Cross Building, 401–407 Calder Street,
and Allison Street, *c.*1890
French iron-crested roof over corner tenement
bay. Rich consoles to window cornices at first
floor. Main cornice on brackets.

415–447 Victoria Road, *c.*1875. Fine example
of a white ashlar terrace of flatted houses, over
projecting ground-floor shops, with iron rails to
flat roof.

Holy Cross RC Church and Presbytery,
109 Dixon Avenue, 1909, Pugin & Pugin
Lively Italian Romanesque, red rock-faced stone.
Basilican plan with elaborate marble interior
features.

CROSSHILL
The north has a similar pleasant tenement
character to adjoining Govanhill but the grain
becomes more open and greener towards the
south, where villas were built later.

Owned by James Rowan in 1795, Crosshill was bought by William (II) Dixon, who bought many estates in Scotland. After his death in 1859, his trustees feued the estate for building. Dixon's son William (III) Smith Dixon gifted a site for a Burgh Hall, to serve two Burghs. The site straddled the boundary between them, with Govanhill in Lanarkshire to the north, and Crosshill in Renfrewshire to the south. One entrance served Govanhill, a second served Crosshill, each Burgh having its own independent facilities, and there was a third entrance leading to the Dixon Halls, which could be used by either Burgh for public functions. Both Burghs were annexed by Glasgow in 1891.

Dixon Halls

Dixon Halls, 656–660 Cathcart Road, 1878, Frank Stirrat
Winner in competition. Set back from the road is this Scots Baronial complex, with characteristic crowstep gables and clocktower with angle turrets and slate pyramid spire (colour page 138). Compare with Stirrat's Renaissance Govan Press Building (see p. 215).

New Bridgegate Church, Dixon Road and Warren Street, *c.*1915, built after war, 1922, Thomson, Sandilands & MacLeod
Scots Gothic, with tower and short spire. Massive traceried west window in red stone. Lavish vestibule, plain interior. Now converted for business use. **Hall** to Dixon Avenue, built 1915.

Holyrood RC School, 60 Dixon Road, 1936, John Burnet, Son & Dick
Long symmetrical brick frontages with large windows to both Dixon Road and Albert Road. Shallow projecting central entrance bay, stone dressings and cornice.

Crosshill Victoria Church, 32 Dixon Avenue, 1891, J B Wilson
Red rubble, perpendicular gothic traceried gallery windows by a prolific Free Church architect. Prominent octagonal stairtower with pyramid cap over open bell stage. Now occupied by studios.

465–505 Victoria Road

465–505 Victoria Road, 8–18 Dixon Avenue, *c.*1890
Ashlar tenement over ground-floor shops, iron-crested French roof over square corner bay. Pilastered top-floor windows, deep main cornice and dentils below decorative cast-iron guttering.

23–45 Albert Road, 318–320 Langside Road, *c*.1850
Dignified white ashlar tenement with regularly
spaced windows and simple classical features.

1 Queen Mary Avenue, *c*.1890
Ashlar classical tenement, channelled at ground
floor with rusticated window heads, architraved
and corniced above. **Nos 10** and **14–32,** *c*.1890.
Long unusual Greek Revival ornamented
tenement, elaborated in groups stepping up the
slope.

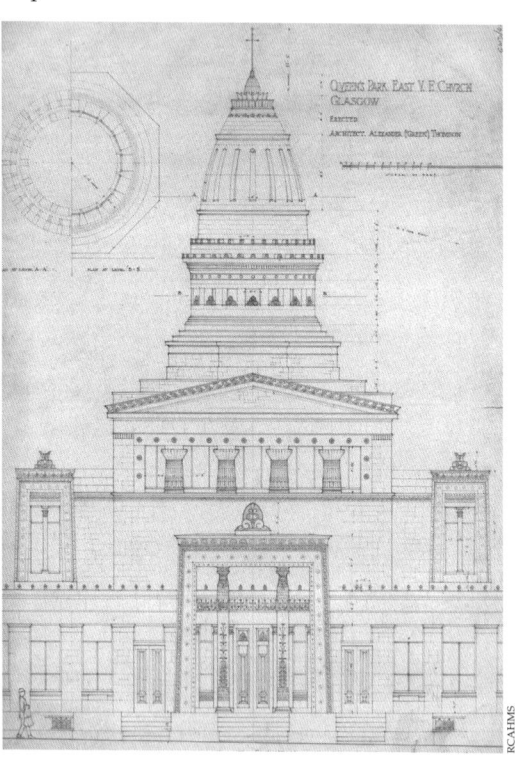

*Queen's Park United Presbyterian
Church, Langside Road, 1867,
Alexander Thomson (destroyed
1943). Greek Thomson's most sublime
monumental design, for Glasgow's
puritanical whig merchants, was
complimented internally by Daniel
Cottier's complex muted scheme of
tertiary colours*

Langside Road
Nos 334–346, *c*.1890. Tenement distinguished by
two groups of four-window bays, with tapering
architraves in Egyptian manner, supporting
pediments and separated by shallow giant
pilasters at centre and ends. **Nos 353–361,**
c.1890. Greek Revival ornamented tenement.
Architraved, pedimented, pilastred windows at
second floor, shops in channelled ground floor.
Tenement building stopped before the climb up
this minor drumlin, to be succeeded in the east
by villas in Albert Road, Crosshill Avenue and
Queen's Drive.

Albert Road
No 82 and **Sunnybank, No 84**, *c.*1890. Pair
of similarly detailed classical villas, central
entrances with high quality sculpted ornament.
Fernbank, No 56 (also entered at 30–32 Crosshill
Avenue), *c.*1890. Alexander 'Greek' Thomson-
style villa, rubble, ashlar dressings, incised
details, fretworked gabled bay.

29–61 and **54–82 Crosshill Avenue**, 1948,
Ronald Bradbury
Local authority housing on corner site in very
English red brick tradition. 1951 Festival of
Britain Award for Merit.

Above *Sunnybank*
Below *29–61 & 54–82 Crosshill Avenue*
Left *St Rule*

St Rule, 30–32 Queen's Drive, *c.*1890
The best of the villas in Queen's Drive, looking
south across Queen's Park and the rise up to
Camphill. Double villa, curved two-storey bay
windows, paired centre porches with fretted
bargeboards.

Crosshill Queen's Park Church, 40 Queen's
Drive, 1872, Campbell Douglas & Sellars
Franco-German Gothic, massive buttressed
square south-east tower with tall octagonal
spire. Douglas's earlier partner J J Stevenson
may have had a hand in the design before he left
for London, but the adventurous spire is more
suggestive of Sellars' hand. Large Geometric
traceried window over wide gable porch. The
clerestory windows helped in the conversion to
flats, 2004.

Below *Balmoral Crescent*

Balmoral Crescent, 78–118 Queen's Drive, 1885,
W M Whyte
Eccentric French Renaissance tenement, with
mansard roof and pedimented dormer windows.
Sculptured heads and figure at Langside Road
corner. Rebuilt behind façade, 1988, McGurn,
Logan, Duncan & Opfer.

Cathcart Road climbs sharply out of low-lying Crosshill, the latter only elevated by the small drumlin at Queen Mary Avenue. On the way uphill towards Mount Florida, we are surprised by the bright **ODS Offices**, Myrtle Park, 2000, Cornelius McClymont Architects. Built on the site of dingy lock-up garages, they comprise an open-plan, largely glazed drawing office, above a meeting room screened from the entrance and stair by an enclosed toilet and kitchen.

MOUNT FLORIDA
On top of the easternmost of the group of three large drumlins, forming the barrier which deflects the White Cart Water away from the Clyde and towards Paisley in the west, is Mount Florida. Started as a suburb of mainly prestigious terraced houses in the 1870s, work stopped for a time following the collapse of the City of Glasgow Bank in 1878. When building resumed in the 1880s, horse-drawn trams had reached the area and four-storey tenements were now constructed to catch blue-collar workers. The pace quickened when the Cathcart Circle Railway was completed in 1887, running 89 trains a day, but Bruce & Sturrock still went bankrupt building it in 1893. The Scott family operated Aitkenhead Colliery on their land at Hangingshaw on the lower eastern edge of Mount Florida during the 19th century.

Cathcart Parish Council Chambers

Cathcart Parish Council Chambers,
183 Prospecthill Road, 1907, Andrew Rennie Crawford & Veitch
Delicate carving on a symmetrical English Baroque front with central entrance dignified by lead-domed cupola. Plain interior now used as Mount Florida Clinic. A formal composition contrasting with the same firm's lively asymmetrical French Renaissance tenements

at Parkhead Cross (see p. 99). The new
Renfrewshire County Council had built a local
office to deal with the Poor Law Relief and other
duties of the former Parochial Board.

149–165 Stanmore Road, *c*.1880
Three-storey white ashlar middle-class tenement
on top of the hill. Channelled ground floor and
bay windows.

Mount Florida Parish Church, 1123 Cathcart
Road, 1884, John Hamilton
Barn-like large sandstone former UP church on
prominent site. Gallery at west end, spire not
built on chunky corner tower.

Hampden Park Stadium, Aitkenhead Road,
1903, Archibald Leitch
Queen's Park FC, the oldest League club
in Scotland founded in 1867, moved to this
site in 1903. Leitch was also designer of the
original stands at both Ibrox and Parkhead.
Redevelopment, 1993, Thomson & McCrae
(colour page 140). All-seat capacity of 52,000,
with sport and other facilities slotted into the
space below the sloping terracing, as done by the
Romans in their amphitheatres.

70–74 Mount Annan Drive, 1906,
Richard Henderson
Superb large stone villa, built on the steep
south- and west- facing slope, with wide bow
window and deep eaves. Henderson combines
the simple detail of Alexander Thomson's late
villa Croyland at Newton Mearns (see p. 169)
with something of the stacked-up composition
of nearby Holmwood. He also designed a simple
factory, with sparse classical features, for William
Park (see p. 190).

Top *70–74 Mount Annan Drive*
Below *Mount Florida Primary School*

Mount Florida Primary School, 1127 Cathcart
Road, 1895, David Barclay
Greek cross plan, red sandstone enlivened by
central pediments on hipped slate roofs.

Battlefield East Church and Hall, 1208–1220
Cathcart Road, 1864, John Honeyman
Early English gothic, the original church, now
the Hall. New larger church, 1912, John Galt.
Traditional red rock-faced Decorated gothic.
Not even the cast-iron columns supporting the
galleries anticipate his pioneering workshop for
the North British Diesel Company (see p. 16).

Kingsway Cinema (demolished)

BATTLEFIELD

Cathcart Road drops again from the shoulder of the Mount Florida drumlin towards Battlefield. Battlefield suburb is a late development on part of Langside estate, replacing an older weaving village with tenements spreading downhill to the River Cart. In 1775, Dr Thomas Brown, while residing at Aitkenhead House, became a partner in the Ship Bank. The next year he purchased 49 hectares (120 acres) of land at Langside and erected a mansion. By the mid-19th century there was a village of 20 to 30 weaving families, redeveloped in 1895 as Battlefield. In 1852, Dr Brown's grandson sold Langside to Neale Thomson, proprietor of the adjoining Camphill estate. Thomson feued land for cottages and villas, Camphill later becoming part of Queen's Park. Development was stimulated by the opening of Langside Station on the Cathcart Circle Railway and then the electric trams.

Kingsway, 1237 Cathcart Road, 1929, James McKissack (demolished)
South American Spanish-decorated cinema on a curved street frontage, designed to evoke romance and mystery; a fairly early work by the designer of many dramatic Glasgow cinemas. It was bought by George Singleton for his Vogue chain in 1950, became a bingo hall in 1965 and was demolished, 2006.

Queen's Park Synagogue

Queen's Park Synagogue, 2–4 Falloch Road, 1924, Ninian Macwhannell
15th-century Venetian Romanesque, red-painted artificial stone, bright painted interior. A late work by a prolific architect.

Grange Road Rest, 55 Battlefield Road, 1914, probably William James Boston
Edwardian baroque tram shelter, shop and public toilets. Cream and green striped glazed tiles, pagoda-like timber roof, domed clocktower. Restored as tearoom, *c*.2000.

Grange Road Rest

Queen's Park School, 73–75 Grange Road, *c*.1874 (demolished)
Two white ashlar blocks, gothic details, one on cast-iron columns over shelter. Two-storey red-ashlar renaissance Higher Grade block, 1900, David Barclay. First-floor windows between outer gables, with dormer heads set above eaves. Incomplete red-ashlar Edwardian baroque block, 1912, Thomson & Sandilands. Intended to replace original buildings but abandoned in First World War. Demolished, 2006.

56 Prospecthill Road, 1876, Salmon, Son & Ritchie
Former Deaf and Dumb Institute, built to replace the first Institution at Parson Street, the sheer size indicates the extent of the infliction. French Gothic foliage decoration and cast-iron crested mansard pavilions, on a hillside climbing towards Mount Florida, built in polychrome stonework with white and red bands and bright pink stones. Became Langside College of Further Education in 1947, then converted to residential use, *c*.2002.

Deaf and Dumb Institute

Langside College Annexe, 1958, Boissevain & Osmond
Crisp modernist extension with brightly coloured glazed brick gables, incorporating new assembly hall, gym and swimming pool.

Langside Public Library, 2 Sinclair Drive, 1913, George Simpson
Edwardian baroque, red sandstone, with pilastered, pedimented central doorway and projecting end bays. Simpson's second baroque library, built soon after Possilpark, also incorporates painted decoration. Painting of *Battle of Langside*, Maurice Greiffenhagen, 1919.

Battlefield Primary School, 44 Carmichael Place, 1912, Macwhannell, Rogerson & Reid
Edwardian baroque, with 17th-century classical details in Dumfriesshire red Corsehill sandstone.

LANGSIDE

The residential district of Langside sits on a steep-sided twin-peaked drumlin, the western summit around Mansionhouse Road and the Camphill summit within Queen's Park. The Infirmary is built in tiers on the east-facing slope, with its entrance near the hilltop. The hill drops very sharply from Mansionhouse Road and Cathkin Road to the River Cart and Millbrae Crescent, skirting the foot of the rise south of the Langside drumlin, with Newlands beyond.

Victoria Infirmary, 517 Langside Road, 1882, Campbell Douglas & Sellars
Competition-winning design. Renaissance administration block, square pavilions with cupolas, linked by colonnade above open arcades. Gable decoration includes Queen Victoria's arms and a puma for medical care. An excellent **Private Patients' Wing**, 1931, Watson & Salmond.

Below Battlefield Monument
Below right The Glass House

The Battle of Langside occurred on 13 May 1568 when, eleven days after her escape from Loch Leven Castle, the army of Mary, Queen of Scots was intercepted by that of her ambitious stepbrother Regent Moray. Moray's army took the high ground at Langside, while Mary's army, under the Earl of Argyll, took the lesser height at Clincart Hill. Argyll attacked first but was routed; the Queen fled to England and her ultimate death. The Memorial pillar was erected in 1887, on the 300th anniversary of her death.

The Glass House, Queen's Park, 1905, Office of Public Works
Long municipal glasshouse ranges about central domed entrance at summit of shoulder. Simpson & Farmer ironwork on red brick base.

18–26 Overdale Avenue, former 1937, Sam Bunton
Former Lighting Department Divisional Control Centre. Modernist, interlocking single- and two-storey silver-gray brick cubes with continuous strip windows. Now a bar and restaurant.

Langside Battlefield Monument, Battle Place, 1887, Alexander Skirving
Elaborate spiral shaft, decorated with thistles, roses and fleurs-de-lis, topped with a lion. Restored 1987.

Langside Free Church, 122 Langside Avenue,
Battle Place, 1896, Alexander Skirving
Greek Ionic temple above entrance porch, in a
'Greek' Thomson-like composition. Skirving had
been Alexander Thomson's chief draughtsman.
Converted to restaurant and bar, 1990s.

25–53 Camphill Avenue, 1903, John Campbell
McKellar
Pompous stepped crescent tenement on steep
westerly slope, Ionic pilastered doorways.

Rawcliffe Lodge, 29 Mansionhouse Road, 1862
Steep iron-crested mansard roofs on chateau
with Scots Renaissance details. Converted to
Carmellite monastery, 1919.

Above *Langside Free Church*
Below *Double Villa, Mansionhouse Road*

63 **Double Villa**, 25 and 25a Mansionhouse Road,
1856, Alexander Thomson
As a developer, 'Greek' Thomson prepared a
feuing plan for Langside in 1853 and this was the
only house he built here. Unique asymmetrical
plan, with separate entrance porches on opposite
sides, designed to look like single large villa.
Squared rubble, ashlar dressings and incised
Greek and Egyptian detail under shallow-
pitch broad-eaved slate roof. Responding to
the change in relative importance of the dining
room, now as much used as the drawing room
for business entertaining, Thomson designed a
new type of continuous glass window behind a
freestanding stone colonade at the dining room.
This was his first experiment in what could be
called an inside-out curtain wall. His interior
decoration for these rooms, with elaborate
cornices and pine-panelled walls, included a
'sun' ceiling in the dining room and a 'moon'
ceiling at the first-floor drawing room (colour
page 139). Decoration restored at no 25a, 1995,
Alexander Page and Mark Baines.

25–53 Camphill Avenue

133

34 Cathkin Road, *c.*1900, possibly C J Menart
Renaissance villa, red ashlar, pilastered door,
pediment above sculptured frieze. **Nos 57–61**,
*c.*1890. Alexander 'Greek' Thomson-influenced
villa, rubble, ashlar dressings, fretwork
bargeboarded gable.

40–46 Millbrae Crescent, *c.*1877, style of
Robert Turnbull
'Greek' Thomson-influenced stepped terraced
houses.

2–38 Millbrae Crescent

64 **2–38 Millbrae Crescent**, 1876, possibly
Robert Turnbull
Long crescent of houses, essentially 'Greek'
Thomson in style, with Greek and Egyptian
details. Two twin-pedimented pavilions, with
ornamental bargeboards, break line of terrace.
Lotus-topped columns to shallow entrance
porches. Some original cast-iron boundary
railings.

Millbrae Bridge, Langside Drive at Millbrae
Road, *c.*1898, possibly James Gibson
Single red segmental masonry arch, granite
balustrades, over River Cart.

Langside Primary School and Lodge,
203–233 Tantallon Road, 1904, Andrew Balfour
Red ashlar Edwardian baroque, with giant Ionic
pilasters and projecting end bays.

South Shawlands Church, 12–14 Regwood
Street, Deanston Drive, 1912, Miller & Black
Red ashlar perpendicular gothic, towerless,
gallery. Chancel stained glass, 1954, Douglas
Hamilton.

NEWLANDS
Leafy residential suburb, mainly of stone-built
semidetached villas with relatively few but large
rooms.
    Newlands House was owned by James
Maclehose in 1795, although the majority
of Newlands, within Cathcart estate, was
agricultural. Newlandsfield Bleach Works were
on the left bank of the Cart, north of Riverford
Road, later becoming a tram depot and now a
supermarket. Auldhouse Retail Park was the site
of the first printfield for calicos and linens in the
west of Scotland. Newlands Road was laid out
in 1895 and speculative villas were built rapidly
up to 1905 when the land was largely developed;
the building boom had fizzled out by 1907.

Below *Newlands South Church*
Middle *14–16 St Bride's Road*
Bottom *St Margaret's Episcopal Church*

Newlands South Church, 2 Langside Drive,
1901, H E Clifford
Perpendicular gothic, Giffnock white rubble,
hammerbeam roof, Art Nouveau interior light
fittings.

Church Hall, 37 Riverside Road, 1898, Stark &
Rowntree
Twin-gabled white Giffnock rubble and ashlar-
dressed front and slate roof.

14–16 St Bride's Road, 1923, Thomas Baird
Symmetrical double villa, unusual circular
porches with bellcast roofs. Delicate glazing
bars and sparse stone carving, Glasgow Style
railings.

**St Margaret's Episcopal Church and
Halls**, 351–355 Kilmarnock Road, 1895,
Peter Macgregor Chalmers
German Romanesque, spire omitted from
north-west tower as completed by Whyte &
Galloway. Furnishings and stained glass, Morris
& Co.; three windows, 1950, Powell & Son; three
windows, 1950, Gordon Webster.

Brackley, Newlands Road

Newlands Road
Dunstaffnage, No 11, *c.*1890. Red rock-faced villa with elaborate side conservatory and belvedere platform on slate roof. If by Thomas Baird, then very different from his Glasgow style of the 1920s. **Carradale, No 29**, *c.*1905, style of H E Clifford. Deep-eaved villa with stone mullioned and transomed windows. **The Oaks, No 40**, *c.*1905. Grand Arts & Crafts villa, with corbelled oriels in white polished ashlar, upper floor harled. **Brackley, No 42**, 1905. Scots vernacular, harled with red sandstone dressings, crowsteps and deep eaves.

Newlands Bowling Club Pavilion, 19 Langside Drive, *c.*1910
Harled pavilion with red-tiled roof carried over timber-columned veranda.

65 **Scott House Old People's Home**, 52–56 Langside Drive, *c.*1890
Nos 52–54 built as two symmetrical cream sandstone, slate-roofed villas, occupied from 1897 as one, 'Hughenden', by Hugh McCulloch, decorator. Fabulous Glasgow Style interiors and stained glass from Wylie & Lochhead. Interiors, *c.*1902, probably E A Taylor, or John Ednie. Music room contains glass, probably David Gauld, of Pre-Raphaelite musicians. Other notable features include Jessie Marion King-style frieze of stencilled maidens. Stair window stained glass of harvest scene with classical maidens carrying fruit, *c.*1898, Harrington Mann. No 56, linked by corridor, is an asymmetrical red sandstone Arts & Crafts villa with baronial details, built for a shipbuilder. Medieval great hall with much timber panelling. Stair window 19th-century stylised flower stained glass.

Top *Dixon's Blazes (see page 3), pictured in the 1840s by
William Simpson;* Middle right *Glasgow Samaritan Hospital
for Women;* Right *Caledonia Road UP Church;* Above *Kidston
Terrace, The Gatekeeper*

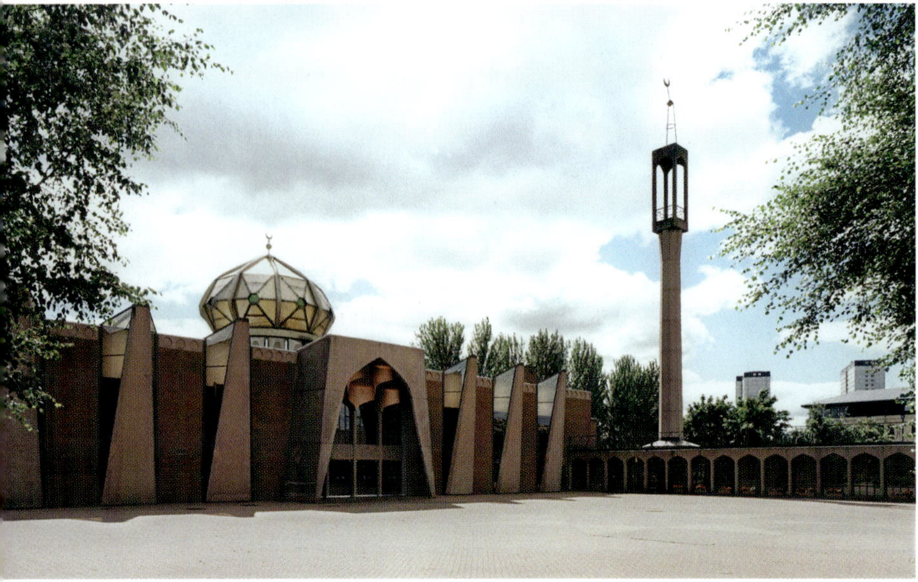

RCAHMS

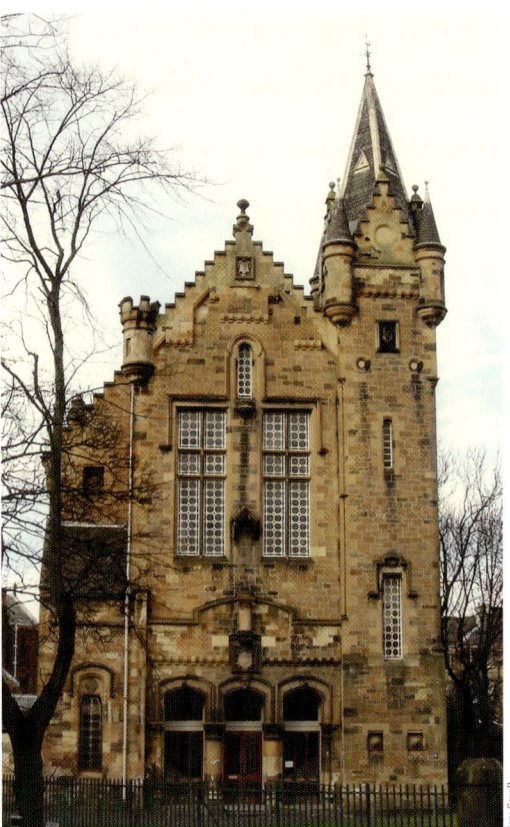

Top *Glasgow Central Mosque*; Right *Dixon Halls*; Below *Gordon Webster Stained Glass, Eastwood Parish Church*

Sam Small

Sam Small

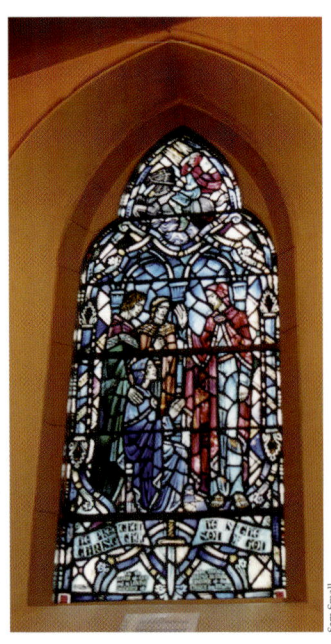

Sam Small

© Mark Baines

Sam Small

Top left *Moray Place*; Top right *Double Villa, Mansionhouse Road, restored ceiling*; Middle *Polnoon Street, Eaglesham*; Below *St Francis Community Centre*

RCAHMS

Above *Carnbooth House*; Right *Langside Public Hall*; Below right *Holmwood House*; Below *Hampden Stadium*; Below left *Greenbank House*

Sam Small

The Beeches, Langside Drive

Langside Drive
Stoneleigh, No 81, *c.*1905, style of H E Clifford.
Rock-faced ashlar villa, steep red-tiled roof and
recessed loggia at first floor. **The Beeches, No
83**, *c.*1900. Magnificent Tudor-style villa, formal
ashlar window details, sculpture above porch
and first-floor recessed loggia.

MERRYLEE
The Renfrewshire farmland of Merrylee in
Eastwood Parish was sold by the Maxwells of
Pollok for a Glasgow housing estate, built in the
1950s and later extended into Mansewood. There
is a ribbon development of stone tenements
along Clarkston Road on the east. Apart from
an excellent church, there is nothing to explore
in the Corporation housing scheme built west of
the Neilston railway line.

Merrylee Parish Church and Halls,
78–80 Merrylee Road, 1912, Peter Macgregor
Chalmers
Scots Romanesque, white stone, stained glass
and green slate roof.

Telephone Exchange, 141 Merrylee Road, 1928,
HM Office of Works, Edinburgh
Cotswold-style, plain rubble building with
mullioned and transomed windows and Tudor
flat-arched doorway.

CATHCART
The large estate of Cathcart belonged to the
family of that name for several hundred years,
before passing to the Semple 'in-laws' in the
16th century. The Earl of Cathcart bought back
the estate and its castle in 1801. The Old Kirkton
was sited below the castle, near the 17th-century
Old Bridge on the main road from Glasgow to

Ayr (bridge rebuilt in the late 18th century). Printfields and bleachfields were located at the Old Kirkton. Papermaking was started by Nicholas Deschamp at Millholm on the left bank of the river in 1729. Millholm briefly became a snuffmill between the 1760s and *c*.1830. The Couper family developed the paper business here in the mid-19th century. The Meal Mill on the right bank of the river became Cathcart Paper Mill in 1812. From 1814 snuff was made in small quantities in a part of the mill, which was closed in 1902. The New Bridge was built half a mile downstream about 1800 when a new road to Ayrshire – now Clarkston Road – was opened, and a new Cathcart Village developed. G & J Weir opened their foundry in 1886 and tenement building went ahead when the Cathcart Railway opened as a spur line in 1884. The Cathcart Circle was completed in 1894 and the trams arrived in 1902. Cathcart was annexed by Glasgow in 1912 and the City bought the rest of the estate in 1927 to form Linn Park.

Cathcart Castle (demolished) & Cartside House

Cathcart Castle, 15th century (demolished)
The keep, about 15 by 9 metres (50 by 30 feet), with vaulted ground and upper floors, had an internal turnpike stair for security and was surrounded by a curtain wall. It fell out of use in the mid-16th century and about 1740 was dis-roofed, prior to a proposed demolition. This was not carried out until 1980, long after Glasgow Corporation had bought the estate to form Linn Park.

Cathcart South Church of Scotland and Hall,
90–92 Clarkston Road, 1893, W G Rowan
Superb former Free Church, in Decorated gothic,
elaborate pinnacled and buttressed front. Large
traceried window with Art Nouveau stained
glass above centre door.

Couper Institute, 84–86 Clarkston Road, 1887,
James Sellars
Vigorous Scots Renaissance with first-floor
Venetian window, stone bracketed balcony and
bell tower with spire. A late Sellars building,
produced while his partner was ill and he was
overworked preparing the 1888 International
Exhibition. **Library and Hall**, 1923, John Alfred
Taylor (J A T) Houston. English baroque, rubble
and ashlar dressings with sculpted details.

New Cathcart Church and Hall, 210–218
Newlands Road, 1907, J B Wilson
Red rock-faced ashlar, perpendicular gothic,
two-storey porch, slim tower linked to Hall,
1899, John Hamilton. Square porch and pyramid
roof.

Weir Pumps Ltd, Cathcart Works,
147–149 Newlands Road, West Range, 1912,
Albert Kahn's Trussed Concrete Steel Co., USA
American functional steel-framed multistorey
foundry. Prefabricated glazed concrete panel
walls, giving more glass than the 1903 concrete
Jessie Street factory (see p. 115). Top floor added,
1949, James Miller. Externally identical east
range built 1948. **Offices & Amenity Block**,
1937, Wylie, Shanks & Wylie. White rendered
Art Deco, showing little of the younger Wylie's
classical training. Art Nouveau wrought-iron
gates. Welfare facilities were becoming popular
with employers. Weirs provided a rest room and
a canteen, plus a lounge, library, cinema and
gymnasium at Cathcart.

New Bridge, Holmlea Road, 1901
Flat segmental-arched masonry road bridge,
with polished red granite balustrades and
voussoirs and cast-iron lamp brackets on piers.
Replacement for 1800 humpback bridge.

Holmlea Primary School, 353–362
Holmlea Road, 1908, Andrew Balfour
Edwardian baroque in red Dumfriesshire ashlar,
with central entry between two-storey plain
ranges and end pavilions.

Top *Couper Institute & Library*
Above *Weir Pumps Cathcart Works*
Below *Weir Pumps Offices*

George Weir and his brother James
started a Consulting Engineers practice
in Liverpool in 1871, moving to
Glasgow two years later. They designed
specialist items for the marine engine
industry, all made by local engineering
firms. In 1886 they opened Holm
Foundry at Cathcart to make auxiliary
equipment for ships. The workforce
had risen to 900 by 1895, when George
retired to Australia. James successfully
obtained orders from the Admiralty
and more from foreign navies. His
son William Douglas Weir succeeded
as Chairman when his father retired
in 1910. During the First World War,
William was employed by the Ministry
of Munitions to secure the supply of
war materials from the west of Scotland.
For this service he was knighted in 1917
and the following year was created Lord
Weir of Eastwood. Created Viscount
Weir in 1938, he was a Director General
in the Ministry of Supply during
the Second World War. He was the
policymaker for the RAF during the
Battle of Britain and for the National
Grid.

Scottish Power, 42 Spean Street, 1912, J J Burnet and Norman Dick of John Burnet & Son
Built as Wallace-Scott Tailoring Institute. Red brick- and ashlar-clad, framed model factory, built around courtyard, extended 1919, windows altered later.

Bridge over River Cart, Delvin Road, *c*.1890
Plate girder, two flat spans, cast-iron decorative parapets, ashlar terminal piers, abutments, central pier with cutwater.

Cathcart Old Parish Church and Session House, 119 Carmunnock Road, 1914, H E Clifford
Perpendicular gothic, completed and opened 1929, Watson, Salmond & Gray. Big buttresses, square tower, simplified hammerbeam roof, stained glass, some by Douglas Hamilton and by R Anning Bell. **Cathcart Old Parish Manse**, No 115, *c*.1914, possibly H E Clifford. Matching grey stone, to north of church, mullioned windows, broad-eaved slate roof. **Cathcart Old Parish Churchyard**, No 118. Roofless tower and west gable, the remaining fragments of original church, 1830, James Dempster. Also in churchyard contemporary **Watchhouse** built into boundary wall and important monuments including: pair of late medieval recumbent slabs; recumbent 1685 Martyrs' slab; **John McIntyre Monument**, 1867, Alexander Thomson, Egypto-Greek domed cylinder; **Thomas Brown of Langside aisle**, 1782, possibly Robert Adam, neoclassical.

Lindsay Tenement, 38–40 Carmunnock Road, 1863, possibly John Baird II
Faintly baronial, crowstepped rubble house, ashlar dressings. First part of a terrace, became a tenement.

Cathcart Old Bridge, Snuffmill Road, *c*.1725
On part of the Gorbals to Carmunnock turnpike road, as well as the route to Ayr. Datestone of 1624 incorporated in 18th-century reconstruction. Large masonry single arch, springs from west bank cliff, low single round arch subsidiary span on east side.

Cartbank, 45 Netherlee Road, *c*.1770
Small Georgian villa with large square bow window, set into the steep river bank; single storey facing drive, two storeys to river. Bowed ends added *c*.1800.

Various Causes have contributed to diminish the quantity of trouts in the Cart, which, it is said, once greatly abounded within. Of those, the use of lime for manure, but especially the crowds of people, who in such a neighbourhood as this, incessantly harass and persecute them, are the chief. Of eels, at all times, there is to be had a plentiful store.
Rev. David Dow, *Statistical Account of Cathcart*, 1793

Cathcart Old Bridge

Holmwood House

66 **Holmwood House**, 61–63 Netherlee Road, 1857, Alexander Thomson
Unique large asymmetrical and picturesque ashlar villa, Thomson's best, for James Couper of Millholm Paper Mills, which were on the river far below. Individual Greek Revival style, deep shallow-pitched slate roofs, magnificent tall lantern, incised and sculptured detail. Almost circular parlour bay window, glass isolated from the stone structure (colour page 140). Extensive major interior work, including the dining room frieze of 21 painted panels illustrating Homer's *Iliad*. Even the dining room sideboard was top-lit! While occupied as a convent between 1958 and 1994, the altar was here. Restoration 1990s, Page & Park. Regeneration of Scotland Commendation, 1999. Ongoing rediscovery and restoration of decorative paintings by Historic Scotland. *National Trust for Scotland, open to the public, guide book.*

The Mansion of Holmwood, ... *with the horizontal lines, low, sweeping roofs and general air of organic unity and, being built in the round, presages the later discoveries of Wright's Prairie houses ... shares the same geometric articulation, the same usage of horizontal regulators, door height inside and the incorporation of outhouses and service buildings into a single building mass, the same integration of houses and garden by die-walls, steps and terraces.*
Andy MacMillan, catalogue to the exhibition *Alexander Greek Thomson, Architect 1816–1875*, Glasgow and London, 1984

MUIREND

There is a steady climb from the River Cart at Newlands to Muirend, although the south bank of the Clyde Valley slopes gently, rising only another 30m (100ft) at the city boundary, some three-and-a-half miles from the city centre. Part of Cathcart estate, Muirend was developed after 1903, when Muirend Station opened, as a suburban speculative development of bungalows.

Muirend Lloyds TSB, 443 Clarkston Road, 1925, A N Paterson & Stoddart
Built as Savings Bank of Glasgow. Tall single-storey renaissance. Iron-balconied Doric framed window and sculpted crest over entrance. Coffered ceiling with elliptical central cupola to banking hall.

Toledo Cinema

Toledo Cinema, 380 Clarkston Road, 1933, William Beresford Inglis
Originally designed for nearly 1,600 seats, Inglis used the technique, pioneered in this country by James McKissack, of invoking a sense of romance and mystery by his Spanish-inspired exterior. The Spanish interior followed the ideas popularised by the American designer John Eberson, to create an 'atmospheric' context for the showing of films of exotic places. Split into three screens in 1982, the American Spanish balcony outside is all that remains now of a sumptuous entertainment palace. The main auditorium was demolished and windows added to the frontages for conversion to flats, *c*.2002. Some reproductions of decorative features from the auditorium are in the new entrance foyer.

Muirend Station, 20 Muirend Road, *c*.1903, style of James Miller
Lanarkshire & Ayrshire Railway. Island platform, Art Nouveau red brick and timber ticket office and waiting room, pierced decorative valance to deep cantilevered canopy.

Linn Park
The park of 84 hectares (207 acres), acquired by the Corporation of Glasgow in 1927, is centred on the undistinguished early 19th-century Linn Mansion. The approach from Clarkston Road crosses the River Cart by the Halfpenny Bridge, while at the north end, entered from Old Castle Road, are the remains of Cathcart Castle.

Halfpenny Bridge

Colin Campbell, a native of Glasgow, was a solder; becoming famous for his campaigns in the Crimea and India, where he sucessfully ended the Mutiny. Created Baron Clyde, he was made a Field Marshall on his return to this country.

Halfpenny Bridge, Linn Park, *c*.1835
Cast-iron depressed arch structure, pierced decorative cast-iron arches, plain cast-iron balustrade, for driveway to Linn Mansion. Oldest complete iron bridge in Glasgow, with 1950s concrete deck.

The Linn Mansion, 20 Linn Park, *c*.1828, enlarged *c*.1852, Charles Wilson
Central gabled porch set in ashlar-dressed rubble. Built for Sir Colin Campbell as a summer retreat.

CLARKSTON
A private housing area was slowly established after the Busby Railway Company opened Clarkston Station in 1866. Glasgow's tramway system was extended outside the city boundary climbing from Muirend, through Netherlee to Clarkston in 1921. Stamperland was then

developed by Mactaggart & Mickel, already
building in the area since 1909. John Lawrence,
building in adjacent Williamwood and
Whitecraigs, entered the Clarkston development
in the 1930s. These were the two biggest, among
four or five Clarkston speculative housebuilders.

Netherlee Parish Church, Ormonde Avenue,
1933, Stewart & Paterson
Red sandstone gothic, perched on a hillock, with
slate roof and large traceried windows at the east
end. Open timber trusses, gallery over east end,
wide nave and low arcades to sides.

Maclaren Place

MacLaren Place, 663–681 Clarkston Road, 1934,
Andrew Wilson
Red ashlar three-storey tenement, with some
delicate Glasgow Style and Art Deco details in
the windows and railings.

Garden Front, Greenbank House

67 **Greenbank House**, High Flenders Road, 1764,
possibly Allan Dreghorn
Dreghorn died in 1764, and the building was
completed the following year for Robert Allason,
grandson of the local farmer, who started as a
baker's apprentice in Glasgow's Gorbals, then
went on to become one of the elite Virginia
merchants. Greenbank, at a height of about
90m (300ft), sits on a rise above Mearns Road,
looking north over the Clyde Valley. With 16
formal rooms, plus large and convenient offices,
Greenbank is one of the few mansions of that
period around Glasgow surviving intact and
is unique in its full symmetrical frontage, with
two projecting wings joined by curved screen
walls in a quadrant (colour page 140). Allason
was also a pioneer in building a formal walled
garden planted with fruit trees and vegetables
rather than flowers and shrubs. *National Trust for
Scotland, gardens open to the public, guide book.*

Flenders Farm Outbuildings, late 17th or early 18th century
Probably an original farmhouse, extended mid-19th century for use as a farmsteading building on Greenbank estate and continuing as a working farm.

Housecraigs Farmhouse, 1794
A single-storey farmhouse, extended in the mid-19th century as another Greenbank estate building, with additional wings. Now residential in a courtyard layout open to Eaglesham Road.

BUSBY
During the 18th century there were corn, meal and waulk mills on the River Cart in the ravine at Busby. In 1780 the Upper or Old Mill became the Glasgow merchant William Fergusson's cotton-spinning mill and about 1790 James Dixon opened another cotton works at the New or Lower Mill, a weaving and finishing business, which survived until 1968. The only other large-scale Busby business, the Busby Print Works of 1796–1901, was across the River Cart in Lanarkshire. The old industries have gone and the whole area has become a lively suburb with local shopping and pockets of new houses everywhere.

Busby Primary School, Church Road, *c.*1900
A tall two-storey renaissance school, with shallow three-storey wings, built on the summit of a hill climbing from the river towards the Eaglesham Road. An inscription reads 'Busby Public School'.

Busby Primary School

EAGLESHAM
The ancient Kirktoun of Eaglesham lies in a hollow south of the steeper rise from Clarkston, and slopes gently downwards to the White Cart Water on the east. The lowest part of Eaglesham is at an elevation of about 162m (530ft), sloping up to over 213m (700ft) on the way to Ballageich Hill and the Bonnyton Moor. Belonging to the Montgomerie family since the 12th century, the village was rebuilt from 1769 by Alexander Montgomerie, 10th Earl of Eglinton. It was not completed for a generation, because some feuars delayed building their new houses, even though the superior gave them the materials. The roofs of the houses were originally thatched, but the owners were later forced, by national building regulations, to adopt slate to restrict

the spread of fire. The street layout is a letter A, with the Lynn Burn running downhill from the apex, in the common green or 'Orry', between the two rows of houses in Montgomerie (originally South) Street and Polnoon (North) Street. The cross-link is formed at the eastern end by Gilmour Street, while the slightly later Cheapside Street extends Montgomerie Street eastwards towards the River Cart and the Lanarkshire boundary. The original village was listed in its entirety as early as the 1960s. It is now a major Conservation Area and practically every building is worth a look.

Eaglesham House, in ruins by 1959 and now entirely demolished, was entered from Floors Road, which runs between Waterfoot on the Glasgow Road and the Humbie Road from Eaglesham to Mearns.

Linn Electronics, 1985, Richard Rogers
A 'clean room' factory built in a simple style, occupying the former site of Eaglesham House.

Polnoon Lodge, Gilmour Street,
late 18th century
Replacement for original house built as a hunting lodge by the 9th Earl of Eglinton, in 1733 before the planned village. A symmetrical two-storey block, with single-storey slate-roofed wings.

Old School House, 53 Gilmour Street, *c*.1790
Neat simple two-storey vernacular house, now in a terrace.

1–47 Polnoon Street
Many single and several two-storey miniature mansions, stepping up the hill from Gilmour Street. Look for Roman Doric columns, arched doorpieces and Georgian fanlights in the grander ones, especially **No 11**, the grandest (colour page 139). Look also for the Art Nouveau detail added at No 45.

3–33 and 52–85 Montgomerie Street
Two similar exceptional groups of cottages, some incorporating shops on the ground floor. Look for date stones and inscribed lintels at Nos 50, 51, 66 and 85; twin consoled doorpieces at Nos 21, 22 and 73; pilastered doorpieces at Nos 32 and 85; and Roman Doric pilastered doorpiece at No 64. The taller **No 34** faced the mill.

In the 'Orry' the Eaglesham Spinning Company, owned by Maclean & Brodie, erected a mill fitted out by the engineers Murdoch & Allan. The 45 ft diameter water wheel used 740 cubic feet of water per minute to generate the 50 horsepower needed to turn 15,512 spindles. The mill employed 200 people and prospered for a few years. The building was destroyed by fire in 1876.
Hugh MacDonald, *Rambles Round Glasgow*, 1854

Above *Polnoon Lodge*
Below *11 Polnoon Street*
Bottom *Montgomerie Street*

Cross Keys Inn, 1 Montgomerie Street and **Cross Keys Cottage**, Montgomerie Square
Part two-storey and part single-storey late 18th-century inn. **2 Montgomerie Street**, part of a terrace, was the Cross Keys Restaurant; all is (2006) closed. **8 Montgomerie Square**, *c.*1790 Single-storey harled house with stone quoins.

Eaglesham Old & Carswell Church

Alexander Montgomerie, 11th earl, revived the ancient Eglinton Tournament in 1839, but the wet weather caused a financial disaster and he had to sell Eaglesham to defray the debts. The Glasgow merchant James Gilmour, whose name is commemorated in Gilmour Street, purchased the Village in 1844.
Hugh MacDonald, *Rambles Round Glasgow*, 1854

Eaglesham Old & Carswell Church,
Montgomerie Street, 1788
Octagonal plan altered 1790 by the 11th Earl of Eglinton. Later classical steeple, housing Mears bell of 1792. Adjacent is a small square detached session house.

1–3 and **6–12 Cheapside Street**
Two groups of 19th-century terraced cottages, some single- some two-storey.

Eaglesham Old & Carswell Manse, 1832
Symmetrical two-storey house, architraved doorpiece, the last house in Eaglesham, set back from the road in its own ground. Across the road is the single-storey plain **Toll House**, 1790s.

Millhall House, early 19th century
Large cottage and stables subsequently altered. Half a mile from Eaglesham and near the site of the Montgomeries' Polnoon Castle, this was the miller's house beside a group of mill buildings and the remains of the Polnoon mill dam on the banks of the Cart.

POLLOKSHAWS ROAD

98–100 Pollockshaws Road, originally Chalmers Free Church

SOUTH GORBALS

98–100 Pollokshaws Road, 1897, Hugh & David Barclay
Baroque aisled and galleried former Chalmers Free Church, stencil décor, stained glass and unusual semicircular portico. Converted to office use, *c.*2005.

Abbotsford Public School, 129 Abbotsford Place, 1878, Hugh & David Barclay
Roman palazzo school and matching house, classrooms on two levels around open hall. Converted to office use, *c.*2005.

St Andrew's Works, 197–243 Pollokshaws Road, 1899, Andrew Myles
A large single-storey red brick electricity generating station, with stone cornice, small pediment and urns over central feature, lesser detail at ends.

600–614 Eglinton Street, *c.*1880
Tenement, with 'Greek' Thomson-style disc detail at second floor. **Nos 656–674**, *c.*1860. Another 'Greek' Thomson-style tenement, with domed and turreted corner tower.

St Andrew's Works

Soon after a provisional Order empowered Glasgow Corporation to supply electrical energy, the City acquired two small electricity generating stations from Muir, Mavor & Coulson in 1892, and they built a new station at Waterloo Street; these were all replaced by two larger coal-fired generating stations at Port Dundas and St Andrews Cross. Coal for the Pollokshaws Road premises was delivered by rail and cooling towers were built on top of the water tanks forming the roof. Generating capacity was greatly increased with Dalmarnock Road power station. The steam turbine generating plant was later removed from Pollokshaws Road, although the building is still a substation.

YMCA, Eglinton Toll

YMCA, 1–15 Maxwell Road, 1894, Robert Miller
Tudor tenement, tall outer gables. Corner
entrance at Pollokshaws Road, leaded glass
panels.

345–363 Pollokshaws Road, 1884
Scots Baronial tenement over shops, rubble,
ashlar dressings, crowstep gables and corbelled
eaves.

St Ninian's Episcopal Church

St Ninian's Episcopal Church and **Hall**,
514–516, 1873, David Thomson
French Gothic, towerless but elaborate apse.
Leaded windows by Heaton, Butler & Bayne;
seven aisle lights by William Meikle & Sons;
stone gothic reredos, 1899, H D Walton; marble
and alabaster, William Vickers; chancel mural,
1901, William Hole.

GOVANHILL WEST
**Sir John Neilson Cuthbertson School and
Lodge**, 35 Cuthbertson Street, 1906, James Miller
English Renaissance with projecting end bays and
hipped roof. Venetian windows enliven wings.

Hutchesons' Girls' Grammar School,
44 Kingarth Street, 1910, Thomson & Sandilands
Renaissance palazzo with baroque details and
two stairtowers.

Strathbungo Parish Church, 603–605
Pollokshaws Road, 1886, McKissack & Rowan
Only the late Scots Gothic tower, with a small
open crown, survives.

Fire Station, 52–58 Allison Street, and
Police Station, Craigie Street, both 1896,
A B McDonald
Lively four- and three-storey Scots Renaissance
blocks, with pediments and crowstepped
gables. Converted to flats, *c*.1990.

St Bride's RC School, 83 Craigie Street, 1894
Built as Strathbungo Public School. Ionic temple
fronts near each end of massive red rock-faced
rubble Board School.

Queen's Park Station, Victoria Road, 1886
Island platform, long wooden building with
glazed bracketed awning and lattice girder
stairs, for Cathcart District Railway.

STRATHBUNGO
Elegant sandstone tenements line Pollokshaws
Road and there are exclusive terraced houses in
the leafy side streets.
    When Sir John Maxwell of Nether Pollok
began feuing the lands of Titwood early in the
18th century to plans by local surveyor, Robert
Ogilvie, Strathbungo was already a crofters'
village. A Paisley weaver, John Houston, set up
a manufactory, employing 80 weavers. Mining
worked shallow seams of the nearby Govan
colliery but had gone by the 1850s and the
two-storey Strathbungo 'lands' were gradually
replaced by tenements from the 1870s.
'Strathbungo Cross' is carved on a tenement
at the corner of Pollokshaws Road and Allison
Street. At the south west of Strathbungo, an
exclusive private residential suburb, Regent
Park, was built behind gates. This development
was started in 1859 by Alexander 'Greek'
Thomson at Moray Place and continued by
other speculative builders. They aimed at
professional men commuting to the city, from
1877 using Strathbungo Station on the Glasgow,
Barrhead & Kilmarnock Joint Railway. The
district was incorporated into Glasgow in 1891.

Above *Hutchesons' Girls' Grammar
School*
Below *Police & Fire Station*

153

Salisbury Quadrant

Lamp Standards, Marywood Square

22–30 Nithsdale Street, *c.*1880
Style of Thomson & Turnbull. Tenement with
simplified 'Greek' Thomson decoration. **No 65,
18–80 Nithsdale Road**, 1879, Robert Turnbull.
'Greek' Thomson-style terraced houses over
shops, very plain, small deep-set windows.
**Salisbury Quadrant, Nos 52–58, 81–95
Nithsdale Drive**, *c.*1880, style of Thomson &
Turnbull. Late Victorian tenement, massive
curved west front to gushet, crude use of 'Greek'
Thomson details.

794–856 Pollokshaws Road, *c.*1850
Four delightful classical tenements, leading to
the park.

3–49 and 4–44 Regent Park Square, *c.*1861
Classical terraced houses, details similar to
nearby tenements, all built before the fashion for
bay windows.

4–50 Queen Square, *c.*1864
Unusually long terrace of classical houses.

Lamp standards, 7–50 Marywood Square, *c.*1880,
Oak Iron Foundry
Seven original cast-iron lamp standards, with
stylised foliage on elegant tapering columns,
sitting on geometric plinths. Gas lamp houses
above ladder supporting arms.

68 **1–10 Moray Place**, 1859, Alexander Thomson
Perhaps the most beautiful of all 19th-century
terraces, this was 'Greek' Thomson's first
speculative development. A serene long classical
colonnaded terrace, two storeys high, visually

154

Sam Small

1–10 Moray Place

stopped by full-height pilastered, Greek pedimented end bays. Viewed from the end, the pilasters of the central range conceal the recessed decorative doors, the frameless windows and even the mutual walls between houses. The deep cornices are decorated with exquisitely carved anthemion (stylised honeysuckle) at eaves level and with Greek key at first floor. Lotus-flower chimneypots can be seen at the rear (colour page 139).

Moray Place
Nos 11–17, *c.*1864, possibly Alexander Thomson. Conventional symmetrical terraced house design, faintly recalling 'Greek' Thomson's adjoining terrace. Pedimented end pavilions, inset pilasters. **Nos 19–25**, *c.*1872. Another speculative builder-designed, two-storey terrace of classical houses with big bows at ends and Greek key ornament between floors. **Nos 27–32**, 1890s. Simplified classical two-storey terraced houses, between advanced Scots Renaissance gable ends, with bay windows, returning in adjoining Gardens.

QUEEN'S PARK
Built before many of the secession churches re-united with the Church of Scotland, this small but expensive and salubrious residential district has many excellent but now redundant church buildings.

Thomas Crawford had built a house at Camphill in 1777 but, when the cotton manufacturer Robert Thomson bought the estate in 1798, the Camphill Mansion was built. His son Neale Thomson bought the adjoining lands of Pathhead Farm

Alexander 'Greek' Thomson (1817–1875) was born at Balfron. Apprenticed to Robert Foote then John Baird, he lived and worked all his life in Glasgow. He designed all kinds of building, contributing greatly to the City's rich Victorian architectural heritage. One of his most successful domestic designs was the monumental Moray Place, outstanding for its purity of proportion and scarcity of ornament. His early work included villas (see Pollokshields and Langside) and his finest at Holmwood (see p. 145), but his churches form his greatest contribution to 19th-century neoclassical architecture (see the former Caledonia Road UP Church, p. 113). He adopted individual features to suit the site for his powerful terraced houses (see Great Western Terrace, p. 30; Westbourne Terrace, p. 31; Walmer Crescent, p. 195). He referred to Romanesque, Assyrian, Egyptian and Indian architecture for dramatic effect.

Above *Former Queen's Park Baptist Church*
Below *Former Strathbungo Queen's Park Church*

from the Maxwells of Nether Pollok, selling them to the City in 1857 for Queen's Park. When it opened in 1862, on the site of the 1568 Battle of Langside, the Park was named after Mary Queen of Scots, not the reigning Queen Victoria. John Carrick, the city Master of Works, who amended Paxton's Park design, prepared a layout of tenement streets centred on Victoria Road. The Camphill Mansion and estate were sold after Thomson's death to Hutchesons' Hospital, then in 1894 to the City, which added them to the Park. Today there is a model boating pond and there is a hill fort, probably of the iron age at Camp Hill. Across Langside Road are the many pitches of Queen's Park Recreation Grounds, totally devoted to football, as well as the Glass House (see p. 132). When the city boundary was extended to the River Cart in 1891, the only open ground was around Clincarthill to the south east.

Bank of Scotland, 697 Pollokshaws Road, *c.*1890
Monogrammed former British Linen Bank, with classical red ashlar tenement over. Octagonal corner above granite columned doorway, adorned by sculpture.

Queen's Drive Building, former Queen's Park Baptist Church, 178 Queen's Drive, 1886, McKissack & Rowan
Romanesque, pair of squat towers with open belfries and pyramid spirelets. Refurbished and modernised 1983, Davis Duncan architects, now converted to offices.

Seventh Day Adventist Church, 174 Queen's Drive, 1886, J B Wilson
Early English gothic, conventional plan, red rock-faced sandstone, with wide porch in buttressed gable entrance front, now converted to flats.

Queen's Park Parish Church, 170 Queen's Drive, 1873, James Thomson
Built as Strathbungo Queen's Park Church and Hall, in decorated gothic, four-stage corner tower with spire behind quatrefoil parapet. Large traceried window over porch, cast-iron columned gallery and barrel-vaulted roof. Stained glass, Daniel Cottier.

144–150 Queen's Drive, *c.*1890
Tenement with bracketed first-floor window hoods above channelled ashlar ground floor. Exceptional oval top-lit stair at No 150.

Gateway to Queen's Park, Victoria Road, 1907,
A B McDonald
Beautiful iron gates, railings and quadrants
supported by Edwardian baroque ashlar piers,
surmounted by superb wrought-iron lamp
brackets.

69 **Camphill Building**, 20 Balvicar Drive, 1875,
William Leiper
Built as Camphill Queen's Park Church, in
Leiper's favourite Normandy Gothic. Good
sculptural detail by McCulloch & Co. of London.
Soaring octagonal spire based on a personal
study of St Pierre, Caen, on massive corner
tower with open belfry stage. Galleried interior,
Leiper stencilled timber vault roof, walls now
whitewashed, leaded glass. Renovated to Baptist
Church, but now closed. **Hall**, 1873, by others to
south.

Above *Gateway to Queen's Park*
Below *Former Camphill Queen's Park Church*
Below left *Camphill House*

70 **Camphill House**, 799 Pollokshaws Road, 1806,
style of David Hamilton
Classical country house, rectangular plan with
hipped slate roof, two storeys above basement.
Continuous cornice, giant panelled corner
pilasters. Painted polished ashlar, sash windows
with slender astragals. Ionic central porch on
north front leads to plaster-vaulted central hall,
with oval staircase off. Converted to Museum of
Costume, 1895, then to flats, 1994.

Camphill Gate, 988–1006 Pollokshaws Road,
1905, John Nisbet
Nisbet adopted the Glasgow Style for his
five-storey symmetrical red ashlar tenement,
with dome-roofed, turreted outer bays. The
first fireproof tenement in Glasgow. **Springhill
Gardens, Nos 912–924**, also by Nisbet, a larger
U-shaped block around common gardens, was
completed slightly earlier.

In 1847, Neale Thomson of Camphill
established Camphill Bakery to supply
wholesome and modestly priced bread
to his own workforce in the Adelphi
Cotton Mills at Hutchesontoun. The
demand was such that he also opened
a shop in Crown Street. In 1854 Hugh
MacDonald reported: *'... at the present
time operations are carried on in four
large bakehouses ... there are no less than
26 ovens, attended by from 46 to 60
bakers ... 500 sacks of flour ... 40,000 to
50,000 quarter loaves ...'* (*Rambles Round
Glasgow*). The bakery was located on
Pollokshaws Road opposite Camphill
House, but the remains are now
hidden behind the tenement known as
Camphill Gate.

SHAWLANDS

South of Camphill proper lay Crossmyloof, in Cathcart Parish. 'Crossmyloof Mansions' is carved on the gushet building at Shawlands Cross. The most popular building in Crossmyloof was the Ice Rink, built in 1907 and rebuilt in 1929 to accommodate 3,000 skaters and spectators. It was demolished in 1986, the site now occupied by a supermarket. The new district of Shawlands was just developing when Crossmyloof was annexed to Glasgow in 1891. 'Shawlands Cross' is carved on the corner building at Skirving Street and Kilmarnock Road. Across Kilmarnock Road were two cinemas, the Elephant, owned by A E Pickard, with its double armchair seats and the Embassy. Both closed in the 1960s and the site is now a bustling shopping centre. Tenements along the Pollokshaws and Kilmarnock main roads contrast with the villas climbing up the hill between.

Below *Tantallon Road*
Bottom *Savings Bank, Pollokshaws Road*

71 **Langside Public Hall**, 1 Langside Avenue, 1847, John Gibson

Rich Italian Renaissance palazzo, with swags, keystone faces, Royal Arms and allegorical figures sculpted by John Thomas of London, who had worked on the Houses of Parliament. Originally the National Bank of Scotland at 57 Queen Street, where the Banking Hall was remodelled, 1856, James Salmon. Rebuilt in Langside Avenue, 1901, A B McDonald. Symmetrical two-storey over basement, rusticated front with Ionic pilasters at ground and Corinthian above. Balustrade protects basement area (colour page 140). 1901 interiors also by McDonald, who retained Salmon's banking hall.

Tantallon Road, 1975, Derek Stephenson & Partners

Early brown-brick three- and four-storey flatted housing development, for housing society. Laid out around formal squares, there are eight-storey pavilion-topped blocks at either end.

Savings Bank, 1110 Pollokshaws Road, 4 Moss-side Road, 1906, Neil C Duff

17th-century renaissance gables, decorative sculptured panels, cornices and friezes, on four-storey red sandstone tenement above bank. Ornamental coved strapwork ceiling to large ground-floor banking hall.

Tusk Restaurant – former Waverly Cinema

72 **Tusk Restaurant and Bar, 18 Moss-side Road**,
1923, Watson, Salmond & Gray
Built as Waverley Cinema; converted 2002,
United Design, to Tea Room, Bar and Restaurant.
Large red ashlar corner block, in diluted 17th-
century classical style. Lead-covered dome above
south-east corner entrance, flanked by giant
Egyptian columns. Sculptured roundels over
inner windows to Frankfort Street. Slate-roofed
attic storey behind main cornice. The same firm's
extension to the City Chambers (see *Central
Glasgow* Guide) was built about the same time.

Shawlands Church, 1114 Pollokshaws Road,
7 Moss-side Road, 1900, Miller & Black
Perpendicular gothic in red ashlar, with
prominent octangular timber roof ventilator.
Hall, 1898, John Hamilton. Arts & Crafts.

Crossmyloof Mansions, 1155 Pollokshaws Road,
10–12 Kilmarnock Road, *c*.1890
Simplified classical white ashlar gushet tenement
with bowed end and balustraded parapet. The
Granary public house at ground floor.

Shawlands Church

Shawlands Old Church, 1120 Pollokshaws
Road, 1885, John Archibald Campbell, of Burnet,
Son & Campbell
Massive Early English gothic, white Giffnock
rubble, towerless, tall open timber roof. Stained-
glass window, 1909, John C Hall. An attractive
early work by a major architect. Compare with
the same firm's Athenaeum Theatre and Barony
Church, of which this is a subtle variant (see
Central Glasgow Guide).

POLLOKSHAWS

Shawhill, another of the barrier drumlins,
pushes the River Cart westwards through
Pollokshaws. Before 1710 Pollokshaws village
was the property of Sir John Maxwell of Nether
Pollok. There was a meal mill on the left bank
of the Cart beside the two-arch Shaw Bridge. In
1782 there were 220 houses in the village, with
331 hand-loom weavers making fine silk gauze
and linen for Paisley manufacturers. There were
also bleachfields along the Auldhouse Burn and
Thomas Baird's dyeworks. In 1798 John Monteith
of Anderston opened a new cotton-spinning mill.
The Burgh, established in 1813, was annexed by
Glasgow in 1912. Of the old Burgh, little more
than a few churches and the Burgh Halls survive,
mainly on Shawhill to the north. The remainder
is almost entirely a Corporation housing
redevelopment of the 1960s and 1970s, with
multistorey towers and slab blocks.

Electricity Substation, Ellangowan Road, Haggs
Road, 1908, W W Lackie
Disguised as an L-plan ashlar villa with
mullioned windows.

Right *14 Hector Road*
Below *War Memorial: St Mary
Immaculate RC Church*

14 Hector Road, *c.*1890
L-plan single-storey Italianate ashlar villa on
the north-east slope of Shawhill. keystoned
tall, round-arched openings, wide bay window,
bracketed eaves.

War Memorial, *c.*1920
Three cast-iron figures, including Christ, set
on an inscribed base, in front of a Corinthian
pilastered wall, supporting a tall arch. In the
grounds of St Mary Immaculate RC Church, on
Shawhill, reached via a steep staircase from the
west.

St Mary Immaculate RC Church and Presbytery, Shawhill Road, 1865, William Nicholson
Decorated gothic nave and aisles, south-east tower. Clinging to the south face of Shawhill near the top. Extended 1900, Pugin & Pugin. Stained glass, 1938, John Hardman Studios.

Clock Tower, Pleasance Street
Only a squat tower and spire remain as a fragment of the old Community Building, 1803, truncated *c.*1895 and 1934. Mixed styles, with classical centre and gothic flanks.

Pollokshaws Old Town Hall

Pollokshaws Burgh Hall

73 **Pollokshaws Burgh Hall**, 2025 Pollokshaws Road, Bengal Street, 1895,
Sir R Rowand Anderson
An eminent Edinburgh architect, who practised infrequently in Glasgow, Anderson was an academic concerned with the revival of traditional Scottish details. In one of his best Glasgow buildings, after the Central Station Hotel (see *Central Glasgow* Guide), he here commemorated the recently demolished Old

*The roads are obsessed with toll-dues,
so much that in going from the south west
of Paisley to Glasgow, a distance of only
three miles, a single horse-gig pays 1s 4d.*
Rev. George Logan, New Statistical
Account of Renfrewshire, 1843

Glasgow College, especially in the bell tower, the main entrance and the 17th-century Scots Renaissance crowsteps and strapwork pediments. Some of the finer features of the Old College are reputed to have been reused. The interior was 'modernised' in the 1960s and 1970s. A Community Trust is undertaking a much-needed restoration, including the large hall, with its original vaulted ceiling and a minimum of classical detail.

Railway Viaduct, Pollokshaws Road, 1847, Neil Robson
Viaduct of three skewed and two straight ashlar arches, rock-faced voussoirs, carrying railway over River Cart north of station. Northmost arch over driveway leads to Pollok House.

Pollokshaws West Station

Pollokshaws West Station, Pollokshaws Road, *c.*1847
Two platform, two-storey brick/sandstone, ground-floor street entrance/first-floor platform entrance, for Glasgow, Barrhead & Neilston Railway. **Railway Overbridge**, Pollokshaws Road, south of Pollokshaws West Station, 1847, Neil Robson, engineer. Single triumphal arch over driveway to Pollok House.

Below *Toll House*
Bottom *Pollokshaws Parish Church*

Old Toll House, 1 Barrhead Road, formerly 1 Cross Street, *c.*1750
Circular, with conical slate roof and large central chimney. Now Council store, within traffic roundabout.

Gallery-access flats, Harriet Place, 1970s
Early brick-faced terrace of five-storey flats. Galleries glazed when pitched roofs added, 1980s.

Pollokshaws Parish Church, 223 Shawbridge Street, 1843
Original Secession church: a Georgian villa with pedimented entrance.

EASTWOOD

In 1812 the Earl of Eglinton sold the barony
of Eastwood to Maxwell of Nether Pollok. As
well as Pollokshaws, some land around the
Auld Kirk of Eastwood and the Auldhouse
Mansion are now in Glasgow, as is the hill of
Mansewood. The remainder of the lands now
constitute East Renfrewshire. There were a
few streets of pleasant bungalows on the hill
of Mansewood before the Corporation built
the adjoining Hillpark housing scheme of deck
access and multistorey flats in the late 1960s.
Across Thornliebank Road, the prize-winning
Eastwood housing scheme was built in the early
1950s.

Below Eastwood Parish Church
Bottom Eastwood Old Cemetery

Auldhouse Court, 1631

Former Auldhouse Mansion. Three-storey
Scots Renaissance L-plan tower house
with crowstepped gables and rubble-built
symmetrical classical front. Extended *c.*1800,
that extension subsequently demolished. New
extension and conversion to flats, 1983.

City Housing, Fyvie Avenue, *c.*1949,
Archibald George (A G) Jury
Designed to satisfy the recommendations of the
Scottish Housing Advisory Committee. Saltire
Society Award, 1951. Prototype for many built
by the Housing Department all over the city and
taken to East Kilbride, where it was adapted by
Francis C Scott (see Crathie Drive, p. 11).

Eastwood Parish Church, 5 Mansewood
Road, 1862, Charles Wilson, completed by
David Thomson
Transitional gothic, west tower and spire. Much
stained glass, 1870s Guthrie & Wells, 1906
J G & C E Stewart, to 1964 Gordon Webster
(colour page 138).

Eastwood Old Cemetery, 200 Thornliebank
Road, *c.*1725
Site of original Eastwood Church until 1781.
Maxwell Mausoleum, 18th century, with fine
marble sculptured panel on east flank. **18th-
century Headstone to Robert Woodrow**, died
1794, Minister of Eastwood, set in an Egypto-
Greek monument by John Mossman, probably
designed by Alexander Thomson. Among
the later are the stone and cast-iron **Smith
Monument** and a tall granite memorial for
John Campbell, writer, who died in 1903.

Thornliebank House

Mansewood, Lawers Road, 1937,
William A Gladstone
Rare small villa by Mactaggart & Mickel's
in-house architect. 1930s streamlined Art Deco
style, with flat roof.

THORNLIEBANK

The village of Thornliebank first developed
industrially in 1778, when Robert Osburn, linen
printer, leased land from Alexander, 11th Earl of
Eglinton, to create a printfield, employing about
50 people. He expanded too fast and became
bankrupt. By 1789 there was a street with a few
cottages in the first hamlet of Thornliebank.
The Glasgow printed calico merchant, John
Crum, bought Osburn's premises, and his sons
Alexander and James were soon employing 847
workers. The family continued to prosper and by
1819 Walter Crum, an internationally renowned
chemist, was in charge. He concentrated the
business on dyeing, especially Turkey Red. His
son Alexander further expanded the business.
Manchester became the headquarters but
Thornliebank remained the Printing Works,
employing up to 2,000 until a major trade
depression caused their closure in 1929. The
Engineering Works continued for a few years but
also closed in 1940.

Thornliebank was a small suburban
community of two-storey semidetached villas
mainly to the east of Main Street until Glasgow
Corporation built their large housing scheme of
cottage flats across the road at Carnwadric in the
1920s. A little further out of Glasgow, the SSHA
built the Arden housing scheme for Renfrew
County in the 1950s. These flats were similar to
Glasgow's Eastwood buildings but had better
landscaping.

*The Mansion House, Rouken Glen,
originally Birkenshaw House, was bought
and completely reconstructed in 1858, by
Walter Crum. Walter's son Alexander
changed the name to Thornliebank House
in 1870. He substantially altered the
building and landscaped the park between
1874 and 1878. His brother sold the
estate to Archibald C Corbett, MP, later
Lord Rowallan, who gifted the estate
and mansion to the citizens of Glasgow
in 1906. Requisitioned by the military
during the Second World War, it was so
badly damaged and then neglected that it
was considered uneconomic to restore and
was consequently demolished in 1963.
Eastwood District Libraries, Crum's
Land – A History of Thornliebank, 1988*

Thornliebank Public School, Main Street,
c.1896, W G Rowan
U-plan stone Tudor gothic sitting on a
promontory. Rowan is better known for his
inventive and exquisitely detailed gothic and
Arts & Crafts churches, such as St Margaret,
Tollcross (see p. 105).

Alexander Crum Library, Spiersbridge Road,
1894, Sir R Rowand Anderson
Built by subscription as a memorial, in
Anderson's Scots Renaissance style. It is now a
branch of the County Libraries, refurbished in
1986.

Dovecot, Deaconsbank Golf Course, possibly 17th century
Circular, rubble-built, eight-pigeonhole group with ledge. It is at the far end of the golf course, near the railway.

GIFFNOCK

With fewer drumlins here the valley floor climbs steadily from Thornliebank through Giffnock and past Broom to reach Mearnskirk at an altitude of about 150m (500ft). Famous for the largest source of building stone in the Glasgow area, Giffnock was entirely agricultural until the first quarry opened in 1835. Alexander Frame Ltd opened a coal pit near Thornliebank in 1850, to be succeeded by Barr & Thornton, who opened a second and deeper pit in 1908. These Giffnock Collieries closed after the General Strike and the mine slag was then used for brickmaking. There was a small Giffnock Forge in this area from 1850 until 1900; The Orchard Lime Mine had kilns on the site of Orchardhill Church, while there were more brick and tile works in the Williamwood area. These had all gone by about 1900. When the Busby Railway opened Giffnock Station in 1864, the first commuter houses were built but the suburban development really started in the 1890s.

Today, a stone-built ribbon development on Kilmarnock Road contains the local shops for a popular suburb of pleasant terraces and bungalows. The total absence of Council housing, prohibited here by Renfrew County to maintain high rateable values, contributes to the popularity.

Orchard Park Hotel, 4 Park Road and Fenwick Road, *c*.1900
Two-storey white ashlar house with Arts & Crafts detail. Octagonal turreted bay, with ogee leaded roof; sculptured doorway; balcony extended from gabled bay and supported on brackets.

Orchardhill Church of Scotland, Church Road, *c*.1899, H E Clifford
Gothic Revival, stone-built with tiled roof and squat tower and stairturret.

Rhuallan House, 1 Montgomery Drive, *c*.1895
Large Victorian villa, renaissance details, large turreted corner bay, with conical roof. After service with the British Legion, it is now East Renfrewshire Council offices.

There were four separate quarries to the east of Fenwick Road, some linked by underground tunnels. To the west lay another four quarries, known as the Burnfield quarries. In 1854 the Glasgow coal mining company, Baird & Stevenson took over the operation, which continued until the stone was worked out in 1912. Beardmore's Forge at Parkhead couped their waste steel slag into the enormous cavities after the First World War and subsequently Derek Crouch Ltd used a magnet to extract scrap metal.
Eastwood District Libraries, *Sandstone to Suburbia – A History of Giffnock*, 1988

Orchardhill Church of Scotland

Sam Small

The Thumb, Fenwick Place

Eastwoodhill, 238 Fenwick Road, *c*.1850s
Two-storey white ashlar renaissance house, built
for William Miller of Netherlee Print Works and
now a nursing home.

The Thumb, Fenwick Place, 1985, Dunlop
Partnership, with Stephen Elliot
Competition win, 40 modern retirement flats in
two five-storey blocks, connected by two-storey
link, in lush landscaped setting.

Giffnock South Parish Church, Greenhill
Avenue, 1929, Stewart & Paterson
Stone-built, slate-roofed Gothic Revival church.
The original church of 1913, now the Church
Hall.

Old Mains, 9 Cadzow Avenue, *c*.1764
Symmetrical two-storey courtyard farmhouse,
with crowstep gables. Plain frontage with
pedimented doorway, the back is much better.

Eastwood House

Eastwood House, Eastwood Park, *c*.1855
Three-storey Tudor mansion; the later two-storey
renaissance wing subsequently demolished.
One-time home of the Weirs of Cathcart, the
Mansion is now a local Council function suite.
Lodge and Gates to Eastwood House, Eastwood
Toll, *c*.1850. Single-storey gatehouse with Tudor
details. Channelled ashlar gatepiers and early
20th-century low quadrant walls carry iron
railings.

Recreation Centre, Eastwood Park

Recreation Centre, Eastwood Park, *c*.1975,
Greenock & Will
Theatre and swimming pool complex built in
simple brickwork, with natural wood finishes in
a leafy parkland setting.

Whitecraigs House, 43 Ayr Road, *c*.1898,
H E Clifford
Enormous two-storey asymmetrical Arts &
Crafts villa, with entrance porch in re-entrant
angle. Excellent period interiors, with panelling,
decorative plaster cornicing and chimneypieces.

MEARNS
The area had seen some small-scale quarrying,
medium-sized bleachfields and printfields
before 1903, when the Caledonian Railway
opened Whitecraigs Station on their line from
Glasgow to Patterton and beyond into Ayrshire.
This was the signal for the start of commuter
suburbs, notably in the area north of the station,
linking up with Rouken Glen Road. To the
south development blossomed, especially in the
renowned 1930s Broom Estate by Mactaggart
& Mickel. This pattern, first on the east of Ayr
Road, extended southwards to join up with
Mearns Cross in the 1960s, then to the east of Old
Mearns Road and later moved into Crookfur, on
the west. The built-up area stops a little south
of Mearns Cross, on the edge of the Fenwick
Moors, which climb above 213m (700ft).

*Coach House & Stable Block, Broom
Mansion (now Belmont House School)*

Belmont House School, Sandringham Avenue,
early 19th century
Former Broom Mansion House. Two-storey
classical mansion, symmetrical main block
with central entrance. Similar extension and
mid-Victorian ironwork porch to left, leading
to modern extension. **Coach House and Stable
Block**, 71 Ayr Road, *c*.1850. Courtyard block,
once entered from the main drive, past gatepiers
and wrought-iron gates from the main road,
leading to the Broom Mansion. Massive coach
doors, between pilasters supporting a pediment.
Originally wooden stalls and cast-iron columns
in stables, now all refurbished and converted to
terraced houses.

*The village of Newton Mearns is a
handsome town, formed of a simple street
on the top of an eminence commanding a
fine view over the country, and with a little
kitchen garden to each house.*
George Craufurd and George
Robertson, *A History of the Shire of
Renfrew*, 1818 edition

*Broom Estate was marketed by 'Mac &
Mick' for its seclusion, its trees, water,
burn, and landscape and its distance from
the city, smog, slums and smoke. It was
at the top end of the speculative market,
and a world away from the mass villas of
[neighbouring] Whitecraigs. There were
to be two sections, area A reserved for
individual strikingly modern flat-roofed
houses designed by James Taylor, while
area B was for houses with pitched roofs.
Apparently Taylor's designs did not sell.*
Charles McKean, *The Scottish Thirties*,
1987

15 Roddinghead Road, 1938, Bill Gladstone
One of very few of Gladstone's villas to survive,
with a pitched roof, in the Broom Estate; **15
Burnside Road** is another.

Kirkhill House

74 **Kirkhill House**, Kirkhill Road, *c.*1870
Two-storey and attic Jacobean-style villa
attached to a simple late 18th-century two-
storey house, now an office suite buried in a
housing development. Good interior woodwork,
including linenfold shutters and doors. Deep
plaster cornices to main rooms, attic originally a
billiard room.

Mearns Castle, Waterfoot Road, mid-15th
century
12m- (40ft-) high tower, with embattled parapet
on corbelled wallhead. Much restored and
combined with new circular building to become
Maxwell Mearns Parish Church, *c.*1970, Walter
Ramsay.

Mearns Kirk, *c.*1813
A two-storey box, with a clocktower, resulted
from the complete remodelling of a late 16th-
century church; recent chancel and wings.

Above *Mearns Castle*
Below *Mearns Kirk*

Kirk House, Humbie Road, *c.*1835
The front faces the garden, the rear can just be
seen from Mearns Road. Two-storey ashlar, slate-
roofed manse, with decorated entry and fanlight.
Gothic panels on original gatepiers to Humbie
Road.

Humbie Bridge over Earn Water, Humbie Road,
rebuilt 19th century
Picturesque single segmental arch a little way
out of Mearns on the road to Eaglesham.

Former Mearnskirk Hospital Buildings

Former Hospital Administration and Residential Buildings, Mearnskirk Road, 1913, J A T Houston
Little remains of the large Mearnskirk Hospital complex designed before but built after the First World War. Late 17th-century English Renaissance style. Built of red brick with white stone dressings and some Art Deco entrances. The Administration Buildings have been converted to flats and all are now incorporated into a large residential complex set within mature parkland.

Croyland, 202 Ayr Road, *c.*1870, Alexander Thomson
Well-proportioned, low-eaved, steep-pitched slate roof over satisfyingly simple ashlar two-storey villa by 'Greek' Thomson. Built long before motorcars made this a major artery, the area is resuming a local character with the new M77 Motorway taking through traffic.

Fa'side, off Ayr Road, 1911, Frank Burnet & Boston
Baronial tower house addition to north wing of late 18th-century two-storey house. Good panelled interiors to tower house, decorative chimneys, plasterwork and some stained glass. John Pollok of Fawside was persecuted as a Covenanter.

Croyland

Balgray House, some way off Dodside Road, by private drive, late 18th century
A small symmetrical but plain Georgian mansion lurks in trees on a rise above the south side of the reservoir.

Over Pollok Castle, late 17th century
Renaissance building for Sir Robert Pollok de Pollok, first baronet, honoured for service to the 'Glorious' (Protestant) Revolution of 1688. MP for Renfrewshire after 1707 Union, Garrison Commander of Fort William in 1715. Destroyed by fire in 1882 and replaced by a Baronial

Many of the farms owned after 1946 by the Fa'side Estate Company had been Pollok property in the 18th century. Robert Pollok the poet, renowned for his *Tales of the Covenanters* and *The Course of Time*, was born in 1798 at North Moorhouse and lived much of his short life at South Moorhouse. Also a minister ordained in 1826, he is commemorated by a bronze medallion on the monument near Loganswell, at the junction of the 1930s Kilmarnock Road (A77) with Mearns Road, the old coaching road from Glasgow, which passed through Clarkston.

Cottage Homes, Crookfur Road

Capelrig House

The Newton lands have changed masters several times since the days of Craufurd. They are at present parcelled out to different feuars. The principal estate in the parish is Capelrig, with a commodious mansion on a small streamlet in a hollow, about a mile and a half north from the Kirk of Mearns.
George Craufurd and George Robertson, *A History of the Shire of Renfrew*, 1818 edition

In 1849, Sir John Maxwell of Nether Pollok bridged the Earl of Eglinton's Glasgow, Paisley & Ardrossan Canal and the railway, to begin St Andrew's Drive, which led south west from his Kinning Park development (see p. 193) towards Pollok. He employed the Edinburgh architect David Rhind to prepare a feuing plan for the south of his estate. The plan took advantage of the contours, with wide drives winding around the hills. Only villas were permitted to the hilly west, trade and industry being confined to the eastern part.

mansion. Requisitioned for an ammunition store during the Second World War and last inhabited in 1944, the mansion was demolished in 1954. The East Lodge, also demolished, once carried the arms of Capt. Thomas Crawford of Jordanhill, who had married a Pollok, while the **West Lodge** survives on the Barrhead road across Balgray reservoir.

Hollytree, Capelrig Road, 1901, John Archibald Campbell
Built as Todhill. Part timbered, Arts & Crafts two-storey and dormered-attic house with small-pane glazing.

Cottage Homes, Crookfur Road, *c.*1968, Sir Basil Spence
Intimate groups of retirement cottages, built for the Linen & Woollen Drapers.

Capelrig House, Capelrig Road, 1769
Symmetrical Georgian mansion, with two-storey wing added 1913. Refurbished by Renfrew County Council after 40 years of neglect and now East Renfrewshire Council offices beside a large school.

ALBERT DRIVE
POLLOKSHIELDS EAST
A very pleasant good-quality stone tenement area, with its own shops and a fringe of industry across the railway; now host to a thriving Asian community. The flatter land to the east of the plan was feued in the 1860s, taken up for tenements (restricted to three storeys), shops, churches and schools. East Pollokshields Burgh came into being in 1880, being absorbed into Glasgow in 1891.

Tramway Theatre, 25 Albert Drive,
522 Pollokshaws Road, 1894, W Clark, engineer
Built as Coplawhill Tram Works and Depot. Red
ashlar front, round-arched brick tram doorways.
Workshops added, 1899; converted to Museum,
1964, and to Theatre and Exhibition space, 1980s;
refurbished 1998, Zoo Architects.

Tramway Theatre

Horse trams were first operated by
Glasgow Tramway and Omnibus
Company from 1871 to 1894, on lines
leased by the Corporation. The latter
had to build its own horse facilities
before the lease ran out and they could
operate the service directly. Stables,
as in private livery stables, were on
the first floor. By 1902 the system
was electrified and workshops were
built at Coplawhill for building and
repairing the city's trams. The first
1,000 electric cars were built there.
The workshops were converted to a
Museum of Transport after the trams
were withdrawn in 1962. The Warwick
Vase, from Hadrian's Villa at Tivoli,
bought by the Burrell Trustees, was
stored here, the only museum floor
strong enough, until moved in 1983 to
the new Burrell Gallery (see p. 187).

Print Works, 46–50 Darnley Street

75 **Print Works**, 46–50 Darnley Street, 1901,
John Gordon and D Bennet Dobson
Built for Miller and Lang, with figure of Minerva
above larger corbelled bay, stone carved
enrichments and unusual lead griffin rainwater
collector. Sinuous with Art Nouveau details
on doors in elliptical arched entry. Stair and
corridor decorated with figured mosaic floors
and enamelled wall panels. Original richly
decorated first-floor office, with wonderful
flowing Art Nouveau leadwork enclosing exotic
stained-glass coloured figures, W G Morton.
D W Sturrock joined the firm in 1902 and
designed the plainer warehouses next door and
at 49–53 Forth Street in 1903.

100–132 Darnley Street, *c.*1895
Former Glasgow Laundry & Carpet Beating
Works. Red sandstone renaissance offices with
big iron-crested pyramid slate roof. Semicircular
windows on the low wings are typical of
industrial buildings of the period.

*100–132 Darnley Street – formerly
Glasgow Laundry & Carpet Beating Works*

St Albert the Great RC Church and Hall,
149–153 Darnley Street, 1886, J B Wilson
Italian Renaissance with Corinthian columns,
sculptured panels and a tall bell tower. Mosaic
floor, panelled gallery, decorative roof tie beams.
Wilson was a prolific church architect, who also
designed the Institute of Shipbuilders, Elmbank
Street (see *Central Glasgow* Guide).

Albert Cross, 165–193 Darnley Street with 50–54
Glenapp Street and 194–198 Darnley Street with
143–147 Kenmuir Street, *c.*1890
Italianate, white ashlar tenements over shops.
Mansard roofs, gabled dormers, giant order
turreted corner bays, originally with drum-
topped cone roofs. Shops were allowed by
the feu titles in a very few streets within East
Pollokshields.

Above St Albert the Great RC Church
Below Albert Cross
Bottom 32–42 Melville Street
Right Pollokshields Public Library

Pollokshields Public Library, 30 Leslie Street,
1904, Thomas Gilmour
Vigorous Edwardian baroque, red ashlar, with
sculpted details, bold extreme end pavilions.
Competition win, revised by A B McDonald.
Interior altered, 1926, some leaded glass, John C
Hall.

Pollokshields Public School, 11 Melville Street,
1878, Hugh & David Barclay
Italian Renaissance palazzo with end pavilions,
the school became an annexe to Albert Road
Academy.

32–42 Melville Street, 1990s, Elder & Cannon
Blockwork-faced four-storey infill tenement.
The low end houses separate the building from
adjoining three-storey tenements of different
styles. Saltire Society Award, 1997.

16–18 Leven Street, *c.*1875. Classical corner tenement.

Tower Buildings, Albert Cross, 199–221 Albert Drive, *c.*1900
Free-style renaissance, white ashlar tenement over ground-floor shops. Shaped first-floor window heads, bay windows and corner tower.

Pollokshields Primary School, 241 Albert Drive, 1882, Hugh & David Barclay
Built as Albert Road Academy. White Italianate palazzo, pilastered mullions, sculpted at first floor. Simpler classical building, Herriet Street, 1901.

Former Albert Road Academy – now Pollokshields Primary School

War Memorial: Pollokshields-Titwood Church

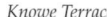

Knowe Terrace

Pollokshields-Titwood Church, 525–529 Shields Road, 1878, Robert Baldie
Mixed gothic, square belfry tower, spire, clock, lavish interiors. Some stained glass in **Hall**, 1874. **War Memorial**, in railed church enclosure, 1921. Anglian, in granite, based on 8th-century sculptured crosses at Bewcastle, Cumbria and Ruthwell, Dumfriesshire.

Knowe Terrace, 553–609 Shields Road, 1874
'Greek' Thomson-inspired details on long terrace, stepped in pairs to slope.

Top *Lorne Terrace*
Above *116-170 Nithsdale Road*
Above right *Shields Road, former Olrig Terrace*
Below *17-57 Fotheringay Road*
Bottom *Sports Hall, Hutchesons' Grammar School*

Lorne Terrace, 256–280 Darnley Street, 84–112 Nithsdale Road, 256–280 Shields Road, 1873, Thomson & Turnbull
White ashlar tenement, completed after 'Greek' Thomson's death. Greek key detail at second floor and rosette frieze; pavilion at Darnley Street corner.

116–170 Nithsdale Road, 1870s
Long white ashlar tenement over shops, architraved and corniced windows, curved east end, circular turret at west.

16–20 Glencairn Drive, 689–707 Shields Road, former Olrig Terrace, 1883
Classical, white ashlar tenement with turreted corner bay.

17–57 Fotheringay Road, *c.*1902, H E Clifford
Red ashlar tenement with Glasgow Style details. A brief use of the style by an architect whose churches were gothic and who pioneered Scots Renaissance for public buildings and English for private houses.

Fotheringay Centre, 2000, Davis Duncan Architects
IT department of Hutchesons' Grammar School, inserted into a Congregational church hall, with new catering facilities and extra classrooms in private courtyard at rear. Glasgow Institute of Architects Award, 2004. **Sports Hall**, Hutchesons' Grammar School, Beaton Road, 1995, Miller Partnership. Colourful framed polychrome brick and glass.

POLLOKSHIELDS WEST
The feuing of St Andrew's Drive started in 1851 and the road was lined with villas by the 1860s. When the area north of Nithsdale Road and east of Albert Drive was built up, the Burgh of West Pollokshields was created in 1875, with a

population of 1,518. Shields Road was extended south of Albert Road in 1870 and more villas were built from the 1880s, by which time there were more than 400 villas. Between 1888 and 1907 James Marr built 58 villas to designs by Alexander Petrie, while George Hamilton built another 68 by Fryers & Penman, who also designed a group of 10 at Whittinghame Gardens, Anniesland. While the architects for many of the villas are as yet unidentified, clearly they followed the fashion published locally by Blackie & Sons in *Villa and Cottage Architecture* (first edition, 1868), or earlier in John Claudius Loudon's *Encyclopedia of Cottage, Farm and Villa Architecture* (first published in 1833). The Burgh of Pollokshields West was also annexed by Glasgow in 1891. Land to the south of Maxwell Park and in the extreme west was developed in the 1890s and 1900s. Haggs Castle was one of the Maxwell residences, built in 1585 on the seven merk lands of Govan, Shiels and Haggs, feued by John Maxwell of Nether Pollok from Archbishop Boyd in 1581, although John had already been a heritable rentaller of these lands before the Reformation.

The picturesque little village of Pollokshields has recently sprung into existence, with a degree of rapidity which fairly rivals the go-ahead Yankee system of town development. This miniature community is composed of elegant cottages and villas, each edifice having its own belt of garden ground walled in, and tastefully planted in front with flowers and shrubs, and in the rear with kitchen vegetables. The greatest variety of architectural taste, moreover, seems to prevail in this rising suburban settlement ... scarcely two of them are similar in design ... each individual proprietor seems to have had his own ideal in 'stone and lime' ... as unlike his neighbour's as possible.
Hugh MacDonald, *Rambles Round Glasgow*, 1854

Sam Small

Pollokshields Burgh Hall

76 **Pollokshields Burgh Hall**, 70–72 Glencairn Drive, 1888, H E Clifford
A former pupil of John Burnet Sr, Clifford followed James Sellars' lead at the Couper Institute and, in his use of monumental Scots Renaissance for civic buildings, was ahead of Rowand Anderson's Pollokshaws Burgh

Halls. This is an asymmetrical composition of 17th-century towers and wings, with an adjoining Jacobean lodge and gate leading to the Maxwell Park drive. **The lodge**, designed to house the Burgh Sanitary Inspector and the Park Gardener, refurbished 1996. An elaborate porch fronts the bulky tower house containing the committee rooms. **The Halls**, altered and extended, 1935, Thomas Somers, and refurbished 1996 by a charitable trust, are to one side; the Upper Hall boasts a Venetian window (colour page 207), and there is much 17th-century style Masonic stained glass in the Lower Hall.

50–52 Glencairn Drive, *c.*1890, possibly Alexander Petrie
Semidetached villa, deep eaves, low end porches, round-headed windows.

Newark Drive
Newark Lodge, No 41, *c.*1890. Asymmetrical villa, steep French roof over projecting bay. Sculpted classical ornament and Egypto-Greek carving to window mullion pilaster capitals. **No 39**, *c.*1880. Asymmetrical villa, deep bracketed eaves, square entrance tower, pedimented and mullioned bay windows, unusual dormered billiard room. **No 37**, 1880s. Ashlar villa, former Barholm, deep-eaved slate roofs, pilastered mullions, balcony with decorative cast iron. **Nos 33** and **27**, *c.*1890. Two neoclassical ashlar villas, former Craigmount and Broxtowe. Iron-crested belvedere and central Corinthian porches. **No 16**, *c.*1880. Italianate ashlar villa, sculpted detail around round-arched window heads, painted Corinthian porch.

161 Nithsdale Road, *c.*1878
Twin pedimented villa in the style of 'Greek' Thomson. Ionic column porch. Converted to synagogue, new side porch, bronze doors, 1928, now School of Islamic Studies.

Pollokshaws West Free Church, 620 Shields Road, 1875, W G Rowan of McKissack & Rowan 'Greek' Thomson-inspired complex, with tower based on Stark's St George's Tron (see *Central Glasgow* Guide) alongside an Ionic temple on a Doric entrance podium. Interior remodelled, 1923, now nursing home. Stained glass, Alfred Webster and Nina Miller Davidson.

Above *School of Islamic Studies, 161 Nithsdale Road*
Below *Pollokshaws West Free Church*

598–612 Shields Road, *c.*1890
Double villa, columned and fretworked open
porches central to each house. Cast-iron window
balconies.

8 Leslie Road, 1880s
Symmetrical villa of unusual design, even in this
area of fierce individuality. Steep bargeboarded
gables, iron-crested bay windows, a semicircular
dormer above the bracketed and hooded central
door.

598–612 Shields Road

The Knowe, Albert Drive

77 **The Knowe**, 301 Albert Drive, 1851,
Alexander Thomson
'Greek' Thomson's earliest surviving villa.
Originally L-plan design in his Italianate
phase, as used the previous year at Craig Ailey,
Kilcreggan (see *North Clyde Estuary* Guide).
Here the tower is a major compositional feature,
between two gables linked by a low roof and an
open entrance porch, with a very low-pitched
roof in front. Although he was to abandon the
arches favoured by his first partner and brother-
in-law John Baird II in 1855, the chimneypots
remained a Thomson signature feature. Interior
largely intact, billiard room added *c.*1899, John
Campbell McKellar. Attractive little **Lodge**,
originally a coach house, with similar details
and ornate timber gates to Albert Drive. Garden
wall and gate to Ayton Road, rebuilt 1873 with
fireclay balustrade and wide gateway.

Albert Drive
No 312, *c.*1875. Villa with window and other
features not unlike nearby 'Green Gables' of
1851, one of four Alexander Thomson villas
demolished in the 1960s to make way for the
Corporation's deck-access flats at St Andrew's
Drive. **No 328**, 1891. Mannerisms inspired by
'Greek' Thomson. Colonnaded first-floor bow
window, with low cast-iron balustraded balcony,

312 Albert Drive

10 Bruce Road

The young architects Boucher & Cousland built themselves a double villa at 35–37 St Andrew's Drive in 1858. James Boucher lived at No 35, while his partner James Cousland was next door at No 37. Not long after Cousland died, Boucher married and moved back to the city centre. The semidetached house, named the 'Swiss Villa', was demolished in 1968. Boucher's retirement house at Coulport was also called 'Swiss Villa'.

now Infant Department, Craigholme School. **No 332**, *c.*1880. Symmetrical villa with distinctive moulding and sculptural detail.

Bruce Road
No 3, *c.*1890. 'Greek' Thomson-influenced ashlar villa, former Carrick House. Broad-eaved slate roofs, fretwork gablehead, pedimented central doorcase and round-arched doorway. **Castramont, No 10**, *c.*1890. Symmetrical villa with steep gabled outer bays and timber mullioned and transomed casement windows. Typical 'Greek' Thomson Egypto-Greek details to gatepiers. **No 18**, *c.*1890, style of early 'Greek' Thomson. Round-arched first-floor windows with channelled voussoirs, on ashlar villa.

25 Maxwell Drive, *c.*1890
Classical villa with Corinthian columned twin bay windows and Ionic doorcase.

55 St Andrew's Drive, 1860s
Former Italianate villa, again early 'Greek' Thomson-style with channelled voussoirs to round-arched openings and iron-crested semicircular ground-floor projecting window, now Briar Ha' Residential Home.

Swiss Double Villa (demolished), St Andrew's Drive

Doralee, 61 and 46 Ayton Road, *c.*1880, possibly William James (W J) Anderson
Renaissance L-plan ashlar villa, pilasters and sculpted detail, full-height bay on right-hand gable.

43 Maxwell Drive, *c.*1880
Large Italianate villa, arched open porch and square corner tower, arched windows, sculpted details, pierced bargeboard, decorative ironwork to balconies at tower.

RCAHMS

Castlehill, Nithsdale Road

78 **Castlehill**, 202 Nithsdale Road, 1870,
Alexander Thomson
Long, low, skilfully massed asymmetrical villa.
The austere unadorned exterior, lacking cosy
domesticity, suits the present use by St Ronan's
Prep School. However, much of the original
idiosyncratic interior decoration does survive
inside, including the Greek motif etched on glass
doors and stylised daisies on cornices.

Sam Small

Ellisland, Nithsdale Road

79 **Ellisland**, 200 Nithsdale Road, 1871,
Alexander Thomson
Tiny but one of 'Greek' Thomson's finest villas.
Rare symmetrical rectangular plan, coarse white
sandstone and low hipped roof, with a row of
antefixae (Greek decorative features) above
the eaves. Original rich interior, comparable

193 Nithsdale Road

with Holmwood (see p. 145), now long since vanished. The main features remain the pair of giant Egyptian lotus-head columns at the central recessed porch, with flanking tall cast-iron lamp brackets. Characteristic lotus-flower chimneypots on end stacks. Low attached boundary wall, with decorative ironwork and Greek detail on gatepiers, like the adjoining St Ronan's.

Wellcross, 193 Nithsdale Road, *c.*1890 Former Carsaig. Ashlar villa, with mullioned and transomed windows. Shallow-pitched double-gabled front with timber carving in gableheads.

197 Nithsdale Road, 1894
White ashlar villa, Corinthian columned porch, balustraded canopy with heraldic shield-bearing lion statue and bracketed eaves. Interior decorative scheme, possibly Stephen Adam & Son, including mahogany stair; carved panel timber chimneypieces, hand-painted hearth tiles and decorative brass canopies; decorative bedroom plasterwork and ornamental ceilings. Exceptional internal stained glass, Stephen Adam & Son (colour page 207): vestibule door, Ceres, goddess of summer; vestibule window, bird scenes and lily pad; arcade over hall archway, female heads; stair window, Elizabethan hawking scene to centre, Shakespeare and Burns portrait heads below, strapwork above and vine swags flanking; upper sashes in first-floor drawing room, probably by Adam Jr; Launcelot and Elaine, King Arthur, Queen Guinevere. Villa subdivided 1977.

Albert Drive
The Hollies, No 352, *c.*1880. Symmetrical classical villa with bay windows in outer bays. Large curved timber brackets support deep projecting eaves of the hipped slate roof. **Park Lodge, No 362**, *c.*1880. Egypto-Greek villa, in style of 'Greek' Thomson, original internal features. Alexander Thomson designed cast-iron railings at boundary with No 360. **Dunmorlie, No 363**, *c.*1880. Symmetrical villa, Ionic doorcase, delicate iron balconies between floors. Art Nouveau extension *c.*1900.

Allerly, 229 Nithsdale Road, *c.*1887,
W F McGibbon
Large Scots Baronial villa for McGibbon himself with bay windows extended up into towers, some sculptural stone details, broad-eaved slate

roofs. **Xaverton House, No 231**, *c*.1880, style of W F McGibbon. Former Oakleigh. Large baronial villa, with bracketed eaves, billiard room lantern, conical-roofed bay window and stone pedimented dormers.

Sherbrooke St Gilbert's Church, 240 Nithsdale Road, 1900, W F McGibbon
Originally a UF church. Thirteenth-century French Gothic with hammerbeam roof. Sculpture of Knox and Calvin within porch. Traceried gable window and flanking buttresses on narrow towers. Interior restored after fire. **Hall**, 1894.

Above *Sherbrooke St Gilbert's (UF) Church*
Left *Sherbrooke Castle Hotel*
Below *31 Dalziel Drive*
Middle *Hazliebrae*
Bottom *Dykeneuk House*

Sherbrooke Castle Hotel, 11 Sherbrooke Avenue, 1896, Thomson & Sandilands
Large Scots Baronial villa, red sandstone with tall tower, perched on the edge of a steep hill. Stained-glass top-lit grand central stair.

The Moss, 28–30 Dalziel Drive, 69 St Andrew's Drive, *c*.1891, probably John Gordon (but possibly Thomas Baird). Renaissance villa with sculpted details, Ionic columned porch linking shallow bay windows, billiard room. **No 31**, 1902, H E Clifford. Large Scots Renaissance villa in white rubble with red tile roof, strapwork entrance and cone-roofed turret. **Hazliebrae, No 38**, 1886, style of W F McGibbon. Tall asymmetrical Scots Baronial villa with crowstep gables, conical slate-roofed tower and triangular pedimented dormers. **Dykeneuk House, No 40**, 1886, style of W F McGibbon. Scots Baronial, chamfered corners and crowsteps. Art Nouveau lights and other interior fittings. Stair window stained glass of Wallace, Bruce and Mary Queen of Scots. **Oak Knowe, No 42**, *c*.1886, style of W F McGibbon. Scots Baronial villa with stone mullions and transoms,

Sherbrooke House

Ardtornish, Sutherland Avenue

crowstep gable and conical slate roof. **No 48**, 1892, W F McGibbon. French L-plan villa, stone mullioned and transomed windows. Fish-scale slate roof on chateau-style tower over entry. **No 58**, 1907, J B Wilson. French Renaissance villa in red sandstone with red terracotta details over openings and at eaves. The Pollokshields drumlins become more obvious here, Sherbrooke Avenue in particular clambering over the steeper slopes.

Sherbrooke Avenue
Sherbrooke House, No 17, *c.*1892. Among the biggest of the Pollokshields Scots Baronial villas. Its square central red sandstone tower is topped by a steep iron-crested French roof. **Balmory, No 21**, *c.*1893, W J Anderson. Arts & Crafts villa in red ashlar-dressed whinstone, with a large round corner tower. **Matheran, Nos 27–29**, 1903, Burnet, Boston & Carruthers. Large Scots Baronial bay-windowed villa with corbelling and a corner tower. Built for Hugh Dunsmuir, it is now the Glasgow School of Occupational Therapy. Decorative plaster above fireplace in open hall complete with a balcony, oak panelling and leaded glass panels.

Ardtornish, 30 Sutherland Avenue, 1892, James Miller
Red ashlar English Tudor villa, with painted timber framing and white stucco. Open loggia to main door, original small-pane glazing.

Tannach

80 **Tannach**, 102 Springkell Avenue, 1992, William Crichton
Elegant large house whose crisp details are sympathetic to the surroundings.

Kelmscott, 110 Springkell Avenue, 1902,
John Nisbet
Scots Baronial and Queen Anne features in Arts
& Crafts villa, with curved bay window, swept
eaves and steep conical roof. Red ashlar ground
floor, white render over and red roof tiles.
Original interior including overmantle tapestry,
Ann MacBeth and stained glass, Oscar Paterson.
The client was J A Mactaggart, who employed
Nisbet to design tenements at Hyndland and
elsewhere in Glasgow.

Kelmscott, Springkell Avenue

Beneffrey, Springkell Avenue

81 **Beneffrey**, 124 Springkell Avenue, 1910,
William Hunter McNab
Large asymmetrical Franco-Scots late gothic
villa by William Leiper's successor. Mullioned
and transomed leaded-pane casement windows,
huge conical-roofed circular turret. Narrow
pedimented gables and tall chimneystacks
as used at West Princes Street, Helensburgh
(see *North Clyde Estuary* Guide) and at Argyll
Mansions, Oban (see *Argyll and the Islands*
Guide). Fine interior, oak panelling, low-beamed
ceilings, carved stone overmantles, high-quality
plasterwork, G Bankart of G Jackson & Sons,
for John Anderson. One of the last villas to be
built in Pollokshields, it became a Strathclyde
University Hall of Residence, and is now
subdivided into three dwellings.

Dunholme, Hamilton Avenue

Dunholme, 110–112 Hamilton Avenue, 1909, James Miller
Cotswold manor, in Lutyens fashion with thin mullions and transoms and metal casement windows. Elaborate renaissance entrance doorcase. Although with shouldered gables and shorter chimneystacks, Dunholme predates his Kildonan, Barrhill (see *Ayrshire & Arran* Guide).

Oaklands, Sherbrooke Avenue

Oaklands, 31 Sherbrooke Avenue and 105 Springkell Avenue, 1902, John Campbell McKellar. Large asymmetrical villa, half-timber cap on square tower. Art Nouveau stained-glass windows, timber gallery and decorative interior plasterwork, for James Donald.

Cairn o' Mount, 34 Sherbrooke Avenue, *c.*1910, H E Clifford
Reticent English Tudor with steep-pitched red-tiled gabled roofs and a big octagonal conservatory.

Redhills, 42 Sherbrooke Avenue, 1902, John Campbell McKellar
Large baroque red ashlar villa for the measurer John Duncanson, who, with John Henderson, later developed tenements in parts of Dowanhill, much of eastern Partickhill and latterly about two thirds of western Hyndland, to John Campbell McKellar's designs after 1898.

Bellsfield House, 35 Sherbrooke Avenue, 103 Springkell Avenue, 1902, Gavin Paterson
17th-century Scots Renaissance in silver rubble, with a complex palette of the usual crowsteps, strapwork pediments, conical-roofed turret and pedimented dormerheads. Now an old people's home.

Bellsfield House, Sherbrooke Avenue

Inchgarvie & Woodmailing, 39 Sherbrooke Avenue, 1903, Burnet, Boston & Carruthers
Large red ashlar renaissance villa, with the architects' customary Glasgow Style touches, for Andrew Biggart.

Haggs Castle

82 **Haggs Castle**, St Andrew's Drive, 1585
Rare genuine L-plan rubble renaissance country
seat of the Maxwells, later of Pollok, until 1595;
the plan typical of houses built during James
VI's minority. Abandoned since 1753, restored,
c.1859, John Baird II, for Pollok estate factor's
house. Distinctive cable mouldings, crowsteps,
slate roofs, original door, elaborate ornament
above. Enlarged circular stairturret and entrance,
c.1890, low baronial wings, c.1900. Divided
into flats, 1940s; converted to Museum, 1972;
returned to residential use, 1990s.

*We proceed to visit the ruins of Haggs
Castle. This ancient and time-worn edifice
with its belt of trees, forms a fine feature in
the landscape for a considerable distance
around. In its better days it has combined
architectural elegance with a degree of
strength necessary to the security of its
inmates in those 'good old times' when the
strong hand was to an inconvenient extent
the law of the land. The place has now a
dark, dismal, and chilly appearance.*
Hugh MacDonald, *Rambles Round
Glasgow*, 1854

POLLOK ESTATE
The lands of Nether Pollok were the property of
the Maxwell family from the 13th century. The
original castle was built by Sir John Maxwell
of Pollok, the second castle was inhabited until
the mid-16th century, and the third was built in
1367. Sir John Maxwell, third baronet, started the
present Mansion in 1747, completing it in 1752.
In 1939 Sir John Stirling-Maxwell drew up a
conservation agreement over the estate with the
National Trust for Scotland, of which he was a
founder member. His daughter gifted the house
and estate to the City in 1966, with permission to
build the Burrell Gallery in the grounds.

*Castle of Nether Pollok, the principal
Manor of an ancient family of the sirname
Maxwell, adorned with curious orchards
and gardens; with large parks and
meadows, excellently well planted with a
great deal of regular and beautiful planting,
which adds much to the pleasure of this
seat. Upon an eminence near to this, stood
the old castle of Pollok, the ancient seat
of that family, where are still remains of a
draw bridge and a fossy.*
George Craufurd, *A History of the Shire
of Renfrew*, 1789

Estate Bridge, Pollok House

83 **Pollok House**, 1752, possibly Allan Dreghorn
Large mid-Georgian mansion with Gibbsian
baroque details; hipped bellcast slate roof,
swags beside upper windows. Original house
raised over semibasement, plain elevations,
rustic corner and keystoned lintels at ground
and first floors. Projecting pedimented
centrepiece to forecourt. Plain rear façade,
wide central Venetian staircase window.
High-quality internal decorative plasterwork
and period furnishings; wonderful library.
Low wings and ogee-roofed garden pavilions
added, 1890 onwards, R Rowand Anderson.
Important collections of Spanish paintings
and six William Blake watercolours. *Glasgow
City Council, managed by National Trust for
Scotland, open to the public, guide book.* **Lodge**,
Pollok House, 97 Haggs Road, 1892, R Rowand
Anderson. Scottish classical with shallow
conical slate roof over a broad semicircular bay
window. **Shawmuir Lodge**, Pollok Avenue,
2060 Pollokshaws Road, 1891, Robert Rowand
Anderson. Scottish classical Lodge with bellcast
slate hipped roof. Tall square gatepiers with
urns and decorative wrought-iron gates.
Estate Bridge over River Cart, 1757. Single
wide segmental arch, balustraded parapet,
roadway widens at abutments. **Stables Range**,
17th to 19th century. **Courtyard Range** on site
of previous house, the Laigh Castle, includes
handsome renaissance gateway (north-west
side) and more 17th-century work incorporated
into later buildings. **Weir, Sawmill and Power
Station**, *c.*1860 for Sir John Stirling-Maxwell.
Weir may be 18th century. Single-storey brick
sawmill with early machinery, although a
turbine replaces the low-breast water wheel.
Late 19th-century Power Station, with Waverley
turbine by Carrick & Ritchie of Edinburgh.

*The seat of Sir John Maxwell, Bart,
of Pollok, is situated in a delightful
position, on the north bank of the River
Cart, a little to the south west of the town
[Pollokshaws]. The house is a spacious
edifice of the plainest architectural
appearance; comfort and commodiousness,
rather than ornamental grandeur, having
been obviously attended to its construction.*
Hugh MacDonald, *Rambles Round
Glasgow*, 1854

84 **Burrell Gallery**, 1972, Barry Gasson,
Brit Andresen and John Meunier
Competition win, to house Burrell's outstanding,
if eclectic, art collection, including two
reconstructed rooms from Burrell's own house
of Hutton (see *Borders & Berwick* Guide). A
modern masterpiece worthy of the collection, set
against the woodlands, which diffuse the light
along one long side. The entrance is through
a medieval stone arch, re-used from Hornby
Castle, Yorkshire, as is the portal leading to the
majestic Courtyard (colour page 207). *Glasgow
City Council, open to the public, guide book.*

PAISLEY ROAD
LAURIESTON
Part of the Old Gorbals, purchased about 1800
from Hutchesons' Hospital by John Laurie, who
tried to rival the West End suburbs by building
such genteel terraces as Carlton Place on the
river frontage and the magnificent Abbotsford
Place.

85 **Laurieston House, 50–53 Carlton Place**, 1802,
Peter Nicholson
Nicholson designed two very long and dignified
neoclassical terraces, punctuated by central and
end pavilions, each with Greek Ionic porches.
John and David Laurie lived in the two houses
of Laurieston House, behind the pedimented
centrepiece, with its bowed and balustraded
porch. Exceptional Italian crafted plasterwork
remains in the vestibule and top-lit staircase. An
ugly mansard roof at **Nos 55–59**, added 1902,
Robert Duncan, was removed during extensive
restorations, 1989, Philip Cocker & Partners. The
huge Victorian replacement for the west pavilion
was reduced by several floors at the same time.
(See also *Central Glasgow* Guide.)

Sir William Burrell (1861–1958)
joined his father's tramp shipping
firm, Burrell & Son, in 1876. Taking
over, with his brother George, on
their father's death, they brought a
prosperous business to international
standing in ship management. They
added to their accumulated wealth
during the First World War, by selling
their fleet to the British Government.
William thereafter amassed a vast
art collection, which he gifted to
Glasgow in 1944, with a subsequent
cash gift to build the gallery. This was
to be some miles away to avoid air
pollution, but modern conservation
methods persuaded his Trustees to
allow Pollok Estate to be the site. The
unique collection of over 8,000 items
of paintings, sculpture, ceramics,
tapestries, stained glass and Oriental
antiquities has become second only to
Edinburgh Castle as the most popular
Visitor Attraction in Scotland.

*The building oozes personality and,
for me, it has a more profound and lasting
impact than the collection, which it houses.
[Goethe] once described architecture as
frozen music, well this particular piece
of architecture is liquid Prozac – and
industrial strength at that.*
Stuart Gulliver, Chief Executive,
Scottish Enterprise, Glasgow, *Prospect
Magazine*, 1990s

Carlton Place from Clyde Street

Bridge Street and Eglinton Street climb steadily some 12m (40ft) up to Port Eglinton and St Andrews Cross, later Eglinton Toll, where the Caledonian Railway passed beneath the road. The railway tracks remain at this elevated level into the Bridge Street and Central Stations. The Glasgow & South Western Railway, arriving along the Paisley Canal route, crosses over the Caledonian lines to continue through Laurieston at high level, before crossing the Clyde and the original tight turn into St Enoch Station. With only infrequent underpasses, the elevated railways in Laurieston and around Tradeston form substantial barriers, which contributed significantly to the collapse of the Lauries' ambitions for a high-class suburb.

65–87 Carlton Place, 1813, Peter Nicholson, completed John Baird I
This near-identical western terrace suffered the loss of the porch at its east pavilion, replaced by a corner entrance, while the west pavilion was demolished c.1856.

Bank of Scotland, 1–3 Bridge Street, 1857, John Burnet Sr
This bank, the first of Burnet's six in Glasgow, occupies a larger footprint than the Baird pavilion it replaced. Figures, rare on buildings of this date, support the coat of arms high above the corner entrance of the Italianate bank. The cornucopias are symbolic of the Edinburgh institution's aspirations, which were accomplished by the Laurieston agent. His rapid growth of their west of Scotland business in trade, manufacturing and shipping made this their most important lending branch in Scotland.

Cumbrae House

86 **Cumbrae House**, 5 Bridge Street, 15 Carlton Court, 1937, Launcelot Hugh (L H) Ross
Art Deco showroom by an architect recruited to work on the Empire Exhibition. Steel frame by Considere Construction, glazed ceramic tile cladding and metal panels between windows. Refurbished and converted to offices, 1988, Houston Bryce Partnership.

20–22 Bridge Street, 1884, probably Bruce & Hay Renaissance-detailed tenement, flats over shops, formerly a Commercial Bank. Original bank exterior with corner entrance.

36–54 Bridge Street, 1888, James Miller
Bridge Street was Miller's first station after
joining the Caledonian Railway staff. Tentative
classical block above two-storey shops, the
arches once led through the tall booking hall to
the platforms at high level. The red sandstone
Caley terminal replaced one of 1841, for the
Glasgow, Paisley & Greenock Railway, the latter
fronted by a massive pedimented portico. The
station was closed in 1905 when the terminus
was moved across river to Central Station.
High-level station converted to residential use
1993.

Glasgow Savings Bank, 63–67 Bridge Street,
*c.*1850, John Gordon
Two-storey Ionic columned bank inserted
below an existing tenement. Large rear domed
banking hall, elaborate plaster cornice, pilasters
and panelled wood doors. First-floor façade
altered, 1888, J J Burnet.

144–150 Norfolk Street, 1898, James Miller
Glasgow Style tenement above modernised pub.
Corbelled oriels and octagonal corner turret,
with playful Edwardian baroque carvings.

Police Training Centre, 71 Oxford Street, 1892,
A B McDonald
Built as a Police Office, with court, cells and
barracks. Classical palazzo façades to Oxford
& Nicholson Streets. Sculpted frieze, a large
armorial wallhead panel above. Above the main
door is a small head of Justice, blindfolded.

The Coliseum, 97 Eglinton Street, 1903,
Frank Matcham
Flemish style, former music hall converted
to cinema, 1925. Octagonal red ashlar corner
tower, topped by former revolving electric
'Coliseum' sign. Exterior re-clad and interior
destroyed by fire 1962. Cinema closed 1980,
subsequently a bingo hall.

New Bedford Picture House, 121 Eglinton
Street, 1932, Lennox & MacMath
Art Deco painted reconstructed stone original
wings, modern entrance. Large neo-Palladian
window with Doric pilasters and colourful
concentric arches on demi-columns. Art Deco
stained-glass stair windows and decor to
cantilevered balcony and boxes. Later another
bingo hall.

Above *Police Training Centre*
Top *Bridge Street Station*

The Coliseum

Port Eglinton

The canal was a busy waterway, as many as 307,270 passengers booking in 1814 between Glasgow and Paisley. The fares were ninepence cabin and sixpence steerage. A couple of boats left Paisley daily for the city, returning the same day. The crew of one of these old time 'packets' was two all told – one at the helm and one on look-out!
T C F Brotchie, *Some Sylvan Scenes near Glasgow*, 1910

TRADESTON
The western part of the Gorbals, bought by the Trades House, when the old barony was subdivided in 1790 (see Little Govan, p. 108). Port Eglinton was established in the area soon after 1805 by the Earl of Eglinton, who had commissioned Thomas Telford to survey a route for his proposed Glasgow, Paisley & Ardrossan Canal, only constructed from Johnstone to Glasgow. The last survivor of Port Eglinton was the former Canal Warehouse at 106–114 Salkeld Street, *c*.1810, David Henry, engineer, demolished in the 1960s. A gridiron of terraced houses was built during the cotton boom between 1790 and 1820, but by 1893 the area had become very commercial and industrialised. It became run-down but is currently undergoing a major redevelopment, with many significant buildings being converted to residential use.

William Park's Motor Car Bodybuilding Works, 40–44 Kilbirnie Street, 1913, Richard Henderson
Albert Kahn's reinforced concrete frame, ashlar walls and large steel-framed windows. Among the few simplified classical features, a segmental arched vehicle doorway. Original R Wayward (London) lift between ground-floor smithy and first-floor paint shop.

Leyland Motors, 140 Salkeld Street, 1933,
probably James Miller
Prominent circular corner tower, Art Deco
strip windows and ribbed faience on fluted
pilasters, more Art Deco columns in vestibule.
A car showroom, recently used as stables by
Strathclyde Police.

Falfield Power-loom Cotton Works, 8–38
Falfield Street, 1821
Red brick four-storey workshop for G L Walker
& Co. Rubble gable, with small bellcote finial,
and adjoining stairtower at corner of Stromness
Street, all cast-iron columns and timber floors.
14–20 Stromness Street, 1861, stone-fronted
three-storey brick extension, part iron framed.
39 Mauchline Street, 1866. A three-storey brick
warehouse, with cast-iron columns and timber
beams, containing a tiled boiler house and an
engine house to power the weaving sheds over.

Leyland Motors

Eglinton Engine Works

Eglinton Engine Works, 25–27 Cook Street,
c.1855
Fitting shop for A & W Smith & Co., Sugar
Machine Manufacturers. Composite structural
frame, originally cast-iron columns with timber
beams and flooring, wrought-iron riveted
replacement beams in the three-storey masonry
block fronting Cook Street. Large door opposite
tall gantried fitting shop, now blocked. Cook
Street commemorates James Cook, the earliest
sugar machine manufacturer, who used
beam engines to power sugar mills in 1815.
181 West Street, single-storey brick engine house,
c.1860. **183 West Street**, *c*.1860. Brick four-storey
patternmaking, fitting and fabrication shops.

Tradeston Paint Mills, 54 Cook Street, 1866
Ashlar paint mill on the corner of West Street,
two storeys extended to three storeys, 1907.
56 Cook Street, 1907, R Thomson. Two-storey
administration and dining block, with central
entrance.

Victoria Grain Mills

Sam Small

Tradeston Street
Clydesdale Paint, Colour & Oil Works, Nos 104–106, 1888, Hugh & David Barclay. Classical pediment with stag's head trademark of Blacklock, McArthur & Co. on four-storey ashlar block. Behind is a two-storey sheet-iron-floored workshop supported on cast-iron columns.
No 118, 1900, W F McGibbon. Venetian red brick warehouse extension to Clydesdale Paint Works, with terracotta stag's head trademark plaques and corner tower. This was built in front of a three-storey varnish factory in the yard, 1896, W F McGibbon. **The Point**, 161–171 West Street, 1876. Two ashlar office and sample room buildings acquired by the Clydesdale Paint Works from James Mills, a dyer. Cart entry to yard, mansard added to one, 1896, also by McGibbon.

Victoria Grain Mills, 155–159 West Street, 133 Wallace Street, 1894, W F McGibbon
Ornate Flemish, red brick with steel and concrete ground floor, iron columns and wooden floors above. Corbelled castellated water tower on corner block, 1896. Converted to residential use, 2002.

8–14 Scotland Street, 65–67 Paterson Street, 1864
Engineering works for James Howden. Two-storey ashlar block with segmental-arched cartway leading to tall single-storey L-plan workshop, with timber kingpost roof. Workshop built around an open yard, with columns supporting two jib cranes. Second office block, 1870, ashlar to Scotland Street, brick, now harled, to Paterson Street.

Glasgow District Subway Power Station, 175 Scotland Street, 1895, John Gordon
Two tall single-storey red brick buildings with steel roof trusses, later incorporated into Howden's Works.

Howden's Main Works, 191–197 Scotland Street, from 1897, Nisbet Sinclair, engineer, with Bryden & Robertson (1907) and later Dykes & Robertson, architects
Flat-roofed single-storey east lodge and taller two-storey red ashlar offices in front of workshop. Two-storey west lodge added 1902, second floor when north-lit mansard-roofed drawing office added to office block, and extended steel-framed works behind, 1907, Dykes & Robertson. Works greatly extended since 1914.

RCAHMS

Scotland Street School

87 **Scotland Street School**, 225 Scotland Street, 1904, Charles Rennie Mackintosh
Severe red ashlar budget school, with sparse Art Nouveau decoration. Standard plan of classrooms stacked above the central hall, cloakrooms at the ends, beyond the pair of glittering glass staircase towers, one each for the girls and boys (colour page 205). Like the stairtowers, evocative of the Loire chateaux which influenced many Scottish castles, the dramatic west gable (the east is now hidden) demonstrates Mackintosh's fascination with Scots Renaissance domestic architecture, as used at the Hill House in 1902 and more famously at the Glasgow School of Art, 1907. The swept-down roof of the Janitor's House, like Windyhill in 1900, is a Voysey device (see *Central Glasgow*, *North Clyde Estuary* and *South Clyde Estuary* Guides). Converted to Museum, 1990s. *Open to the public, guide book.*

KINNING PARK
Sir John Maxwell of Nether Pollok had his estate surveyor, Peter Macquisten, prepare a residential feuing plan in 1834. The development was not successful to begin with and the area later became industrialised, although Kinning Park did become a Police Burgh about 1871, annexed by Glasgow in 1905.

Vulcan Tube Works, 126 Cornwall Street South, *c.*1871
Plain classical office and warehouse, for Cruickshanks, Low & Co. Long ashlar-fronted rubble block, fanlight over cornice at pilastered entrance.

Until recently a beautiful rural spot, the principal features in the landscape being green fields, waving trees and lovers' walks, with here and there a charming mansion house. Kinning House Burn meandered its way till it joined the waters of the Clyde, not far from the Park House Toll, where the road diverges into two branches, the one leading to Paisley, the other to Govan and Renfrew.
Francis H Groome, *Ordnance Gazetteer of Scotland*, 1892

Above *Kinning Park Pumping Station*
Below *Angel Buildings*

On Paisley Road there were tolls at Bridge Street; 'Park House', or Paisley Road Toll; 'Two Mile House', a coach stage near today's junction with Broomloan Road; 'Halfway', or Three Mile House, an ancient hostelry, replaced in 1790 and again about 1900; and Crookston Toll, before leaving Glasgow and crossing the County boundary into Renfrewshire. The Paisley Road toll rental was £143 in 1781 and £1,806 13s 4d in 1840, while the Renfrew Toll rental was £263 in 1794 and £778 in 1840. Steam cars were using Govan Road in 1878 and both tolls were abolished when horse trams were introduced on Paisley Road the next year.

In 1801 the Glasgow lawyer John Bennet purchased Ibroxhill from the Hill family, owners since the 1750s. He built a new house called Ibroxhill, which he sold to a Glasgow merchant, John McCall, in 1816. The land was later acquired by Glasgow Corporation, who converted the mansion into a tearoom in 1905 before demolishing it in 1914.

Kinning Park Pumping Station, 100 Seaward Street, 1909, D & A Home Morton
Tall terracotta brick pumphouse with round-headed windows, semicircular above. White-glazed brick inside, ridge ventilators.

Old Toll Bar Public House, 1–3 Paisley Road West and 2–4 Admiral Street, *c.*1860
Classical tenement over public house. New pub front conceals 1892 ornate interior. Gilded bar fitments, etched windows, richly painted inner doors with cornucopias. Painted and gilded mirror adverts by Forrest & Son, Glasgow for David McCall.

Angel Buildings, 2–20 Paisley Road West and Govan Road, *c.*1885, Bruce & Hay
Dutch Renaissance tenement over restaurant. Elaborate roofscape of tall slate-clad pyramids and carved stone dormers. A winged angel above a tall wooden bellcote dominates the view from the east.

Toll Gate Pier, north-side piazza, junction of Govan Road and Paisley Road, *c.*1800
Cast-iron toll gate pier, gifted by Old Glasgow Club, 1934.

News International, 71 Milnpark Street and 124 Portman Street, 1873
Built as Kingston Engine Works for Smith Bros, Engineers & Ironfounders, founded 1866. Classical red and yellow brick, round-headed windows, large eliptical door, cylindrical iron columns, open brick arcade to erecting shop, travelling crane.

Kinning Park Colour Works, 73 Milnpark Street, *c.*1892, Bruce & Hay
Ornate red and white brick office and laboratory for Hird Hastie, with round-headed windows and pedimented segmental doorways.

IBROX

Best known for the Stadium, which is surrounded by a mixture of small and very large flats in stone tenements, including some by the Corporation Housing Department. The smaller groups are undergoing refurbishment by several Housing Associations. The area, with some Asian residents and close to the new Glasgow Arc Bridge, is becoming very popular.

Lorne Street School, 58–62 Lorne Street, 1892, Hugh & David Barclay
Lively red ashlar Italianate school with central hall. Ionic frames to first-floor windows, fluted pilasters over.

252–256 Paisley Road West, 2–6 Harvie Street, 1882, probably James Sellars. Refined Italianate corner tenement over shops and dreadful pub front. Ogee lantern and finial above corner turret.

Walmer Crescent

88 **1–15 Walmer Crescent**, 1857, Alexander Thomson
Complete three-storey and basement, straight faceted terrace following crescent plan, with terminal pavilions. With its Schinkel-type continuous second-floor pilastered window band, Walmer Crescent anticipates Moray Place of 1859 (see p. 154). With three-storey square projecting bay windows rising from the basement, this is 'Greek' Thomson's most austere design, although one of his grandest and most imposing.

Turning towards Govan, by way of Paisley Road, we find workmen busy erecting a fine bank of houses, intended by the builder as attractive residences for the bein' middle class of Glasgow. This is Tulliallan Place. Some distance farther on, the road crosses a sluggish burn by means of an old bridge, and then immediately to our right, we come to the isolated but handsome sweep of Walmer Crescent, exclusively occupied by rich city merchants of those days. To the right and about a quarter of a mile off the road, we see Middleton House, standing in the midst of a wood of elm, beech and fir – a typical gentleman's country house.
T C F Brotchie, *A History of Govan*, 1873

Bellahouston Academy Annexe, 423 Paisley Road West, 1875, Robert Baldie
Long symmetrical baronial front, with central tower and the usual crowsteps, oriels and iron-crested mansard roof. Built as a private boarding school, altered 1903 to standard Board School. Better known for his gothic churches, Baldie also designed the baronial offices for the Carron Iron Works, 1875, demolished 1980s (see *Falkirk & District* Guide).

494–498 Paisley Road West, *c.*1825
White ashlar classical tenement.

Bellahouston Academy

Ibrox Parish Church, 67 Clifford Street, 1862, James Smith, completed by Melvin & Leiper
Built as Bellahouston Parish Church. Geometric gothic with stained glass in every window, corner tower. **Halls**, 1885, W F McGibbon. Like a 17th-century tower, but gothic.

28–68 Ibrox Terrace, *c.*1850, style of Charles Wilson
Very long Italianate terrace with featured centrepiece.

520–532 Paisley Road West, 1881, McKissack & Rowan
White sandstone tenement, 'Greek' Thomson-style details, including continuous stepped moulding over first-floor windows.

Ibrox Methodist Church, 534 Paisley Road West, 1867, Angus Kennedy
Originally a UP church. Two-storey gothic box with Early English door and tower. Chancel and transepts, 1896, Bruce & Hay. Converted to climbing centre, 1990s.

Glasgow Engineering Works, 143 Woodville Street
Built for Blair, Campbell & McLean, coppersmiths, now Maritime House. East Block, 1900, Robert A Wightman. Flemish-style brick, central gabled two-storey offices, recently harled, fronting finishing shops. West Block, 1910, Arthur Hamilton. Steel-framed three-storey brick workshops. Pedimented entrance, Art Nouveau-detailed staircase and bay window.

Ibrox Stadium, 100–170 Edmiston Drive, 1928, Archibald Leitch & Partners
Tall renaissance red brick stand to Edmiston Drive, with central entrance and end pavilions, for Rangers FC. Then the largest, most lavish stand ever built, with 10,000 seats. Extended, 1994, Gareth Hutcheson. Club and executive upper deck, with catering and private boxes, and lower front deck, supported on 141m (462ft) girder beam. Brick and glass block corner stairtowers.

Ibrox Stadium

Sam Small

Sports Complex, Hinshelwood Drive, *c.*1990, Strathclyde Regional Council, Department of Architecture and Related Services
Broad-striped brick walls and steel frame, facing entrance to Ibrox Stadium. Profiled sheet roofing with top lighting.

DUMBRECK

A very popular and attractive inner suburb of
stone villas, which are not quite so big as those
in adjoining Pollokshields West.

The Glasgow merchant William Waddrop built
the house Dumbreckhill after he acquired the
estate in 1790. Dumbreck was inherited by his
nephew Robert Scott of the Thistle Bank.

Craigie Hall

89 **Craigie Hall**, 6 Rowan Road, 1872,
John Honeyman
Designed for Joseph MacLean, son of William
MacLean of Plantation (see p. 210). Renaissance
ashlar mansion with central Ionic columned
entry and balustraded window over. Classical
colonettes to bay window on garden front.
Sumptuous neoclassical ceilings, cornices and
embossed frieze, painted dados and inlaid
Honeyman tiled floors. Outstanding rusticated
marble walled entrance hall with Corinthian
columns. Lion mask frieze to staircase, marbled
columns to first-floor screens and gilded
guilloche detail to first-floor corridor architraves.
It was acquired about 1890 by Thomas Mason, a
Pollokshields villa builder, who had it extended
and new internal fittings provided in 1892, by
John Keppie and Charles Rennie Mackintosh
(Honeyman & Keppie). Pavilion with coat
of arms above Art Nouveau bay window.
Exceptional fittings included Art Nouveau
overdoors, tulip friezes and open pediments
in hall. Fitted library cases, with swelling
colonettes and sinuous shelving. Elaborate wood
fittings in drawing room. Mahogany organ case
and elaborate chimneypiece in music room.
Other remarkable fittings include Lalique Art

Hazelwood House

Deco light fittings, Art Deco mirror fireplaces, bathroom fittings and stained-glass windows. Restored and converted to serviced offices and function rooms, 1980.

Hazelwood House, 52 Rowan Road, 1882, James Milne Monro
Jacobean villa, now nursing home. Symmetrical south front with gabled outer bays and Tudor-arched door on east front.

BELLAHOUSTON
The Rowan family, old church rentallers, obtained a charter from James VI after the Reformation, granting perpetual rights in their land. James Rowan of Maryland, a descendant, purchased the Bellahouston estate in 1726. When his descendant Thomas died in 1824, the estate passed to Moses Steven (Buchanan Steven & Co.) of Polmadie, a relation by marriage. Two years later Steven bought Wearison from the trustees of Henry Ritchie of Craigton. Steven then bought the adjoining Dumbreck House from Robert Scott of the Thistle Bank and changed its name to Bellahouston. After he died in 1871, his sisters set up a Trust, which feued part of the estate for middle-class houses along the south side of Paisley Road West and sold the remainder of the estate in 1892 to Glasgow Corporation for Bellahouston Park. The 1938 Empire Exhibition was organised in this Park by the Government to help revive the Scottish economy. There were over 100 large temporary buildings and many smaller ones, all dominated by Tait's Tower. Only the permanent Palace of Art remains *in situ*, while Tait & Ross's Engineering Pavilion was taken to Prestwick, where it is part of the Scottish Aviation Industries works (see *Ayrshire & Arran* Guide). Much of the Park is now devoted to sports facilities, including a dry ski slope on the side of the drumlin where Tait's Tower once stood.

Many of the central Glasgow works of James Milne Monro (1840–1921), one-time President of the Glasgow Institute of Architects, have been demolished. His most famous building, the former Grand Hotel, St Andrews (until recently Hamilton Hall, and now being reconstructed as The Grand Club), is seen by TV millions behind the 18th green of the Old Course (see *The Kingdom of Fife* Guide).

90 **House for an Art Lover**, Bellahouston Park, 1988, Andrew MacMillan
Adaptation of an incomplete 1901 competition design by Charles Rennie Mackintosh. Started by Graham Roxburgh for a serviced office complex, completed by Glasgow City Council, now leased to Glasgow School of Art as a postgraduate study centre and to a restaurant. The Music Room is frequently a popular venue for concerts (colour page 207).

Palace of Art, 1121 Paisley Road West, 1938,
T S Tait and L H Ross
Sole *in-situ* survivor of Empire Exhibition. Art
Deco block of halls, around open landscaped
court. Concrete block walls, profiled sheet roof
and large rooflights (colour page 208). Some
decorative ironwork, including staircase lamp
brackets. Converted to community use, 1951,
Glasgow Corporation. Refurbished 2002, as a
sports training centre of excellence.

Palace of Art

Bellahouston Sports Centre, Bellahouston
Drive, *c.*2000, Glasgow City Council
Indoor facility to complement the many outdoor
pitches and other sports facilities in the Park.

MOSSPARK
Part of the ancient Cardonald lands was
purchased by Glasgow Corporation in 1908 from
Arthur Baird of Blantyre & Lennoxlove. The area
was absorbed by the City the next year and in
1921 became one of its finest municipal housing
schemes of two-storey cottages and terraces,
built around another drumlin.

Craigton, another part of Cardonald, was
acquired in 1746 by John Ritchie, father of James
Ritchie, one of the 'tobacco lords' and an original
partner in the Thistle Bank. The estate was sold
before 1843 to Henry Dunlop, who had sold on
to Graham Hutcheson prior to a destructive fire
in the 1850s.

In 1816 John Snodgrass leased
the Mill of Cardonald for 19 years
from the Stewart Lord Blantyre, a
descendant of the Stewarts of Darnley.
Snodgrass produced peasemeal and
barley meal. When he died in 1837,
his three sons formed the company
of J & R Snodgrass, building a second
mill at Port Dundas and later another
at Washington Mills, Anderston, to
become one of the largest millers and
flour merchants in Glasgow, today a
part of Allied Mills.

The National Projectile Factory,
operated by Weir of Cathcart, was built
on 10 hectares (24 acres) of the former
Craigton Estate during the First World
War. After the war, the site was sold
to Wallace Farm Implements Ltd, who
made the 'Glasgow' tractor. Closed in
1924 due to cheaper American imports,
the building was then used to produce
Weir prefabricated houses. They made
3,000 houses, of which 40 were erected
at Robroyston, but the works closed
in 1928.

Craigton House (demolished)

Mosspark Baptist Church

Mosspark Parish Church, 167 Ashkirk Drive, 1927, Thomson, Sandilands & MacLeod
Substantial towerless red sandstone gothic church. Open decorative timber roof, white stone pulpit, communion table and font.

Mosspark Baptist Church, 155 Corkerhill Road, 2001, Davis Duncan Architects
Flexible open-plan sanctuary space. Steel frame enclosed in polymer-rendered brick wall facings.

CARDONALD & CROOKSTON

Cardonald was given to Sir James Stewart, an illegitimate son of the first Earl of Lennox in the 15th century. In 1702 another Stewart Earl of Lennox sold Crookston to James Graham, later to become the first Duke of Montrose. His son sold Crookston and Darnley in 1757 to Sir Walter Maxwell of Pollok. In the 1810s the Earl of Eglinton's canal passed through Crookston. A small quay was formed at Ross Hall but a proposed branch to Hurlet was never built.

*Through Cruikston's Castle's lonely wa's
The wintry wind howls loud and dreary
Robert Tannahill, Cruikston Castle, 1808*

Moss Heights

Moss Heights, Berryknowes Avenue, 1949, A G Jury
Modernist local authority housing, at 10 storeys, the first multistorey flats in Glasgow. Built on the steep slopes of Craigton, part of Cardonald, the flats enjoy superb views.

Cardonald Parish Church, 2141 Paisley Road West, 1888, Peter Macgregor Chalmers
Plain Early English gothic, red sandstone, modest, stained glass. Chalmers added a side aisle to the first church, 1899.

Crookston Station

Crookston Station and Cottage, 21 Lochmaben Road, 1884
Single-storey station with a lattice girder footbridge for Glasgow & South Western Railway. Stationmaster's house with deep bracketed eaves.

Ralston Avenue
Struan, Nos 81 & 85; Dunard and **Raeberry,**
Nos 97 & 101; Westfield and **Auldersyde,**
Nos 109 & 113, three 1870s double villas with
'Greek' Thomson-style gables, broad eaves and
bargeboards.

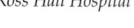

Ross Hall Hospital

Ross Hall Hospital and Lodge, 197 Crookston
Road, 1877
Baronial mansion for James Cowan of
Hawkhead. Red sandstone with customary
crowstep-gabled main front, conical-roofed
circular turrets and extravagant sculptural
details. Jacobean interiors and stained glass,
some 1886, W & J J Keir. Matching Lodge with
conical-capped gatepiers, castellated quadrants
and heavy decorative wrought-iron gates.
Extension, 1982, Spence & Webster. Shiny glass-
and aluminium-clad Ward Block, linked to main
building by space-frame canopy.

The Ross family of Hawkhead sold
their land at Ross Hall to Peter
Murdoch, a Glasgow merchant, in
the late 18th century. Murdoch's
family then sold the estate to James
Cowan in the early 1870s. Cowan
was a Barrhead man, owner of a
carriers business, Cowan & Co. He
built Ross Hall in 1877, and after he
died in 1907 the house was bought
by Frederick Lobnitz, the head of
a shipbuilding firm, Lobnitz & Co.
They made dredgers and rock-cutting
equipment for the Suez Canal. Lobnitz
was knighted for wartime services
under William Weir. In 1959 the firm
was taken over by Weir's and in 1982
the house was purchased for a private
hospital.

Crookston Castle

Crookston Castle, 170 Brockburn Road, *c.*1390
The second oldest remaining building in
Glasgow, after the Cathedral, Sir John Stirling-
Maxwell presented the Castle to the National
Trust for Scotland in 1931 as its first property.
A remnant of a massive stone tower house, set
high on a hill. Very unusual plan, continental,
comprising central three-storey rectangular
block of ashlar-dressed rubble framed by four
taller square towers, one surviving to wallhead.
Beautifully built, it is now a consolidated ruin,
cared for by *Historic Scotland. Historic Scotland,
open to the public, guide book.*

Tradition whispers of newly married
Queen Mary and Darnley spending
happy times at Crookston, while Burns
later put words of lamentation in
Mary's mouth:
*Now blooms the lily by the bank,
The primrose down the brae,
The hawthorn's budding in the glen,
And milkwhite is the slae,
The meanest hind in fair Scotland
May rove their sweets amang,
But I, the Queen of a' Scotland,
Maun lie in prison strang*
Robert Burns, *Lament of Mary Queen of
Scots, on the approach of Spring*, 1790

The small mining village of Hurlet, on the left bank of the Levern, was in the earl of Glasgow's Hawkhead estate. The 200-hectare (500-acre) Hawkhead, or Hurlet coal seam, extended beneath Hawkhead, Househill and Nether Pollok estates. The pits, already in decline, did not reopen after the 1926 General Strike, when the district was incorporated into Glasgow. Coal and building stone were supplied by canal and railway to Glasgow. Large-scale alum and copperas works were established in the 19th century, both at Hurlet and at Nitshill, providing mordents to fix colour dyes.

Another mining community, across the River Levern, was located some distance from Hurlet at Nitshill, on Househill lands. The estate was acquired in 1646 from the Stewarts, by the Dunlops of Dunlop in Ayrshire. About 1700 they sold to John Blackburn, a merchant investor in the disastrous venture of the Company of Scotland's colony at Darien, Panama, whose son Andrew became a partner in the Glasgow Arms Bank. In 1750 Andrew sold to another banker, Robert Dunlop, a founding partner in the Ship Bank. Robert was a younger son of James Dunlop of Garnkirk. Nitshill also supplied Glasgow with coal and stone.

The [railway] engine whirls us past the red hills of the Hurlet, amid sights and scents unholy, past Nitshill, with its quarries, and belching volumes of smoke.

Hugh MacDonald, *Rambles Round Glasgow*, 1854

Leverndale Hospital, 510 Crookston Road, 1890, Malcolm Stark
Hilltop former Hawkhead Asylum, Elizabethan towers and bay windows. Extended, 1903, H & D Barclay. Now a charred ruin after fire.

POLLOK
A Glasgow Corporation Housing Scheme built on land acquired in 1935 from the Maxwell family of Nether Pollok. Maxwell, a founder member of the National Trust for Scotland, sold the land on condition that a low-density development with cottage house types be adopted.

36–42 Lyncross Road, 2002
Two and three-storey terraced housing, in place of the Council-built properties.

St James' Pollok Church, 183 Meiklerig Crescent, 1893, H E Clifford
Red ashlar perpendicular gothic, with aisle arcades, open timber roof and gallery stairturret. Originally Pollokshields Titwood Church, moved and rebuilt, 1951, Thomson, McCrae & Saunders, now the Village Reading Centre.

Craigbank Secondary School, Damshot Road, 2001, Glasgow City Council
Reconstructed concrete frame and walls reclad with coloured render and new blue and charcoal panels have created a new St Paul's RC High School. The campus incorporates state-of-the-art classroom IT facilities, high-tech drama studio and a sports complex.

The Wedge, 1066 Barrhead Road, Pollok Roundabout, 2005, Chris Stewart
A sedum-planted roof is novel, especially in this part of Glasgow, but the café and community facilities are popular!

NITSHILL
Nitshill expanded after 1848, when the Glasgow, Barrhead & Neilston Railway opened a station and by 1860 the population was 1,000. Nitshill was brought into Glasgow in 1926 and a large housing estate was built on the hills post 1945. There is little left of the original settlement and nothing of note in the housing scheme.

Salterland Viaduct

Salterland Viaduct, Salterland Road, *c.*1847,
Neil Robson
Glasgow, Barrhead & Neilston Railway viaduct
over Levern Water. Three rusticated ashlar
block arches, all with brick soffits, two wide and
skewed, the eastmost a simple round arch over a
minor road.

East Hurlet House, 1554 Barrhead Road, *c.*1763
Two-storey vernacular house, with one- and
one-and-a-half-storey wings. One-time home of
Charles Macintosh, inventor of the waterproof
coat, the interior contains re-used panelling from
Curling Hall, Largs.

DARNLEY
The earl of Lennox granted lands to Stewart
of Minto in 1472 and Darnley remained in that
family's possession until 1938, when Glasgow
purchased the land for a housing estate. The
South Nitshill Estate was built there in 1957 and
Darnley Estate in the 1970s.

Glen Clunie, Gallery Access Housing, *c.*1970,
City Architect
Built on a hilltop, with long views.
Refurbishment for City Housing, 2000, Zoo
Architects.

Above *Glen Clunie*
Left *Darnley Mill*

Darnley Mill, 500 Corselet Road, *c.*1644
Scots Renaissance, crowstepped group of much-
altered cottages, with conical- roofed circular
north-east tower, for Stewarts of Darnley.
Extended and incorporated in restaurant, *c.*1999.

When the Clyde was deepened, the old floodplains were raised. Dredged material was dumped behind the new retaining walls, to create flat and level land from the city centre to Shieldhall and beyond.

GOVAN ROAD
KINGSTON

Shipbuilding moved down river as Glasgow Harbour developed. Kingston Dock opened behind Windmillcroft Quay in 1867, but was too small to attract a railway connection. Filled in during the early 1960s, it is now the site of the south end of the Kingston Bridge. In the first half of the 19th century, manufacturing and then warehousing dominated the area after the Scottish Co-operative Wholesale Society (SCWS) built their huge empire south of Kingston Dock from 1872.

Clyde Place, 1861, Andrew Duncan, Clyde Navigation Trust Engineer
Small mooring posts and a cobbled wharf on timber piles are all that remain of Clyde Place Quay; transit sheds demolished, 2002.

Kingston Model Lodging House, 38 Clyde Place, 18 Centre Street, 1878
Four-storey ashlar front with ornate carved panels at second floor, carried on cast-iron frame. Converted to warehouse, 1927.

Westcars Saab Showroom

Westcars, West Street, 2000, McEwan & Smith
Sleek and elegant steel and glass car showroom.

D & D Warehouse, 100 Centre Street, 1981, Elder & Cannon
Banded polychrome brick enclosure, a light-hearted foray into postmodernism by a young practice (colour page 205).

Warehouse, 56–64 Kingston Street, Centre Street, 1878
Tall ashlar-fronted brick warehouse with dormer hoists behind, for William M Hayman, contractor.

The Co-operative movement developed rapidly after the 1860s and the wholesale side needed production space as well as warehousing. Most of the Glasgow workshops were located at Shieldhall (see p. 225). Founded in 1868, the Scottish Co-operative Wholesale Society was regarded as a thrift institution, alongside the Savings Bank and Friendly Societies. Thrift was a virtue extolled by the propagandist Samuel Smiles in his *Self Help* of 1859 and encouraged by the State.

SCWS, 120–130 Morrison Street, 1872, J Spence
The earliest of the Scottish Co-operative Wholesale Society's warehouses is a Victorian classical block, inscribed 'SCWS Unitas' over the Paisley Road entrance. Extended with more elaborate detail, 1873 and completed, 1876 with the narrow gusset gable, topped by a clock. Later the Society's Funeral Service, the Society had outgrown the warehouse site within a decade, now unused.

© Captain Marcus Maclean

RCAHMS

RCAHMS

Top *Plantation House, in the background of Maclean family portrait by an unidentified artist*; Above *Tower of the Winds*; Below *D & D Warehouse*; Left *Scotland Street School*

Sam Small

Above *Glasgow Science Centre;*
Right *Scottish Exhibition & Conference Centre*

Top left *Burrell Gallery;*
Top right *Upper Hall, Pollokshields Burgh Hall;* Middle right *Stained Glass, 197 Nithsdale Road;* Bottom *Music Room, House for an Art Lover;* Middle left *Pollok House*

© Burrell Collection

Sam Small

RCAHMS

Sam Small

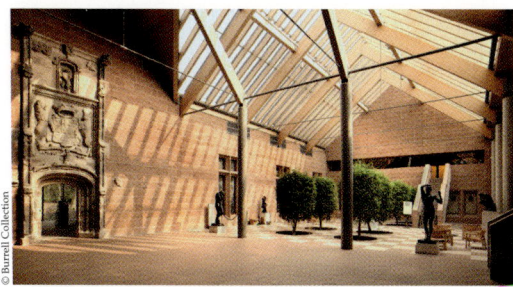

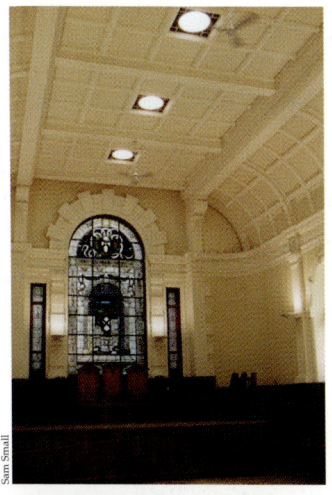

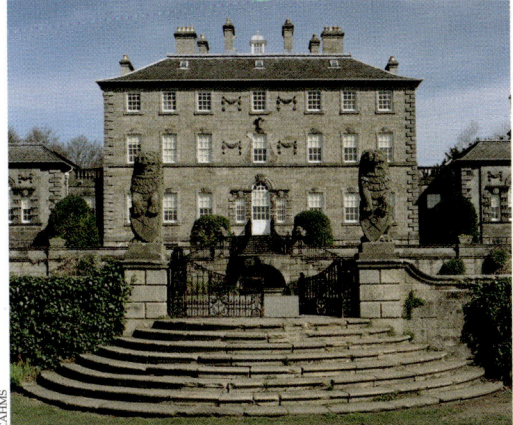

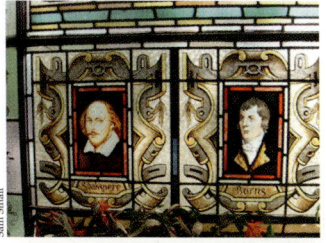

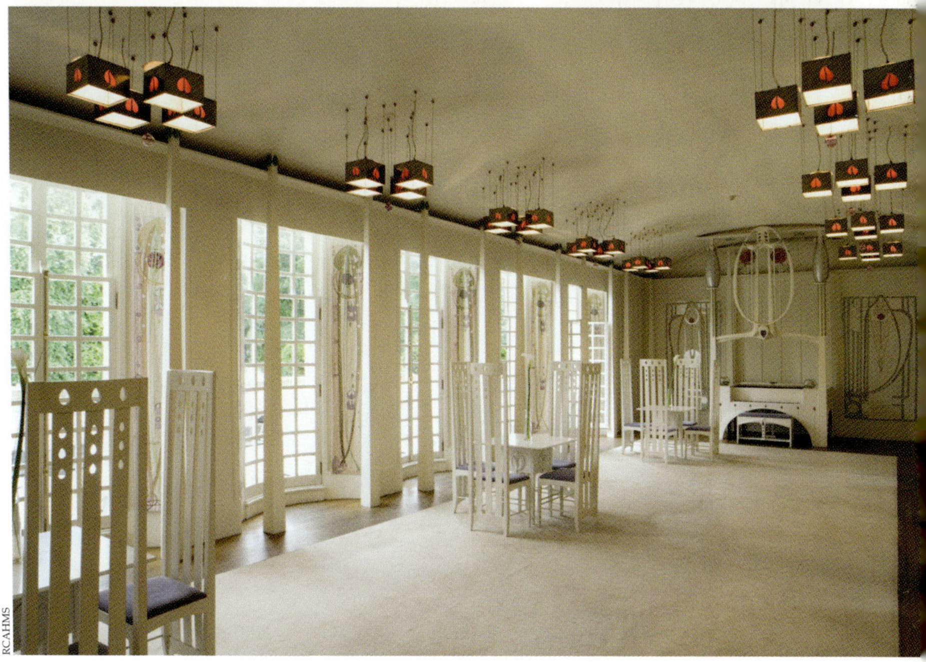

RCAHMS

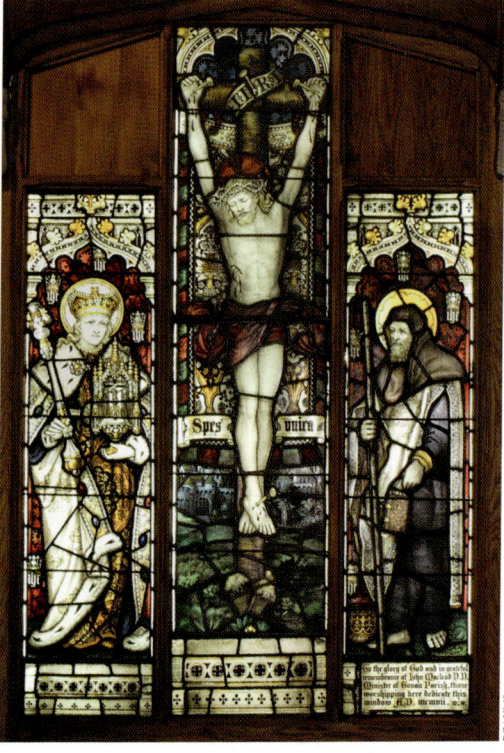

Top left *Pearce Institute*; Top
right *Interior by Basil Spence of Scottish
Pavilion, Empire Exhibition*; Right
*Stained Glass by Burlison & Gryllis,
Stevenson Memorial Chapel, Govan Parish
Church*; Above *British Linen Bank,
Govan*; Middle left *Palace of Art*

SCWS Head Office, Co-operative House

Co-operative House, 95 Morrison Street,
1886–93, Bruce & Hay
The SCWS Head Office complex was built in
several stages; the first started at the corner of
Wallace Street and was entered at 44 Dalintober
Street. Above their Flemish Renaissance
warehouse, Bruce & Hay sited the elaborately
panelled Co-op Hall, with its Corinthian
columns and hammerbeam roof, while behind
was another panelled Committee Room.
Alongside, at 34 Dalintober Street, in 1888, they
added a five-storey crowstep-gabled warehouse,
topped by a carved lion and shield. This building
linked through to 19–37 Carnoustie Street, where
a Jacobean storage and production building,
1891, also Bruce & Hay, occupied the rest of the
block through to Wallace Street. In 1893 Bruce
& Hay won a competition for the last part, the
real headquarters. A symmetrical landmark with
elaborately detailed French Renaissance four-
storey pavilions, capped by distinctive square
domes. Said, although denied at the time, to be
their unsuccessful design for the City Chambers.
Complex converted to 80 loft apartments and
family homes, with ground-floor shops, bars and
restaurants, around new courtyard. Workshops
and studio spaces also provided, 1997, Glass
Murray Architects.

SCWS Warehouse, 53 Morrison Street and 33
Dalintober Street, 1919, James Ferrigan
A five-storey warehouse, built after the First
World War, around three sides of a brick
lightwell. Beaux Arts, with granite Doric
columned main entrance and giant Ionic
pilasters through third and fourth floors.
Venetian windows above each end pavilion
cornice, adorned with seated statues, urns and
mansard roofs.

Bruce & Hay designed many red
and white brick industrial buildings,
including Hydepark Bakery, Anderson
for Bilsland Bros and for UCBS at
McNeil Street, Hutchesontoun, both of
which were fronted by red sandstone
renaissance offices, like those for
D & W Henderson at Meadowbank,
now cocooned and awaiting new use.

Kingston Library, 330–346 Paisley Road, 1901,
Robert William Horn
Built as Kingston Public Halls. Edwardian
baroque ashlar front, with central entrance,
decorative frieze, giant pilasters and scrolled
pediment. Large hall above small hall. Rebuilt
after fire, 1948.

Plantation House (demolished)

PLANTATION

In 1783 John Robertson, a sugar and cotton
merchant as well as cashier of the Glasgow Arms
Bank, bought Craigiehall estate and renamed it
Plantation. Twenty years later it was sold to John
Mair, a Paisley mason. Then in 1829 the estate
was acquired by William Maclean, a Glasgow
merchant and Deacon Convenor of the Trades
House (colour page 205). James Salmon laid out
the estate for feuing *c*.1860 but development was
delayed over arguments about the new dock.
By the late 19th century the area around Princes
Dock was covered by workers' tenements.
Glasgow Harbour Tunnel was opened in 1895,
linking Plantation to Finnieston.

Glasgow Harbour Tunnel Shaft & Rotunda,
1 Plantation Place, 1888, Wilson & Simpson,
engineer
One of two domed brick rotundas built over
24m- (80ft-) diameter shafts accessing twin
horse-drawn vehicular and one pedestrian
tunnel under the Clyde. The South Rotunda,
with Corinthian cast-iron columns and slate and
glass roof, now awaiting a new use.

Glasgow Harbour Tunnel Rotunda

91 **Tower of the Winds**, Govan Road, Mavisbank
Road, 1894, John Burnet, Son & Campbell
Hydraulic Pump House, the former Prince's
Dock Hydraulic Power Station. Romanesque
corbelled cornice atop tall pump room (colour

Tower of the Winds – the former Prince's Dock Hydraulic Power Station

page 205). Castellated tower, another water accumulator, with original hydraulic equipment. Stump, a mere third, of the octagonal brick chimney, crowned with red ashlar sculpted frieze of the 'Four Winds'. Converted to office use, *c*.2005.

Pacific Quay: Masterplan, 2005, Gareth Hoskins Riverside redevelopment, on site of 1988 Garden Festival, the infilled Prince's Dock.

Finnieston Bridge

92 **Glasgow Arc**, or Finnieston Bridge, 2002, Gillespies, with Halcrow, consulting engineers Four-lane – two dedicated to public transport – fixed bridge, plus footpaths and cycle-ways, all suspended from a striking concrete arch.

Queen Elizabeth Tower, Mavisbank Gardens, *c*.2004, RMJM
Adjacent to the Finnieston Bridge, a block of 72 flats above underground car parking, with a dramatic tower at the east. Penthouses with roof gardens step down towards the west.

BBC Scotland

1 Pacific Quay, 1997, Parr Partnership
High-specification speculative office
accommodation, 9,150 square metres (30,000
square feet), over three floors with central
service core. Glass and metal cladding with
aerofoil roof over simple box.

BBC Scotland, 2001, David Chipperfield
Competition win, an outwardly simple, square
six-storey glass box, entered from a new Civic
Square facing the Glasgow Science Centre. Large
ground-floor studios and open-plan offices
stepping above a central naturally ventilated
atrium to provide public space with access to the
secure areas. Executive architect, Keppie Design.

Scottish Media Group, 2004, Parr Partnership
New facilities for Scottish Television, in an
elegant rectangular box.

Glasgow Science Centre

93 **Glasgow Science Centre**
Two striking titanium-clad geometric buildings,
Imax Cinema and Science Centre, 1995, Building
Design Partnership
Competition-winning scheme includes space-
framed Imax, cantilevering slightly towards
canting basin. Science Centre, a bi-directional,
diagonal span, tilted D-section, of 11,500 square
metres (28,500 square feet) on four floors, fully
glazed north face overlooks river (colour page
206).

Rotating Tower, 1992, Richard Horden
Competition win intended for St Enoch's Square,
shelved for lack of funds and built with the
Science Centre. Aerofoil section triple-columned
tower, freely rotating, with lift to viewing
platform. The whole complex, now floodlit,
looks superb at night from the north bank.

Queen's Dock, 1882, James Deas
The opening of the Queen's Dock and the
railway spelt the end of Stobcross House and
Finnieston. Cut and built in Giffnock stone, the
Dock transformed the area into a city service
centre, legacies of which are still evident. It was
filled for the Scottish Exhibition Centre (see
below). Only the **Finnieston Crane**, 1932, by
Cowans Sheldon, now recalls the mercantile
bustle. The crane could load railway engines
and tanks on to cargo ships, which is said to
be one reason for its survival. Otherwise the
engineering works have gone.

Clyde Auditorium

Scottish Exhibition & Conference Centre, 1984,
James Parr & Partners.
Red and grey wriggly metal glandular volumes
flanking a central, top-lit atrium, created upon
the Queen's Dock to contain party-political
conferences, prestigious trade exhibitions,
concerts, and the annual Carnival. Most easily
identifiable by its **Clyde Auditorium**, 1997,
Norman Foster & Partners – better known as
'the Armadillo' – popularly named from the
eight distinctive overlapping aluminium clad
shell roofs (colour page 206). With concrete block
internal walls, this is industrial construction. With
over 3,000 seats, this state of the art conference
centre is bigger than the Royal Concert Hall
and one of the top conference venues in Europe.
Large glass entrance at open end and covered
link to the Crown Plaza Hotel. (See also Johnny
Rodger, *Contemporary Glasgow*, 1999 Rutland
Press.) **Crown Plaza Hotel**, formerly Forum, by
Cobban & Lironi, 1989, is a tall, staggered blue-
glass tower, with a large white podium.

Old Houses, Govan Ferry

GOVAN

In 1575 Govan was described as *'A gret and ane large village upon the Watir of Clyde'*. By 1790 the population of 2,518 was mainly salmon fishers, weavers or engaged in other rural occupations. Even into the 1830s Govan was a quiet semi-rural location, although there had been a colliery at Drumoyne, south of Elder Park. By the 1840s shipbuilding and the attendant railways had destroyed the quiet.

William Hamilton started feuing Middleton estate for building in the 1840s. He sold 4 hectares (10 acres) to Alexander Reid for tenements but only a few were built along Paisley Road West before the 1890s, when Archibald Stewart & Company completed them. Tenement building had begun in 1866 at Greenfield, feued by the Good family, and at Helen and Robert Streets the same year. In 1896 the Glasgow Subway Workshops were opened at Broomloan Road. More Hamilton lands, including J & G Thomson's Clyde Shipyard and Cessnock Bank Villa, were bought by the Clyde Navigation Trust to construct Cessnock Dock, later Princes Dock, which opened in 1897. The dock, with three mooring basins, three graving docks and large timber stores, was used to export Lanarkshire coal and to import iron ore and limestone.

By 1904 the population of Govan had reached 90,908, living in tenements, and it was the fifth largest Burgh in Scotland when annexed by Glasgow in 1912. There were three ferries

The Hamiltons held a merk land of Govan from the archbishop in the 16th century, later feuing their land. In the late 18th century, the cotton merchant James Hamilton of Mavisbank was owner of about 16 hectares (40 acres) of Meikle Govan. He also acquired 19 hectares (46 acres) of Partickhill, which his grandson had to give up to his creditors.

McArthur & Alexander founded a shipyard at Water Row, to the east of Govan, in 1839. It later became Robert Napier's Old Yard. On the west side of Govan, Charles Randolph and John Elder, who had already purchased Napier's Old Yard, opened a new yard on the former John Cumming Fairfield estate in 1864. When John Elder died, William Pearce became sole owner of the yard and changed the name to the Fairfield Shipbuilding & Engineering Company, building fast Atlantic liners and warships. In 1968 it was merged in the unsuccessful Upper Clyde Shipbuilders, then in 1972 became, with Stephen's and McConnell's, Govan Shipbuilders. The firm was nationalised in 1977, later bought by Kvaerner Govan and today is part of British Aerospace.

across the Clyde: the Highland Lane passenger ferry to Kelvinhaugh; the Water Row vehicular Govan ferry to Ferry Road, Partick; and the Govan Wharf passenger Govan Ferry West to Meadowside.

Govan Town Hall, 401 Govan Road, 1897, Thomson & Sandilands
Magnificent large Beaux-Arts composition. Govan's second Municipal Offices and Council Chamber, now local Public Halls and Glasgow Social Work Department. The main entrance, a central-arched frontage on Govan Road, is flanked by busts of former Councillors and a Provost. The Italianate Summertown Road entrance leads to the Concert Hall, decorated with cartouches of music and drama and a carved frieze by Archibald McFarlane Shannan, who sculpted Mrs Elder a little later (see p. 222).

Govan Graving Docks, Stag Street, 1869, 1883, 1894, James Deas
Outstanding complex, unique in Scotland, comprising three dry docks and associated quays. The longest dock (1894) – 268m (880ft) long, 25m (83ft) wide and 8m (26.5ft) deep – held the largest vessels afloat or could be divided to take two smaller vessels. Dock bases and ground surfaced with heavy-duty whinstone setts. Dock walls, stepped sides and quay edges built to last in grey granite. Retaining walls and ramp sides in white sandstone. Workshops in ashlar or polychrome brick. Dock equipment of steel caisson gates, two with folding bridges, hydraulic capstans at dock entrances, bollards, hydraulic pump and sluice houses. Scotch derrick crane, A & W Smith. An 1889 weighbridge. Closed, minor buildings deteriorating, awaiting new use.

Govan Press Building, 577–581 Govan Road, 1889, Frank Stirrat
Red ashlar renaissance offices fronting printing works, with busts of Gutenberg, Scott, Burns and Caxton, also of Mr & Mrs Cossar, the owners.

Napier House, 638–646 Govan Road, 1898, W J Anderson
Glasgow Style red ashlar former seaman's lodging house over shops. Experimental non-reinforced concrete construction. Govan Road section heightened, 1905, George Simpson, for telephone exchange.

Thomas Lucas Paterson of the Dowanhill Estate Company bought land at Langlands and the large Ronald estate at Broomloan in 1852. He had feued less than half of his 25 hectares (62 acres) before his financial crisis of 1873 stopped further development.

Govan Town Hall

Smith & Rodger constructed the Middleton Iron Ship Building Yard, on Hamilton lands, upriver from Napier's Old Yard. Later owned by the London & Glasgow Shipbuilding & Engineering Company Ltd, Middleton Yard together with Napier's New Yard further east, called Govan East Iron Shipbuilding Yard, was taken over in 1912 and extended by Harland & Wolff of Belfast. Subsequently called Govan Shipyard but closed in 1962, the site became the first phase of a 1970s riverside housing scheme, with streets named after Napier. The former Harland & Wolff engine works in Govan Road, 'The Shed', was used for large-scale shows in the 1990s.

Detail of Govan Press Building

215

Govan Savings Bank

Govan Burgh Chambers, 18–20 Orkney Street, 1866, John Burnet Sr
Classical, painted ashlar with channelled rustication and central arched entry. Corinthian pilasters to recessed first-floor courtroom windows. Extended, 1899, as Police & Fire Station, now cocooned.

Broomloan Road Nursery School, 71 Broomloan Road, 1875, Alexander Watt
Built as Broomloan Road Public School. White ashlar, Italianate with round-headed windows and projecting gabled end pavilions.

Summertown Centre, 1894, H & D Barclay
Built as the second of the school buildings for Broomloan Road Public School. Central-hall-plan, square building, rusticated red sandstone ground floor with prominent central entrance bay. Window mullions Doric on ground floor, Ionic at upper.

Govan Savings Bank, 705–707 Govan Road, 1904, Eric A Sutherland
The standard bank site was required to be on a prominent corner. Here Sutherland enhanced the corner site with an elaborate elongated stone drum, the only feature not of conventional classical architecture. After flirting with the Glasgow Style and then Art Deco for his cinemas, Sutherland returned to a simplified classical palette for his later banks. Carved coats of Royal Arms, Richard Ferris.

New Govan Church Hall, Govan Cross, 784–796 Govan Road, 2–4 Greenwell Street, 1873, Robert Baldie
Built as St Mary's Church. Geometrical gothic with trefoil tracery in flat gabled facade, tower in extension. Horseshoe gallery on cast-iron columns.

John Aitken Memorial Drinking Fountain, Govan Cross, 1884, Cruickshank & Co., Denny Iron Works
Cast-iron drinking fountain of a boy on a rock, in an upturned dish. Cast-iron fish-scale dome roofed canopy, on hexagonal arcade, embellished with inward-facing mythological beasts, carrying plaques of the Arms of Govan and of Masonic and Oddfellow symbols. Dedicated to John Aitken, a local doctor who became the Burgh Medical Officer of Health.

5–9 Water Row, 1897, William Tennant. Former YMCA, symmetrical delicate classical red ashlar façade with central Venetian dormer window above the entrance.

Above *Former YMCA, 5-9 Water Row*
Left *British Linen Bank*

94 **British Linen Bank**, 816–818 Govan Road, 1–3 Water Row, 1897, John Gaff Gillespie of James Salmon & Son
Simple composition with exuberant Glasgow Style external decoration, on a conventionally constructed tenement. Designed at the same time that Gillespie's colleague and future partner, James Salmon Jr (son of William Forrest Salmon and grandson of James Salmon Sr), devised the subtle Art Nouveau interior for the same bank at Main Street, Gorbals (see p. 110). The ground-floor classical stone façade features lively Art Nouveau capitals by the Dutch sculptor, John Keller (colour page 203). The corner entrance is embellished with a trireme's prow and two 'BLB' sails, flanked by two 'Winged Winds' by another friend of William Forrest Salmon, Francis Derwent Wood, the young English sculptor who had just been

awarded the Gold Medal of the Royal Academy Schools. The entrance is topped by a remarkable lead-covered open crown of thorns.

Pearce Institute

95 **Pearce Institute**, 840–860 Govan Road, Pearce Street, 1892, R Rowand Anderson
For a Working Men's Club gifted to the people of Govan by Lady Pearce, in memory of her late husband and in silent acknowledgement of the source of her wealth – shipbuilding, Anderson provided a large early 17th-century Scots Renaissance palace (colour page 208). Two linked main blocks contain four large halls, restaurant, billiard room, gym and cookery demonstration room. The Dutch-gabled west block, with the barrel-vaulted MacLeod Hall at first floor, has a projecting ogee-roofed stairtower to the west. Above the tea room, in the lower link block with its clock and corbelled cast-iron balcony, is the gothic vaulted Lithgow Hall. The richly carved main entrance in the crowstepped east block leads up a large stair to the Fairfield Hall, with its oriel window at the back and the Stephen Hall above. There are original Art Nouveau suspended light fittings in the top-lit billiard room at the front.

Statue of Sir William Pearce, 801 Burleigh Street, 1894, Onslow Ford
Blackened bronze figure, holding a plan, on a tall granite base. Pearce was the shipbuilder who created Fairfield's, the leading shipyard on the Clyde.

Cardell Halls, 801–805 Govan Road,
2–4 Burleigh Street, 1894
Chunky Scots Baronial gusset building, with
broken pediment at Govan Road and strapwork
to Burleigh Street. Sculpted cat on cornice at east
front. Built as a Temperance Headquarters, it is
now a pub!

Govan Parish Church

96 **Govan Parish Church**, 866–868 Govan Road,
1883, R Rowand Anderson
Huge Early English gothic, cruciform plan
under a single roof, chancel extended, 1906.
Plain exterior with cross finial and angled gable
buttresses. Anderson had reverted, from the
current hall-like church plan, to the traditional
multi-cell cruciform plan, but put a new single
roof over all. Splendid interior devised by the
Rev. Dr John MacLeod, to provide a glorious
traditional setting for worship. Anderson
had made ample provision for stained glass,
the major element in MacLeod's plans. Kerr
windows, 1891 below the Choir Gallery; above,
1902, Heaton, Butler & Bayne, probably chosen
by Commissioner R Malcolm Kerr. Steven
(Bellahouston) Memorial Chapel; side windows,
1893, Burlison & Grylls (colour page 208);
east window, 1894, Clayton & Bell. Baptistery
windows, 1898, Shrigley & Hunt. MacLeod was
dissatisfied with all their designs and finally
prevailed on his original choice, Charles Eamer
Kempe, who would normally only accept
Episcopal commissions, to make the remainder of

Govan Sarcophagus, drawn by John Honeyman

the church windows. **Early Christian sculpture** – best in Scotland. St Constantine's Sarcophagus, AD 576, decorated with interlace, beasts; buried in churchyard at the Reformation, discovered in 1885 and returned to the church. Pagan 'Sun Stone', a swastika and mounted bagpiper; 'Cuddy Stane', Jesus on an ass; Govan Cross Shaft, interlace and horseman, top missing; five Viking hog-backed tombstones; 17 Celtic stones, Celtic crosses added, adapted as gravestones, 17th, 18th centuries. All are now inside the church. **Govan Old Parish Burying Ground**, surrounding the church, the heart-shaped burying ground, containing 16th- to 19th-century monuments, clearly a location of rare antiquity.

St Anthony's RC Church, 831 Govan Road, 1877, John Honeyman
Byzantine red ashlar with round-headed doorway and dogtooth mouldings. Square tower and open arched belfry. Good interiors and stained glass.

881–887 Govan Road, **2–4 Shaw Street**, 1900, Frank Burnet & Boston
Glasgow Style tenement above modern public house. Red ashlar with projecting corner bay and corbelled balcony at third floor. Oriels, balconies and dormers on both streets add to the fantastic roofscape.

Lyceum Cinema, 908 Govan Road, McKechnie Street, 1937, C J McNair
On the site of an earlier burned-out music hall-turned-cinema, the new Super Cinema seated 2,600. Art Deco faience and glass below wide canopy around corner entrance. Brick upper walls each side of the curved and finned moulded glass block corner feature. Original features in circular foyer and 1938 projection equipment. Latterly a bingo hall, now awaiting a new use.

Lyceum Cinema

Abraham Hill's Trust School, 65–69 Golspie
Street, 1874, James Thomson of Baird &
Thomson
Severe Italianate two-storey L-plan charity
school. Three-storey bell tower over Doric
columned central arched entrance. Doric
pilastered entrance porch on smaller north front.

Entrance to Fairfield General Offices

97 **Fairfield General Offices**, 1030–1048 Govan
Road, 1889, Honeyman & Keppie
Long classical red sandstone office block; wide
projecting central entrance bay with 'Modern
French' detail. Pilastered first-floor windows
to open-plan drawing offices. Doric columned
tower at west, brick rear. Built for Fairfield
Shipbuilding & Engineering Co., the pedimented
doorway supports mermaids in an arched
panel. Flanking, on trireme podia, shipwright
and mariner sculptures. Cornice above
entrance supports balustraded balcony, in a
Corinthian columned, pedimented temple, with
large stained-glass windows. Mosaic-floored
vestibule, ornate wrought-iron stair balustrade.
Carved wooden fireplace and portrait of Sir
William Pearce in panelled boardroom.

The Honeyman & Keppie partnership
lasted from 1889 until John Honeyman
retired in 1901 to make way for their
assistant Charles Rennie Mackintosh
to be made a partner. During those 12
years, the workload was dominated
by the efforts of Mackintosh. Apart
from the Fairfield offices, John
Keppie's major contributions were
the posthumous completion of James
Sellars' Anderson College of Medicine
(see *Central Glasgow* Guide), Sellars
Memorial at Lambhill Cemetery, 1889
and the four-storey Hide, Wool &
Tallow Market at Greendyke Street,
overlooking the Green, 1890. These
were followed by the interiors for the
Glasgow Art Club, in Bath Street, 1892
and extensions to Lilybank House,
1895.

Fairfield Engine Works, 1048 Govan Road,
*c.*1868, Angus Kennedy
Giant classical brick façade, with twin pilasters
and blocked arches, to Elder Street, fronting
91m (300ft) square, four-bay workshop. The
two western erecting shop bays, 1906 and
1916, Sir William Arrol, were built to match the
demolished boiler shop, 1889, Andrew Myles,
further to the east. Cast-iron internal frame and
double mezzanine galleries on box girders, part
removed 1938, and travelling crane over. Glazed
ridge on slate roof carried on king posts.

*Fairfield Fitting Out Basin showing
Titan Crane, 1930*

Titan Cantilever Crane, 1911, Sir William Arrol
200-ton, uprated *c.*1941 to 250-ton, giant
cantilever Titan crane on east quay of Fairfield
fitting-out basin. Lattice girder tower on roller
track. Asymmetrical cantilever track jib, with
motor room and counterweight at short end.

Elder Park, remnant of Linthouse Mansion,
*c.*1825, style of David Hamilton
Ionic portico, pair curved flights of steps,
segmental-arched doorway, fanlight, parts
of flank walls. Re-sited 1921, when mansion
demolished. **Cottage**, vernacular survivor,
converted as park amenity.

Portico of Linthouse Mansion, Elder Park

Statue of John Elder, 1888,
Sir Joseph Edgar Boehm, sculptor
A tall granite pedestal, with classical detail and
plaques, carries the bronze standing figure,
holding his invention, the compound steam
engine.

Statue of Mrs John Elder, Elder Park, 1905,
Archibald McFarlane Shannan, sculptor, cast by
Singer, bronze founder
Bronze seated figure, wearing Glasgow
University Hon LLB robes, on a raised granite
plinth, enclosed in wrought-iron railings.

Shannon was among the sculptors employed
by Rowand Anderson to adorn the front of the
National Portrait Gallery in Edinburgh.

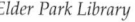

98 **Elder Park Library**, 228a Langlands Road, Elder
Park Street, 1901, J J Burnet
Elegant Edwardian baroque, the shallow
colonnaded portico follows the shape of a small
dome above the otherwise inconspicuous entry.
Pedimented pavilions to rear, original interior
with deep cornices and a coffered segmental-
vaulted ceiling.

Elder Park Library

Elder Cottage Hospital

99 **Elder Cottage Hospital**, 1a Drumoyne Drive,
Langlands Road, 1902, J J Burnet
Rich late 17th-century English Renaissance,
remarkable bracketed and arched entry hood
over columned central porch, a sculpted
panel over. Bellcast roof and gabled dormers,
details typical of many smaller country houses
influenced by Wren. **West Block**, No 2a, *c*.1902,
J J Burnet. Harled building, with half-timber
Tudor gables, broad eaves and bargeboards.

223

Linthouse Mansion (demolished)

Next morning, I went [from Erskine] to Glasgow but was compelled by a mistake about horses to go, with the vulgar, by a steamer!
Henry, Lord Cockburn, *Circuit Journeys*, 1840

Above *Linthouse St Kenneth's Church*
Below *Alexander Stephen House*

LINTHOUSE

The David Hamilton-style Mansion was built in 1791 on the 8-hectare (20-acre) Spreul estate of Linthouse. It became the residence of Michael Rowand, cashier of the Ship Bank. Alexander Stephen moved his shipyard across the river, then to Linthouse in 1869. The firm was actually founded at Burghead in 1750. The yard was later merged into Upper Clyde Shipbuilders (UCS), but closed in 1970 and the site is now occupied by an industrial estate. Stephen used the mansion for his offices until 1921, when the house was demolished and the porch re-erected in Elder Park. The estate was developed for housing after the shipyard was opened.

Linthouse St Kenneth's Church, 9 Skipness Drive, 1899, James Miller
The red ashlar classical nave front, with baroque canopied entrance, is strangely flanked by battered towers in the Arts & Crafts style Miller was using in his villas at the time. The composition was much better developed a few years later at St Andrew's East Church (see p. 86). Original **Hall**, linked by arch to church, has small-pane mullioned windows. Twin-gabled Church Officer's House. Alterations and West Hall, 1933, Keppie & Henderson. Detached from Linthouse proper by Clyde Tunnel approaches.

Alexander Stephen House, 21 Holmfauld Road, 1914
Simple classical office block, for Alexander Stephen, shipbuilder. Red brick on ferro-concrete frame, treated as pilaster strips. Wallhead balustrade to flat roof over main cornice. Off-centre entrance door, with sidelights and fanlight. Offices to south, larger windows to workshop on other side.

SHIELDHALL

The early 18th-century house at Shieldhall belonged to Alexander Oswald. The Shieldhall estate was sold to Robert Cassels for housing about the time Stephen's shipyard arrived in 1869. Peter Paterson's 18th-century Merryflats estate, to the south of Linthouse, became the site for Govan Poorhouse, built in 1872. Becoming also a hospital and asylum for the combined parishes of Govan and Gorbals, until 1930, it is now part of the Southern General Hospital. Much of the Shieldhall estate was purchased by the Scottish Wholesale Co-operative Society in 1881 for an industrial estate. The Cabinet Works were the first to be built in 1884 and more were being built up to 1930. After Cassels' misfortune, the Trustee for his creditors sold a site in 1913 to John Woyka & Co. Ltd for a timberyard and in 1927 they laid out streets and sewers for housing. About that time Fairfield's built a Clubhouse and Sports Pavilions at Shieldhall. King George V Dock was opened in 1931.

Govan Municipal Fever Hospital, Merryflats, *c.*1860, possibly John Honeyman
The hospital still contained 54 beds when Glasgow Corporation took over in 1912, but Merryflats was later extended, as Shieldhall Hospital.

Southern General Hospital Administration Building, 1345 Govan Road, *c.*1868, James Thomson, of Baird & Thomson
Built as Govan Parish Poorhouse. Unlike fever hospitals, the supervision of the poor was the responsibility of Parish Boards. The Institution opened in 1872 and the following year, on the combination of Govan with Gorbals, or Little Govan, Parish, the latter closed its existing Gorbals facility and moved into the Govan premises, which were rapidly expanded. The first part, a long symmetrical French Renaissance building, with many mansard turrets adorned by iron crests and a bell tower complete with a clock, became the centrepiece of the Combination Poorhouse. It is now entered through the Doric portico of the low central wing.

Shiels House, 612 Old Renfrew Road, *c.*1830
Simple classical ashlar mansion, with a square-columned porch. Gutted and roofless, at serious risk.

Robert Cassels was one of three founding partners of the Glasgow Iron Company in 1845. They started the St Rollox Works, another at Motherwell, then steel works at Wishaw. By 1872, when Cassels was managing partner and James Stewart Reid, the major shareholder, was his other partner, the Glasgow Iron & Steel Company employed over 4,000 men. After investing in Paterson's Dowanhill, Cassels bought the feuing estate of Shieldhall, again borrowing heavily from the Company. In 1887, when Reid demanded repayment of the loan, Cassels had to resign, sell his share in the Company and transfer title of Shieldhall to Reid as security for £80,000.

Southern General Hospital Administration Building

There was a colliery at Craigton Farm, one of many on the Glasgow coalfields, which stretched from Broomloan Road and Helen Street in Govan to Govanhill. Most were worked out by the early 19th century, but at this one some remnants survived and were not built over until very recently.

Drumoyne Primary School, 200 Shieldhall Road, 1947, John McNab

Symmetrical U-plan, with tall central, Edwardian baroque, ashlar entrance block. Framed red brick and glazed panel classroom wings now concealed by modern extension.

Luma Tower (former lightbulb factory)

100 **Luma Tower**, 510 Shieldhall Road, 1936, Cornelius Armour, SCWS architect

1930s modernist former lightbulb factory. Rectangular block, with three levels of offices and an iron-railed flat roof walkway to the left; two-stage, glazed lamp test tower, off-centre, over a curved staircase. To the right a two-storey manufacturing hall with tall first floor. Extended and converted to residential use, the tower to an office suite, 1995, Cornelius McClymont Architects. Saltire Society Award, RIBA Award, Civic Trust Award, 1997. Supreme Award for Regeneration of Scotland, 1998.

Ian Paterson, Glasgow City Council, Town Planning Conservation Department; **Maureen Goodfellow**, The Royal Incorporation of Architects in Scotland; **Dr Irene O'Brien**, Glasgow City Archives; Staff of the Mitchell Library; **Veronica Fraser**, Royal Commission on the Ancient and Historical Monuments of Scotland; **Dr Deborah Mays**, Historic Scotland; **Prof. Michael Moss**, Glasgow University Archives; **Gordon Urquhart**, formerly of Glasgow West Conservation Trust; **Rosemary Carmichael**; **Andrew Jackson**; **Rosalind & Geoffrey Jarvis**; **Helen Leng**; **Dr E D Livingstone**; **Marcus MacLean**; **David H Mann**; **Susan Skinner**, **Caroline Torres, Gill Cloke, Alastair Harper**; **Alan Ferdinand**, Four Acres Charitable Trust. Especial thanks to **Rebecca M Bailey** for facilitating the funding.

References
The following list for further reading includes the principal sources which have been used in this publication:

The Baillie Magazine; **Brotchie, T C F** Borderlands of Glasgow; **Brotchie, T C F** History of Govan; **Brotchie, T C F** Some Sylvan Scenes near Glasgow; **City of Glasgow** Book of Glasgow, Civic & Empire Week, 1931; **City of Glasgow District Council Planning Department** The Cathcart Heritage Trail; **Corporation of Glasgow Housing Department** Reviews of Operations, 1919–1937 & 1919–1947; **Donnelly, Michael** Glasgow Stained Glass; **Eunson, Eric** The Gorbals, An Illustrated History; **Finnie, Stephen & Thomson, Pat** The Good and the Bad, A History of Garngad; **City of Glasgow** Municipal Glasgow, Its Evolution and Enterprises; **Glendinning, Miles, Macinnes, Ranald & Mackechnie, Aongus** A History of Scottish Architecture; **Gault, Rob & Linda** The Govan Heritage Trail; **Gomme, Andor & Walker, David** The Architecture of Glasgow; **Groome, Francis H** Ordnance Gazetteer of Scotland; **Herbert, Beatrice W H** The Carmunnock Heritage Trail; **Historic Scotland** List of Buildings of Architectural or Historical Interest; **Horsey, Miles** Tenements and Towers; **Hume, John** Industrial Archaeology of Glasgow; **Laird, Ann** Hyndland; **Macdonald, Hugh** Rambles Round Glasgow; **Marshall, Ian & Smith, Ronald** Queen's Park Historical Guide and Heritage Walk; **Napier, James** Notes and Reminiscences of Partick; **Oakley, Charles** Official Handbook and Industrial Survey; Old Country Houses of the Old Glasgow Gentry; **Reed, Peter** Glasgow, The Forming of the City; **Rush, Sally Joyce** The Stained Glass Windows of Govan Old Parish Church; **Simpson, William** Glasgow in the Forties; **Small, David** Bygone Glasgow; **Small, David** Quaint Bits of Old Glasgow; **Smart, Aileen** Villages of Glasgow, Volumes 1 & 2; **Smith, Ronald** The Gorbals Historical Guide and Heritage Walk; **Smith, Ronald** Pollokshields Historical Guide and Heritage Walk; **Spalding, Bill** The Story of Partick, Part 1; **Statistical Accounts of Parishes** Old 1790s; New 1840s; Third 1950s; **Taylor, Charles** Partick Past & Present; **Urquhart, Gordon** Along Great Western Road; **Widdows, Tom** James Mckissack – Cinema Architect.

Godfrey, Alan Reprints of Old Ordnance Survey Maps with Historical Notes: **Hillhead**, Susan McGann; **Partick**, Dr Gilbert T Bell; **Maryhill**, R H J Urquhart; **St Rollox**, Andrew Stewart; **Springburn**, Mark O'Neill; **High Street**, Jane MacLean; **East End**, Dr Gilbert T Bell; **Glasgow Green**, Elspeth King; **Parkhead**, Andrew Jackson; **Central Glasgow**, John C Clayson; **Govan**, G J Cassidy; **Pollokshields**, Robin Urquhart; **Bellahouston**, Irene O'Brien

Stenlake, Richard Old Photographs (mainly from the Collections of Members of the Strathclyde Postcard Club): **Bygone Partick**, Bill Spalding; **Bygone Partick 2**, Bill Spalding; **Partick Remembered**, Bill Spalding; **Old Cowcaddens, Possilpark & Lambhill**, Andrew Stuart; **Old Springburn**, Andrew Stuart; **Old Dennistoun**, Andrew Stuart; **Old Riddrie, Millerston & Stepps**, John Hood; **Old Parkhead**, Charles MacDonald; **Old Shettleston & Tollcross**, Rhona Wilson; **Old Baillieston, Garrowhill & Easterhouse**, Rhona Wilson; **Old Bridgeton & Calton**, Eric Eunson; **Old Cathcart, Langside and Mount Florida**, Eric Eunson; **Old Govan**, Bill Spalding; **Old Cardonald**, Bill Spalding.

ACKNOWLEDGEMENTS

City of Glasgow Archives **Abridgements of Seisins**; City of Glasgow Archives **Glasgow Dean of Guild Court Records**; City of Glasgow Archives **Partick Dean of Guild Court Records**; City Of Glasgow Archives **Glasgow Iron Company Papers**; City of Glasgow Archives **James Reid Stewart Trust Papers**; City of Glasgow Archives **Shieldhall Trust Papers**; Faculty of Procurators, Hill Collection **Dowanhill Feuing Plan**; Glasgow City Marketing Bureau; Glasgow University Archives **Dowanhill Estate Company Papers**; Glasgow University Archives **T L Paterson Trust Papers**; Glasgow University Unpublished Thesis, 1970: Simpson, Michael Anthony **Middle Class Housing and Growth of Suburban Communities in the West End of Glasgow: 1830–1914**; McArthur, John **Plan of the City of Glasgow, Gorbells and Caltoun: 1778**; Scott Sutherland School of Architecture Unpublished Thesis, 1978: Morrison, Andrew Keith, **The Development and Architecture of Kelvinside, Glasgow**; National Archives, Scotland **Court of Session Records**; National Monuments Record of Scotland **Villas Designed & Executed by Boucher & Cousland, Architects, Glasgow**; Registrar General of Scotland **Census Enumeration Records**; Richardson, Thomas **Map of the Town of Glasgow and Country Seven Miles Around: 1795**; Post Office Directories **Glasgow and Suburban, with Maps by Joseph Swan and John Bartholomew: from 1778**.

Poem on page 109 from *Swing, Hammer, Swing* by Jeff Torrington, published by Secker & Warburg. Reprinted by permission of the Random House Group Limited.

PICTORIAL GLOSSARY

1. Architrave (projecting ornamental frame)
2. Astragal (glazing bar)
3. Barge (gable board)
4. Basement, raised
5. Bullseye, keyblocked (circular window with projecting blocks punctuating frame)
6. Buttress (supporting projection)
7. Caphouse (top chamber)
8. Cartouche (decorative tablet)
9. Cherrycocking (masonry joints filled with small stones)
10. Channelled ashlar (recessed horizontal joints in smooth masonry)
11. Chimneycope, corniced
12. Chimneycope, moulded

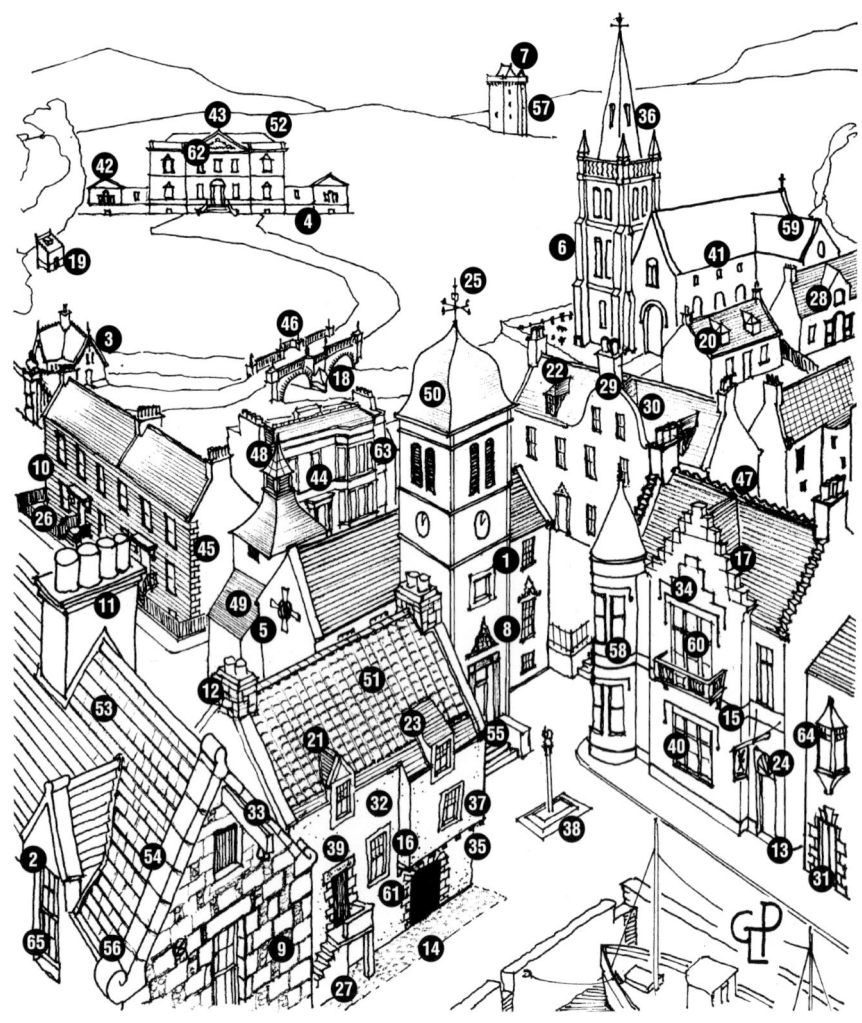

13. Close (alley)
14. Cobbles
15. Console (scroll bracket)
16. Corbel (projection support)
17. Crowsteps
18. Cutwater (wedge-shaped end of bridge pier)
19. Doocot, lectern
20. Dormer, canted & piended
21. Dormer, pedimented (qv) wallhead
22. Dormer, piended (see under 'roof')
23. Dormer, swept wallhead
24. Fanlight (glazed panel above door)
25. Finial (crowning ornament)
26. Fly-over stair
27. Forestair, pillared
28. Gable, wallhead
29. Gable, wallhead chimney
30. Gable, Dutch (curved)
31. Gibbs doorway (framed with projecting stonework)
32. Harling
33. Hoist, fishing net
34. Hoodmoulding (projection over opening to divert rainwater)
35. Jettied (overhanging)
36. Lucarne (small dormer on spire)
37. Margin, stone
38. Mercat Cross
39. Marriage Lintel
40. Mullion (vertical division of window)
41. Nave (main body of church)
42. Pavilion (building attached by wing to main building)
43. Pediment (triangular ornamental feature above windows etc)
44. Portico
45. Quoins, rusticated (corner stones with recessed joints)
46. Refuge (recess in bridge parapet)
47. Ridge, crested
48. Roof, flared pyramidal
49. Roof, leanto
50. Roof, ogival (with S-curve pitch generally rising from square plan and meeting at point)
51. Roof, pantiled
52. Roof, piended (formed by intersecting roof slopes)
53. Roof, slated
54. Skew (gable coping)
55. Skewputt, moulded (lowest stone of skew, qv)
56. Skewputt, scroll
57. Stair jamb (projection containing stairway)
58. Stringcourse (horizontal projecting wall moulding)
59. Transept (transverse wing of cruciform church)
60. Transom (horizontal division of window)
61. Voussoir (wedge-shaped stone forming archway)
62. Tympanum (area within pediment qv)
63. Window, bay (projecting full-height from ground level)
64. Window, oriel (corbelled bay qv)
65. Window, sash & case (sliding sashes within case)

Drumchapel

Garscube

Knightswood

Lambhill

Anniesland

Maryhill

Jordanhill

Ruchill

River Clyde

Scotstoun

Hughenden

Kelvinside

Possil

Westbourne Gardens

Hyndland

Broomhill

Dowanhill

Woodside

Whiteinch

Partickhill

Port Dunda

Glasgow Harbour

Partick

Linthouse

Little Govan

Shieldhall

Govan

Kingston

Lauriesto

Ibrox

Plantation

Cardonald

Tradeston

Gorbals

Crookston

Bellahouston

Kinning Park

Hutchesontoun

Pollokshields

Mosspark

Dumbreck

Strathbungo

Govanhill

Polmad

Queen's Park

Crosshill

Pollok

Pollok Estate

Shawlands

Mount Florida

Pollokshaws

Langside

Battlefield

Cathcart

King's Park

Newlands

Muirend

Nitshill

Cro

Darnley

Merrylee

Thornliebank

Cas

Giffnock

Eastwood

Carmun

Clarkston

Busby

Mearns

route continues to south side of Mearns route continues to Eaglesham

ingburn
Robroyston
Balornock
Barmulloch
Millerston

Rollox

rngad
Riddrie
Cranhill
Easterhouse

nnistoun
Carntyne
rove

Shettleston

Bridgeton
Baillieston
Parkhead
almarnock
Tollcross
Mount Vernon

Daldowie
Carmyle
River Clyde

— Route followed in text
Area covered by Central Glasgow guide
— City of Glasgow council boundary

N

5 km

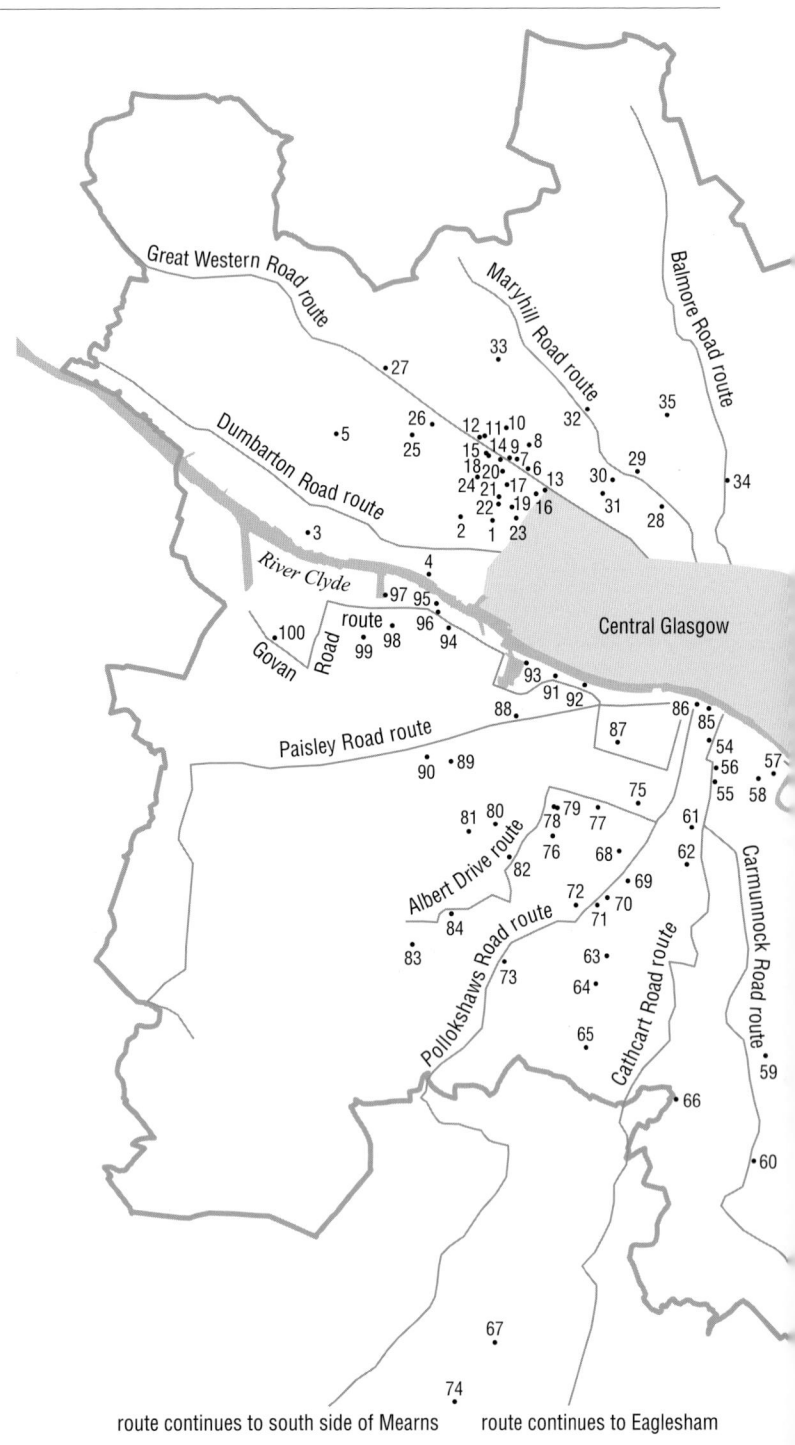

route continues to south side of Mearns   route continues to Eaglesham

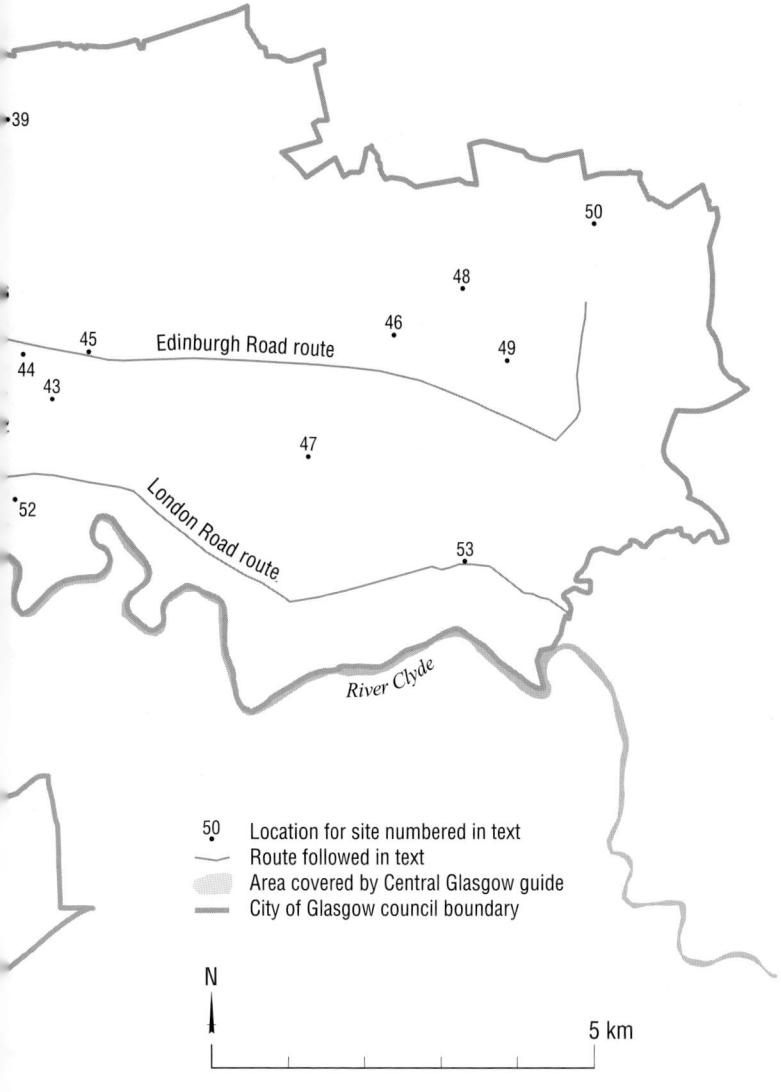

•39

50

48

46

45
Edinburgh Road route

49

44
43

47

London Road route

•52

53

River Clyde

50 Location for site numbered in text
— Route followed in text
      Area covered by Central Glasgow guide
      City of Glasgow council boundary

N

5 km